# THE
# REFERENCE
# SHELF

# NICARAGUA AND
# THE UNITED STATES

edited by ANDREW C. KIMMENS

## THE REFERENCE SHELF

Volume 59 Number 2

THE H. W. WILSON COMPANY

New York    1987

# THE REFERENCE SHELF

The books in this series contain reprints of articles, excerpts from
books, and addresses on current issues and social trends in the United
States and other countries. There are six separately bound numbers in
each volume, all of which are generally published in the same calendar
year. One number is a collection of recent speeches; each of the others
is devoted to a single subject and gives background information and discussion from various points of view, concluding with a comprehensive
bibliography. Books in the series may be purchased individually or on sub-
scription.

**Library of Congress Cataloging in Publication Data**

Main entry under title:

Nicaragua and the United States.

(The Reference shelf ; v. 59, no. 2)
Bibliography: p.
1. United States—Foreign relations—Nicaragua.
2. Nicaragua—Foreign relations—United States.
I. Kimmens, Andrew C.    II. Series.
E183.8.N5N49   1987        327.7307285        87-8148
ISBN 0-8242-7050-5

Printed in the United States of America

# CONTENTS

PREFACE ......................................... 5


I. A LONG INVOLVEMENT

Editor's Introduction ............................. 6
Richard C. Schroeder. Roots of Current Antagonism ...
...................... Editorial Research Reports     6
Conor Cruise O'Brien. The Protomartyr ..............
.................................. Atlantic Monthly    12
David Haward Bain. The Man Who Made the Yanquis
    Go Home ................... American Heritage      16


II. U.S. POLICY IN THE 1980s:
   SUPPORT FOR THE COUNTERREVOLUTION

Editor's Introduction ............................. 36
William M. LeoGrande. The United States and Nicara-
    gua ............... Nicaragua: The First Five Years  37
George P. Shultz. Nicaragua and the Future of Central
    America ............ Department of State Bulletin   61
John P. East. Is the Reagan Administration Policy to-
    ward Nicaragua Sound? (Pro) ... Congressional Digest  70
Edward M. Kennedy. Is the Reagan Administration Poli-
    cy toward Nicaragua Sound? (Con) ................
    ......................... Congressional Digest      75
The Case for the Contras .......... The New Republic   81
Robert Leiken. Reform the Contras . The New Republic   88
Edgar Chamorro with Jefferson Morley. Confessions of a
    'Contra' ..................... The New Republic     95
Eldon Kenworthy. United States Policy in Central Amer-
    ica: A Choice Denied ............. Current History  109

III. THE NICARAGUAN RESPONSE:
    DEFIANCE AND WOUNDED NATIONAL PRIDE

Editor's Introduction .............................  121
Forrest D. Colburn. Nicaragua under Siege ...........
..................................Current History  122
Thomas H. Stahel. An Interview with Miguel d'Escoto
    Brockman, Foreign Minister of Nicaragua .. America  132
Saul Landau. The Way of the Sandinistas ...Progressive  144
Nicaragua's Sovereignty and Independence Should Not
    Be Jeopardized by Military Activities, International
    Court of Justice Declares ........... UN Chronicle  154
Abraham D. Sofaer. The United States and the World
    Court ...............Department of State Bulletin  168
Thomas M. Franck. Icy Day at the ICJ ..............
..............American Journal of International Law  178
Sergio Ramírez Mercado. The Unfinished American
    Revolution and Nicaragua Today ................
........................... Nicaragua under Siege  185
Alvin Levie. Statements by Rollin B. Tobie, Ana Maria
    Lopez, and Modesta Martinez ...................
.................. Nicaragua: The People Speak  195


IV. SOLUTIONS: INCREASED HOSTILITIES OR A MODUS VIVENDI

Editor's Introduction ............................  204
Shirley Christian. Epilogue .......................
............... Nicaragua: Revolution in the Family  205
Contadora: Peace Process in Central America .........
.................................. UN Chronicle  212
Susan Kaufman Purcell. Demystifying Contadora .......
.................................. Foreign Affairs  220
Max Singer. Losing Central America ..... Commentary  241
Maria Elena Hurtado. Chasing Rainbows: A Futile
    Search for Regional Peace ..... World Press Review  249


BIBLIOGRAPHY ......................................  252

# PREFACE

No part of U.S. foreign policy during the first half of the 1980s has proved more contentious and divisive than opposition to Nicaragua's 1979 Sandinist revolution. The cornerstone of this policy is U.S. military assistance (sometimes under the guise of "humanitarian aid") to the counterrevolutionary insurgency, and this hostile step has tended to freeze the positions of the antagonists.

The terms of the debate have remained remarkably stable for a political situation so obviously filled with passion: Ronald Reagan's administration has nowhere shown itself more loath to compromise; Daniel Ortega Saavedra's junta, although appearing surprisingly agile in influencing world opinion, has no less firmly resisted all U.S. demands—foremost among them that it negotiate directly with the counterrevolutionaries and not with their backers in Washington. Neither has any consensus emerged in the United States: from the beginning of the decade never more than four out of ten of the U.S. public have supported aid to the "Contras," even though this is a major foreign-policy initiative of the most popular president in years.

The origins and salient features of the U.S.-Nicaraguan imbroglio and the political debate it has aroused are the subject of this volume. Section I inquires into the history of U.S. involvement in Nicaragua and the history and personality of the eponymous hero of the Sandinista revolution. Section II examines the anti-Sandinista policy of the Reagan administration, including the debate over the nature and aims of the Contras. Section III considers the Nicaraguan government's reaction to this externally supported threat to its existence, along with the arguments surrounding Nicaragua's suit against the United States before the International Court of Justice. Section IV outlines the possible outcomes of the current impasse, and looks particularly at the peace efforts of the Contadora group of nations.

ANDREW C. KIMMENS

March 1987

# I. A LONG INVOLVEMENT

## EDITOR'S INTRODUCTION

The somber history of U.S. influence in Nicaragua is little known in the United States, although many Nicaraguan school-children can no doubt recite by heart the major events of more than a century of involvement—sometimes directly—by their powerful North American neighbor. The articles in the first part of this book summarize the history of this involvement, focusing particularly on the arguments surrounding the prolonged U.S. military presence in Nicaragua in 1912–25 and 1926–33 and the dominant figure of the latter period, General Augusto César Sandino.

The first article, by Richard C. Schroeder and reprinted from *Editorial Research Reports*, is a concentrated history of U.S. involvement in Nicaragua from the Walker affair of the mid-1850s to the end of the Somoza family's dictatorial rule in 1979 and the coming to power of the Sandinista National Liberation Front.

The second article, from *The Atlantic Monthly*, is by the Irish writer Conor Cruise O'Brien and describes General Sandino's career as a staunch opponent of U.S. military interference in Nicaraguan domestic politics and the strong appeal of Sandinism in today's Nicaragua. D. H. Bain's account of Sandino's rebellion against his American-backed countrymen, reprinted from *American Heritage*, concludes this section.

## ROOTS OF CURRENT ANTAGONISM[1]

Nicaragua is the largest (57,143 sq. mi.) and least densely populated (pop. 2.9 million) of the five Central American nations. A

[1]Reprint of a chapter from *Decision on Nicaragua* by Richard C. Schroeder, a contributor to *Editorial Research Reports*. *Editorial Research Reports*. vol. 1 no. 8, 1986, pp. 154–59. Copyright 1986, Congressional Quarterly Inc. Reprinted with permission.

veritable backwater in Spanish colonial days, Nicaragua—together with Guatemala, El Salvador, Honduras and Costa Rica—threw off Spanish rule in 1821 and for a brief period was part of the Mexican Empire under Augustín Iturbide. With the dissolution of the empire in 1823, Nicaragua became one of the five units of the United Provinces of Central America. The Central American union broke apart in 1838. From that point on Nicaragua was nominally, if not always effectively, independent.

The early days of the Nicaraguan republic were marked by a fierce political struggle between two cities and two political parties: the Liberals of León, the old colonial capital, and the Conservatives of Granada, the country's commercial center. Pervasive foreign interference, a fact of Nicaraguan life, has persisted to modern times. The principal outside influence came from the British, who had established outposts on Nicaragua's Caribbean coast during Spanish colonial rule, and from the United States, initially in the person of Commodore Cornelius Vanderbilt, who held a concession for a transport service from the Caribbean along the San Juan River and Lake Nicaragua and then overland to the Pacific—the quickest and cheapest way to travel from the U.S. East Coast to California.

The rivalry between Nicaragua's Liberals and Conservatives spawned a bizarre episode in the mid-1850s that has colored U.S.-Nicaraguan relations ever since. Central America at that time was the target of bands of "filibusters," bands of private adventurers from New York, Baltimore and New Orleans who rented themselves out to different political factions for military action against opponents. In 1855, the American filibuster William Walker contracted with the Nicaraguan Liberals to aid them in a civil war with the Conservatives. Walker landed with a force of 58 men and, astonishingly, handily defeated the Conservatives. His ambition did not end with that mission, however. Walker proclaimed himself commander in chief of the Nicaraguan army and in 1856 had himself "elected" president of Nicaragua, managing to gain diplomatic recognition from the United States.

The turn of events alarmed the Liberals and strengthened the Conservative cause. Walker also incurred the hostility of Commodore Vanderbilt by trying to take over Vanderbilt's transit company. Vanderbilt bankrolled the Nicaraguan Conservatives who, aided by Conservative troops from other countries, renewed their offensive against the American intruder. With the tide turning against him in 1857, Walker agreed to a truce and prudently left the country under the protection of an American naval officer. Walker made two more attempts to lead expeditions into Central America and on his second try landed in Honduras where he was captured by a squad of British marines, handed over to the Hondurans, and shot to death.

Although his filibustering was a failure, Walker's intervention left its mark on Central America. It thoroughly discredited Liberal movements throughout the isthmus and in Nicaragua the Liberals were frozen out of power for the next three decades. Moreover, the spectacle of Walker and Vanderbilt, two Americans, struggling for mastery of a supposedly independent Nicaragua aroused bitter antagonisms which later action by the United States would intensify.

### American Intervention since 19th Century

Following the Walker episode, Nicaragua settled into a period of relative tranquility known as the Thirty Years. A Liberal revolt in 1893 brought José Santos Zelaya to the presidency, which he held for the next 16 years. Santos Zelaya was a dictator who ruled Nicaragua with an iron hand, but his regime brought relative prosperity and a significant degree of modernization to the Nicaraguan economy. Santos Zelaya was also a firm believer in Central American integration, managing even to establish a brief union (1896–98), called the *Republica Mayor* (Greater Republic), between Nicaragua, El Salvador and Honduras. His great mistake, however, was antagonizing the United States.

The Spanish-American War (1898) had given the United States a colonial domain, and a new taste for exercising influence outside its borders, especially in its own hemisphere. Consciously or unconsciously, Santos Zelaya's integrationist zeal clashed with the new international spirit in the United States. The Nicaraguan leader also irritated Washington by refusing to grant the United States canal-building rights that would have included U.S. sovereignty over a slice of Nicaraguan territory. Instead, the United States maneuvered the independence of Panama from Colombia and secured the same canal-building concession it had sought from Nicaragua. As recounted by Professor Thomas W. Walker:

. . . Washington eventually let it be known that it would look kindly on a conservative overthrow of Zelaya. In 1909, when the revolt finally took place in Bluefields, Zelaya's forces made the tactical mistake of executing two confessed U.S. mercenaries. The United States used this incident as an excuse to sever diplomatic relations and to send troops to Bluefields to ensure against the defeat of the Conservatives. Though he held on for a few more months, Zelaya was ultimately forced to accept the inevitable, to resign, and to spend the rest of his life in exile.

Engineering the overthrow of a hostile Central American president was in keeping with the terms of the Roosevelt Corollary to the Monroe Doctrine. As enunciated by President Theodore Roosevelt in 1904, the Corollary held that the United States might, under certain circumstances, exercise an "international police power" in the Western Hemisphere. "Of course that view completely reversed the meaning of the original Doctrine [of 1823]," comments historian Walter LaFeber. "[President] Monroe and [Secretary of State John Quincy] Adams had originally intended it to protect Latin American revolutions from outside (that is, European) interference." In succeeding years, the Roosevelt Corollary would be invoked in Nicaragua time and again.

### U.S. Occupation; Sandino and Guerrilla War

When Santos Zelaya resigned, the United States refused to accept another Liberal government and the Conservatives returned to power. In 1912 U.S. Marines were once again sent into Nicaragua to help quell a rebellion by the Liberal leader Benjamin Zeledon. With the Marines fighting side by side with the Conservatives, Zeledon was captured and killed. This time the Marines were not withdrawn, but stayed on until 1925, under the guise of protecting U.S. lives and property. Although small in number—only about 100 Marines were stationed in Nicaragua during this period—and called a "Legation Guard" by the United States, they assured that real political power was centered in the U.S. diplomatic mission in Managua.

Shortly after the Marines pulled out in 1925, the Liberals rebelled again. So the Marines returned in 1926, this time staying until 1933. In 1927, President Coolidge sent Henry L. Stimson, the future secretary of state, to Nicaragua to work out a compromise settlement between the Liberals and Conservatives. In the ensuing election of 1928, the Liberals regained the presidency, but the United States continued to make political and economic decisions. It was during the second Marine occupation that the United States organized, trained and armed a new Nicaraguan military force, the National Guard, to control the endless bickering between the Liberals and Conservatives. By the time the United States made its final withdrawal from Nicaragua in January 1933, the Guard had come under the command of an ambitious, English-speaking politician, Anastasio Somoza García. He and his sons were to rule Nicaragua for more than four decades.

The 1927 agreement between the Liberals and Conservatives did not end insurgency in Nicaragua. Resistance to the United States and to the National Guard was led by a charismatic and tactically brilliant field commander, Augusto César Sandino. When frontal assaults proved futile and costly, Sandino turned to harassment and hit-and-run forays. He cultivated the support of peasants in the rural areas for supplies, information about government troop movements and occasionally emergency manpower in military encounters.

The National Guard and U.S. Marines responded with aerial bombardment of "hostile" towns and forced resettlement of entire peasant villages—measures that built more support for the rebel cause. Despite the rapid buildup of U.S. forces in Nicaragua—some 5,000 Marines were thrown against Sandino's men in 1930 and 1931—Sandino was still "as great a threat . . . as he had been at any previous point in his career" (Richard Milett, *The Guardians of the Dynasty: A History of the U.S.-Created Guardia Nacional de Nicaragua and the Somoza Family* [1977], p. 32) when the Marines finally left Nicaragua.

To the United States, Sandino was a "bandit," or worse still a "communist." To many Nicaraguans, however, he was a nationalist hero who led the struggle against foreign occupation. To National Guard Commander Anastasio Somoza, Sandino was a threat to Somoza's plans for long-term domination of Nicaraguan politics. After the Marines departed, Sandino signed a preliminary peace agreement with the Liberal government. But early in 1934, when Sandino arrived in Managua to negotiate a final truce, he was treacherously ambushed and assassinated, almost certainly on the orders of Somoza.

*Somoza Era and the Sandinista Revolution*

By 1936, Somoza had consolidated his control not only of the National Guard but of the Liberal Party as well. In that year, Somoza ran for the presidency and was elected without opposition,

assuming office on Jan. 1, 1937. For the next 42 years, the Somoza family ruled Nicaragua as its own private *finca* (ranch). In
the brief periods when Somoza or one of his sons did not hold the
presidency, a Somoza commanded the National Guard and a pli-
able surrogate did his bidding in the national palace.

In 1956, the elder Somoza was assassinated and immediately
succeeded in the presidency by the head of the National Assembly, his older son, Luis. In 1963 a Somoza-family factotum, René
Schick, was installed as president and died in office in 1966.
Schick's successor was the commander of the National Guard,
Anastasio Somoza Debayle, the younger son of the late dictator.
With the exception of a brief time in 1972, when Nicaragua was
governed by a Somoza-controlled junta, the younger Somoza
held the presidency until forced out by an insurrection on July 17,
1979.

The long period of Somoza rule was based on absolute control of the National Guard and the Liberal party, and close ties
to the United States.* The Nicaraguan economy grew steadily
under the Somozas, with agriculture leading the way until the
mid-1960s when industrial activity assumed greater importance.
But as the Nicaraguan economy expanded, so, too, did the wealth
of the Somoza family. They became the country's largest landowners and major investors in industries. When the revolutionary
Sandinista government seized power in 1979, it took over Somoza family holdings worth half a billion dollars, including 20
percent of the country's arable land and 154 commercial and industrial establishments. Observers point out that this was only
what the family left behind; perhaps as much wealth was shipped
out of Nicaragua to the United States and Europe before the Somoza regime fell.

The instrument of destruction of the Somoza dynasty was the
Frente Sandinista de Liberacion Nacional (FSLN), the Sandinist
Front for National Liberation, named for the old guerrilla fighter. The Front was founded in 1962 but became a serious challenge to the government only in the 1970s. Popular discontent
with the Somoza government began to surface in the wake of a
devastating earthquake in 1972. The Somoza family seized on the
disaster to siphon off millions of dollars of disaster relief funds.

*Both Somoza sons were educated in the United States. Luis attended Louisiana State University, the Universi-
ty of California and the University of Maryland. Anastasio was a graduate of the U.S. Military Academy, in 1948.

By the mid-1970s, the Sandinistas were waging open guerrilla warfare in several parts of Nicaragua, and the government responded by committing atrocities which only built further support for the guerrilla cause. Pedro Joaquin Chamorro, editor of the newspaper *La Prensa*, and a staunch opponent of the Somoza government, was assassinated in early 1978. President Somoza was widely believed to be responsible for the death, although he denied complicity. The murder consolidated opposition to the regime, not just among the poor and the peasantry but among the influential middle class and the business community. An unprecedented general strike swept the nation that Jan. 24, and by early March it was apparent that the Somoza regime was in serious trouble for the first time. In June of the following year, the Sandinistas launched their "final offensive," and on July 19, 1979, the president and the other members of the family still in Nicaragua fled the country.

---

## THE PROTOMARTYR[2]

---

Sandinismo is apparently regarded in Washington as an ideology essentially alien to Nicaragua but cunningly decked out in some kind of Latin American fancy dress. I don't know whether they really believe these things in Washington, or whether they only pretend to believe them, but if they do believe this one they are in fundamental error, and are headed for more unnecessary trouble. Sandinismo is a thoroughly Latin American ideology, with deep roots in Latin American history, and specifically in the history of Nicaragua. Far from being an alien phenomenon in Nicaragua, Sandinismo is a native response to alien domination: the alien domination in question being that of the United States. Perhaps that is the basic reason why Sandinismo, viewed from Washington, looks so alien.

Augusto C. Sandino (1895–1934), the eponymous hero of this ideology, became a national hero to the Nicaraguans for the same basic reasons as those for which Joan of Arc became a national

[2]Conor Cruise O'Brien, a contributing editor of *The Atlantic Monthly* and the pro-chancellor of Dublin University. Excerpt from "God and Man in Nicaragua," *The Atlantic Monthly*, August, 1986. pp. 66–69. Copyright © 1986 by The Atlantic Monthly Inc. Reprinted by permission.

heroine to the French: he fought the foreigners who had invaded his country, and he was murdered by the servants of those same foreigners. (English historians, in the case of Joan, and American ones, in the case of Sandino, may define the issues differently; but I am talking about how the issues appear to *nationalists* of France and Nicaragua, which is what matters in considering Sandinismo.)

The particular foreigners whom Sandino fought, at the head of a small but resolute band of guerrillas, were the U.S. Marines, who were in Nicaragua from 1912 to 1933, at the invitation of Nicaragua's Conservative faction. Sandino fought the Marines, with varying fortunes, from 1927 to 1932. He was successful to the extent that the Americans were unable either to subdue him or to buy him off—the latter being unusual at the time in Central American politics, civil or military.

The last of the Marines left Nicaragua on January 2, 1933. They left not because they had been defeated by Sandino—as the simpler sorts of Sandinista rhetoric suggest—but because U.S. policy had changed, in favor of something subtler. But Sandino probably had quite a lot to do with the change in policy. The indomitable guerrilla leader had been news throughout the world and had caught the imagination of nationalists not only in Latin America but as far away as China. The publicity was judged to be bad for the United States, and it was possible to protect U.S. interests by other means. The means consisted of the Nicaraguan National Guard, selected and trained—and originally commanded—by U.S. Marines. The new commander of the National Guard, selected by the U.S. minister in Managua, was Anastasio Somoza García, the founder of the dynasty that was to rule Nicaragua until the revolution of 1979.

On February 21, 1934, Sandino and two of his generals, after dining in Managua with Juan Bautista Sacasa, then the President of Nicaragua, were abducted by members of the National Guard, driven out to Managua airfield, and shot by firing squad. Two years later Somoza—who had been at a poetry reading when Sandino and his comrades were shot—ousted Sandino's host, Sacasa, and made himself President.

A marked feature of Sandinismo, as mentioned, is its cult of heroes and martyrs. Sandino himself is the supreme hero and the protomartyr. *¡Bienvenido a la Patria de Sandino!* says a large sign at Sandino Airport, Managua, recalling the scene of the original martyrdom. There are portraits of him everywhere: a skinny, morose little man, invariably wearing a ten-gallon hat and looking like a figure out of a 1920s cowboy movie. You see sketches of him in chalk on rocks along the Nicaraguan country roads: just lines, like a matchstick man, identifiable only by the hat. And in at least one place an economical artist paid homage to Sandino by the simple hieroglyph

Sandino's status as a martyr may appear a bit anomalous, since Sandino was not a Christian, although he did believe in God. Like many mavericks in the twenties, he was a theosophist and a spiritualist. But Christian Sandinistas of today insist that whatever Sandino *thought* he was, he was indeed a true Christian martyr: one who fought and died for the God of the Poor. He refused to call himself a Christian because the most eminent Nicaraguan "Christians" of his day—like the Bishop of Granada, who blessed the U.S. Marines—were in the service of the enemy. These, however, were not really Christians at all but worshippers of Mammon. Had Sandino lived to see the advent of liberation theology, he would have proclaimed himself a Christian revolutionary. And on that last point, at least, I think the Christian Sandinistas are probably right.

To the U.S. media of his day, of course, Sandino was no kind of hero or martyr, Christian or other, but a bandit and a Red. A bandit he certainly was not. The question of whether he was a Red is more complex. In several ways he *was* a Red. In his Mexican years—1923 to 1926—he associated with Communists and other revolutionary ideologues and picked up some of their outlook and vocabulary. He was not a Marxist—no one who was into theosophy and spiritualism could reasonably be described as a Marxist—and although he did often use the language of class war, I think it clear that for him the class struggle was secondary to the national struggle. This appears in the fact that Sandino stopped fighting once the Marines had been withdrawn. The *social* structure in Nicaragua was not changed by the departure of the Marines. The fact that Sandino spent his last evening on earth with the very "moderate" President Sacasa seems to indicate that social conditions did not arouse in Sandino the same elemental passions that drove him on, over five years, to fight the foreign foe on Nicaraguan soil.

The primacy of nationalism also appears in the incident that—according to Sandino's own account—led to his departure from Mexico and return to Nicaragua. A Mexican revolutionary acquaintance of his, dismissing the possibility of revolution in Nicaragua ever, said that every Nicaraguan was a *"vendepatria."* The mere thought of being taken for a *vendepatria*—a man prepared to sell his country—was so unbearable to Sandino that he determined to return to Nicaragua and raise an army to fight the U.S. Marines. And the expression *"vendepatria"* is even now the most deadly insult in the lexicon of the Sandinistas. It is the word with which they brand people like Archbishop Obando.

In general, all Sandino's most passionate utterances, all those that are treasured by contemporary Sandinistas, are expressions of exalted nationalism. I could cite a number of examples, but there is one that sums them all up. This consists of the four words of Sandino's that are the national motto of Sandinista Nicaragua: *¡Patria Libre o Morir!* Give me liberty or give me death.

The second hero and martyr in the Sandinista pantheon is the poet Rigoberto López Pérez, who in 1956 killed Anastasio Somoza García, at a party in León, and was then shot down by Somoza's bodyguards. President Eisenhower called López "the murderer of a friend of the United States"; of course to Sandinistas he is not a murderer but the executioner of Sandino's murderer. López's deed and fate were an inspiration to Sandinismo's third hero and martyr, who was also its leader and principal ideologue, Carlos Fonseca Amador, a founder, with Silvio Mayorga and Tomás Borge, of the Frente Sandinista de Liberación Nacional in 1961. (Both Fonseca and Mayorga were later killed by the National Guard.)

In long "Notes" that he wrote on López, Fonseca quoted Machiavelli's epithet for tyrannicides: *rarísimos.* Fonseca also quoted some of López's own poetry, including the lines

> Nicaragua is getting back to being
> (or may be for the first time)
> a free country
> without affronts and without stains
> [*una patria libre*
> *sin afrentas y sin manchas*]

According to Fonseca, the words "or may be for the first time" have "an extraordinary revolutionary transcendence" in their context. It is, I believe, this sense of national humiliation (Fonseca himself wrote of *la patria humillada*) that supplies the basic drive of Sandinismo. Up to July, 1979, the Sandinistas fought to wipe out what they regarded as the humiliation of their country. And since July, 1979, and especially since Ronald Reagan became President, they have been fighting to avert the reimposition of national humiliation on their country. And to Sandinistas, national humiliation is precisely what Reagan insists on when he refuses to negotiate with them, and tells them to negotiate with the contras. It is not in the nature of Sandinistas to negotiate with contras. *Not* negotiating with *vendepatrias* is what their tradition and their whole intellectual, moral, and emotional formation are all about. *Patria Libre o Morir.*

## THE MAN WHO MADE THE YANQUIS GO HOME[3]

Rear Adm. Julian L. Latimer stood on the bridge of his flagship, the USS *Rochester*, as it nosed into the harbor of Puerto Cabezas, on Nicaragua's northeastern Mosquito Coast. It was Christmas Eve, 1926, and the fifty-seven-year-old West Virginian had been called abruptly away from family festivities at the Canal Zone naval station at Balboa.

Rear Admiral Latimer could see Puerto Cabezas clearly: with its sawmill and rows of workers' shacks, it looked like a Georgia lumber town. But it was owned lock, stock, and barrel by the Standard Fruit Company, which used it as a shipping point for the mahogany produced by the company's vast plantations in the interior. American-owned the town may have been, but the *Rochester* was there, along with two other warships, the *Cleveland* and the *Denver*, because Puerto Cabezas currently was occupied by people the U.S. State Department viewed as hostile.

A civil war between Nicaraguan Liberals and Conservatives, erupting in the aftermath of the country's 1924 election and a

[3]Reprint of an article by David Haward Bain, author of *Sitting in Darkness* and other works, from *American Heritage*, v. 36, no. 5, August–September 1985, pp. 50–61. Copyright © 1985 by David Haward Bain. Reprinted by permission of the author.

subsequent coup, had drawn Washington's attention when deposed Liberals appealed for outside aid to help reestablish their "constitutionally elected" coalition government. Led by Dr. Juan B. Sacasa, the Liberals had been able to enlist only one ally—Mexico. Rather than helping their cause, this sealed their fate. The Coolidge administration was squabbling heatedly with the ruling Mexican Liberal party over Mexican laws curbing foreign ownership of property and restricting *gringo* oil leases. Among certain circles in the United States, such economic nationalism was nothing but "bolshevism."

The *Rochester* and its accompanying warships owed their presence in Nicaraguan waters at least outwardly to the call of Adolfo Díaz, a Conservative who had been installed as president with American approval. He was disliked at home because he was unable to rule without the presence of U.S. Marines. During a term of office fourteen years before, Díaz's call for *Yanqui* help had cost a thousand Nicaraguan lives and millions in state debts. This time, invoking a highly questionable threat, Díaz claimed that the Liberal army had been beefed up by "three hundred Mexican bolsheviks." The U.S. State Department quickly responded—citing the "spectre of a Mexican-fostered Bolshevistic hegemony intervening between the United States and the Panama Canal."

Rear Admiral Latimer might have expected only a short postponement of his Christmas celebration as his squadron anchored in the harbor opposite the building that housed the Sacasa government. The Liberals had abandoned their initial capital, in the Caribbean port of Bluefields, only days before—at first sight of the warships. And now on this Christmas Eve it seemed that they were also to lose control of Puerto Cabezas. As swarms of bluejackets trooped through the town searching Sacasa's residence and posting sentries every few yards, Latimer declared that, effective 4:00 P.M. Christmas Day, everything "within rifle range" of American properties would be "neutralized." The action was not an intervention in the internal affairs of Nicaragua, he explained; it was simply a measure to protect American lives and property.

Dr. Sacasa—who still called himself president—protested the "bellicose display," saying that he had no quarrel with Americans or designs on their holdings. But he and his ministers and generals looked on, powerless, as bluejackets disarmed all Nicaraguan soldiers left within Latimer's neutral zone. Seven hundred tons of weapons and ammunition, purchased earlier by the Liberals in New Orleans, were confiscated and piled alongside the harbor— destined to be dumped in the bay.

Before this could be done, an unlikely squad of six Liberal soldiers and a group of port prostitutes stole over to the pile of confiscated weaponry. They managed to grab thirty rifles and six thousand cartridges. Their leader, an unprepossessing little man whose name was Augusto César Sandino, had, a few weeks before, floated in a dugout canoe for nine days down the Coco River from the interior highlands to secure some weapons for his irregulars. Of all the officers in the Liberal ranks, Sandino alone planned to ignore Admiral Latimer's directive to disarm, beginning a pattern of defiance that would bedevil and divide the United States for six bloody and costly years. In weeks Latimer's force of 16 warships, 215 officers, 3,900 soldiers, and 865 Marines would prove insufficient to effectively occupy Nicaragua. By then the name Sandino had already come to stand for more than just the man.

Augusto César Sandino was born on May 18, 1895, in the Toltec village of Niquinihomo, in southwestern Nicaragua. His father, don Gregorio, owned a small farm on which he grew coffee and raised cattle. Doña Margarita Calderón, his mother, was part Indian, and young Augusto inherited his *mestizo* complexion from her. From his father he inherited a passion for Liberal politics.

Augusto attended primary school before the revolution that culminated in the first Marine occupation in 1912. As a teenager, his education over, he had begun to manage some of his father's lands when he witnessed the body of the popular Liberal revolutionist, Benjamin Zeledón, being brought in tied feet foremost to his horse by soldiers of President Díaz.

Sandino was compelled to leave Nicaragua in 1921 after a personal dispute with a village official (some said later Sandino had killed him). He worked in Honduras briefly, then as a laborer in Guatemala for United Fruit—his first close acquaintance with *Yanqui* imperialism—and later in Mexico.

Mexico at that time had become a magnet for political exiles from all over Latin America. The impressionable young Sandino drank in their debates on the merits of a Central American Union, the need for laborers' organizations, and the popular Lib-

eral notion of regaining control over isthmian resources. He also
looked into various kinds of spiritualism. The blend of politics
and mysticism would plant in him a conviction that he was
"called" to perform great acts.

From Sandino's perspective, his radicalization (he would call
it his "illumination") becomes understandable. Nicaragua's first
grievance about American intervention came in 1855, when a
half-crazed Tennessee adventurer named William Walker led a
private army to Nicaragua with the aim of establishing himself as
the leader of a *gringo* paradise, with slavery its economic mainstay.
He actually ruled the country for two years until some Central
Americans stood him up before a firing squad.

American interest in the country increased dramatically as it
became apparent that an isthmian canal was not only possible but
necessary. Washington helped depose two presidents, selected
two others, and snuffed out at least one revolution by landing Marines in an occupation that lasted twenty years. Long after the
Panama Canal had opened, there were plans afoot to dig another
sea lane across southern Nicaragua. The Wilson administration
had forced through a treaty granting the United States exclusive
and perpetual rights to construct such a canal. A token sum of
three million dollars was appropriated by Congress for these
rights—but the money was turned over to American banks to
partially satisfy the enormous Nicaraguan debt. One of Sandino's
first manifestos spoke of the "robbery" of canal rights.
"Theoretically," he wrote, "they paid us three million dollars.
Nicaragua, or rather the bandits who then controlled the government with the aid of Washington, received a few thousand pesos
that, spread among Nicaraguan citizens, would not have bought
each one a sardine on a cracker . . . ."

By early 1926, while Sandino pored over political tracts with
the urgency of the newly converted, the United States had extensive influence throughout Central America, perhaps nowhere as
much as in Nicaragua. The republic's resources, considered underdeveloped, lay in the land: coffee, banana, and sugar plantations, minerals, vast tracts of mahogany and pine forests, and
ample grazing land for cattle. North Americans owned or managed the lumber and gold-mining industries, most of the financial
institutions, including the Nicaraguan National Bank, the rail-
road, and the customs house. Two American fruit companies

controlled between them some three hundred thousand acres of plantations.

When Sandino learned in 1926 that the newly elected Liberal president of Nicaragua had been intimidated into resigning and that American gunboats had moved in, he decided to end his own exile and return home to help organize resistance. Withdrawing three thousand dollars of his savings, he got a job at an American-owned mine in the northern Nicaraguan highlands of Nueva Segovia and started organizing the miners. At first he sought to dissociate himself from the traditional Liberal politicians, who were distrusted because they habitually betrayed the poor, but later he decided he could succeed only by joining up with the Liberals. He heard of Sacasa's move to Puerto Cabezas and of the seven hundred tons of imported weapons. Sandino traveled from the Segovias down to the sea, and thence to the Liberals' stronghold. He arrived a few weeks before Admiral Latimer's warships.

The appearance of a scruffy young irregular from the mountains did not visibly impress the urbane Dr. Sacasa nor his war minister, José María Moncada. Graying, convivial, and pro-American, a former schoolmaster and journalist, General Moncada knew Sandino's father well, from local political work, and viewed Augusto as something of a backslider. The young man had adopted a jaunty guerrilla's outfit, the most striking elements being his large, shovel-shaped Stetson cowboy hat (which dwarfed his prematurely lined face), bandoleros crossing his chest, and a formidable pair of riding boots. For his part, Sandino thought Moncada possessed questionable Liberal credentials, as the elder general had served in Díaz's cabinet during his earlier administration. Thus Sandino did not react well when the "renegade conservative" haughtily turned down his plea for arms.

Moncada irritated him further by telling him, after Sandino had stolen guns from the confiscated pile, to return to the mountains—and to leave the rifles behind. Other Liberal leaders temporarily defused the situation, and Sandino left for San Rafael del Norte in the Segovias. News of his flamboyant action at Puerto Cabezas was already becoming mythical among the ranks of Liberal soldiers. In time the legend would tell of Sandino not only going hungry to feed his troops and the poor but also dreaming clairvoyant dreams and sending forth mysterious "waves" that psychically linked his fighters. But in 1927 the legend was young—more concerned with moral righteousness and *machismo*.

Soldiers began migrating from the Sacasa-Moncada forces to be with Sandino, who had grown disgusted with the traditional *politicos* and had decided the revolution would have to be saved from them. Sacasa was only inept, he felt, but the more ambitious Moncada bore watching. "Moncada will at the very first opportunity sell out to the Americans, " he wrote in early 1927.

The minister of war's personal ambition was soon unveiled. Not only Sacasa but also his sworn enemy, the Conservative Díaz, told the Americans they would abdicate their leadership in favor of a third man, and General Moncada began to maneuver himself into the spotlight. Inevitably he clashed with Sandino, the commander of the only other organized Nicaraguan army. Soon after Sandino left Puerto Cabezas, he defeated a large Conservative force at El Bejuco, capturing thousands of rifles and millions of cartridges, and Moncada's ill-equipped soldiers began showing up among the *Sandinistas*. Furious, Moncada attempted, unsuccessfully, to have Sandino killed.

Meanwhile, President Díaz's foreign aid continued to arrive. On February 21, the Navy Department announced that 5,414 American servicemen were on duty in Nicaragua or on their way there. Washington began to sell munitions on credit to the bankrupt Díaz government. None of this sat well with Sen. William E. Borah of Idaho, chairman of the Senate Foreign Relations Committee, who had long been voicing doubts about entanglements in Latin America. Decrying a U.S. "mahogany and oil policy" that put protection of property above questions of right and wrong, Borah demanded that the troops be recalled.

Patiently the administration repeated the rationale: the intervention was strictly "neutral"; communists in "Mexico and other Latin American countries" were committing anti-American acts, and citizens' lives and property were endangered. Increasingly the Monroe Doctrine was cited. In April, President Coolidge spoke, promising to protect United States citizens wherever they might be. He added, "We are not making war on Nicaragua any more than a policeman on the street is making war on passersby."

Coolidge's soothing words fell upon uneasy ears. Walter Lippmann, then writing for the New York *World*, complained that the United States had "neither been honestly neutral, nor have we honestly intervened. We have combined the worst features of both policies." The *London Spectator* commented, "The United States is finding out, as we found out long ago, how slippery is the slope of imperialism."

Plainly Coolidge did not enjoy what was going on. Marines, simply by their presence, were coming under fire. To avert a political and military disaster, the President appointed Henry L. Stimson, a former Secretary of War, to mediate between the embattled parties. But the peace conference, which began on May 4 outside Managua, satisfied no one but the United States. Under threat of American force, the armies of both Díaz and Sacasa were instructed to disarm. Díaz would complete his term, followed by an American-supervised election. Stimson (it was whispered) obtained Moncada's cooperation by promising him the presidency in 1928.

Sandino began to suspect Moncada when a Liberal war council convened to vote on the disarming. Moncada assured his subordinates that this defeat was actually a victory, since the 1928 election would doubtlessly return them to power. Of twelve Liberal generals, only Sandino refused to commit himself, turning down promised rewards of money and land. The chilly relations between the two men worsened when Moncada angrily blurted out, "And who made you a general?"

"My comrades in arms, señor," answered Sandino. "I owe my rank neither to traitors nor to invaders." Again a confrontation was averted by those present, and when Sandino asked permission to consult with his guerrillas, Moncada let him go in the naive hope that the young officer would disarm in the mountains.

"I spent three wretched, depressed days in the Común heights, wondering what attitude I would take," Sandino recalled. "I didn't want my soldiers to see me weeping. . . . Finally I broke the chain of doubt and resolved to fight, feeling I was the one called to raise Nicaragua's protest against the sellout and that bullets were the only defense of our sovereignty."

Stimson, assured by Moncada that Sandino would disarm, proclaimed the civil war ended. The Díaz government secured a one-million-dollar loan from a New York bank to offer any Nicaraguan ten dollars for each surrendered rifle or machine gun. American planes took to the skies to drop leaflets announcing this across the entire country. In the highlands Sandino learned of the reward and immediately moved his men farther into the mountains, away from temptation. Nevertheless, in that poor country, many deserted. When Moncada grew worried about Sandino's extended silence, he sent as an emissary don Gregorio Sandino to remonstrate with his son. "In this world," the father warned, "saviors end up on crosses, and the people are never grateful." But it was the father's mind that was changed, and don Gregorio wrote to his other son, Sócrates, urging him to join Augusto.

It soon became apparent to all that Sandino was unmovable. He signaled his defiance by raiding the American gold mine at San Albino, in which he had once worked. Gold and cash receipts he appropriated for the cause were less important than the dynamite he seized. It would be used to manufacture crude "Sandino bombs" from sardine tins.

American reaction was swift. The American legation in Managua accused him of "audacious and vicious acts of banditry," and Capt. G. D. Hatfield demanded that the Nicaraguan present himself to the small Marine garrison at Ocotal for surrender. Otherwise, he wrote, "You will be proscribed and placed outside the law, hunted wherever you go and repudiated everywhere, awaiting an infamous death: not that of the soldier who falls in battle but that of the criminal who deserves to be shot in the back by his own followers."

"I will not surrender," replied Sandino's letter. "I want a free country or death."

On July 16 he led a small band of *Sandinistas*, augmented by nearly eight hundred unarmed peasants, or *campesinos*, against Hatfield's little garrison. Guerrillas quickly overran Ocotal except for the two-story adobe city hall and the municipal square it commanded, where they were halted by the Marines' machine guns. The battle raged for more than half a day until five American planes arrived to bomb and strafe the attackers, who fled into the jungle.

News of the engagement created a small furor in America. First reports contrasted Marine losses of one dead and two wounded to the *campesinos'* three hundred casualties. President Coolidge praised the Marine aviators for their heroism, but other Americans were horrified. The Illinois governor Edward Dunne dispatched an open letter to the President that blasted the use of airplanes against troops having no antiaircraft guns or planes of their own. The liberal weekly *The Nation* wrote: "The United States created the anarchy which it is now attempting to suppress. . . . What law excused the use of American Marines on Nicaraguan battlefields or of American bombing planes for mass murder?" At least two senators, Borah and Walter F. George of Georgia, denounced Coolidge's Nicaraguan policy.

A few days after the battle of Ocotal, telegraph operators in Central America intercepted a proclamation from Sandino. His motive in attacking the garrison was to show that the *Sandinistas* were not bandits, he said. "We prefer death to slavery, for the peace obtained by Moncada is not the peace that can give liberty to men . . . ."

Rear Admiral Latimer, having been honorably relieved of his Central American command, reported to Washington. "Conditions in Nicaragua today are better than when the revolution started," he said. "The recent activity of Sandino has no political bearing or significance." The State Department promised the "bandit" would be "annihilated."

The Nicaraguan highlands, where the *Sandinistas* were hiding, were historically impossible to govern effectively even in peaceful times. Some thirty thousand square kilometers in all, the Segovias were reached from the Caribbean coast by crossing a succession of inland swamps, which were replaced as one moved west by thickly forested plains that rose to overgrown mountains. One river, the Coco, drained the mountains, and it was unnavigable except by rafts or Indian canoes.

Months of search and foray by American troops through the *cordillera* ended in the last days of 1927. Col. L. M. Gulick, commander of the 2d Marine Brigade, learned through spies of Sandino's whereabouts—on a nearly impregnable mountain in the Segovias called El Chipote. Harold Norman Denny, a *New York Times* correspondent, described the territory: "Chipote was a mile-high mountain overgrown with forests looming above the valleys at its base like the prow of a titanic battleship," he wrote. "Its flanks extended back fifteen miles and in the center of this triangle was the house in which lived Sandino, surrounded by a small picked bodyguard. The prow of the mountain was studded with trenches and machine gun nests, and at the top were quarters for men and storehouses for supplies. Sandino, the neighboring Indians said, had boasted that it never could be taken."

An American Marine patrol along with a detachment of the Nicaraguan National Guard and a large convoy of pack mules were dispatched by Colonel Gulick to attempt to storm the mountain. It was a tragic blunder. The patrol was surprised on a cliffside trail, and its captain was badly wounded in the first attack. The men rallied, taking their dead and wounded with them as they pushed forward to a level place where they held off waves of attackers. A reinforcing column fought its way to their side on January 1, 1928. The combined force was besieged in a hamlet called Quilali for a week by Sandinist snipers in the overlooking hills.

With five killed and twenty-three badly wounded, the beleaguered Marines appealed for aid in an ingenious way. They had no radio, so they strung wires between poles to which were attached messages. Airplanes snagged these with grappling hooks. In an era when aviation exploits made headlines daily (it was only seven months since Lindbergh had flown the Atlantic), what followed thrilled the world. A pilot, C. F. Schilt, volunteered to rescue the wounded. A single lane ran through Quilali, and the Marines widened this by demolishing the adjoining board-and-adobe houses with their bare hands until an airstrip was created. While a brother aviator strafed the surrounding hills to keep the Sandinist snipers down, Lieutenant Schilt dived into the town ten times to evacuate the wounded. It was a feat that won him a Congressional Medal of Honor.

The bravery of American aviators and ground troops notwithstanding, the incumbent Republican administration wished Nicaragua would go away. A Pan-American conference opened on January 16, 1928, in Havana, and as a contemporary historian wrote, "The sharpest debates that had ever occurred in the history of Pan-American conferences took place in a special subcommittee to which [the question of American intervention] was referred." The attacks against the United States were led by El Salvador and Mexico, and to a somewhat lesser extent by Argentina and Chile. Even the representatives of pro-American countries acknowledged that Sandino had a wide appeal across Latin America. His dispatches and manifestos, printed word for word in many newspapers, touched Latino nerves rubbed raw by years of foreign domination. Among some elements in Latin America, Sandino's symbolic eminence was approaching that of the two great liberators, Bolívar and Martí.

Sometimes Sandino's program was obscured by an inchoate pan–Latin Americanism, but behind the rhetoric lay two goals: Latin ownership of natural resources, and education and jobs for the poor. Above all, Sandino believed that nothing could be accomplished until U.S. forces were out of Nicaragua.

"When [the Yankees] speak of the Monroe Doctrine, they say, 'America for Americans,'" Sandino wrote. "Fine, well said. All of us born in America are Americans. But the imperialists have interpreted the Monroe Doctrine as 'America for the Yankees.' Well, to save their blond souls from continuing in error, I propose this reformulation: 'The United States of North America for the Yankees. Latin America for the Indo-Latins.'"

By the time the conference ended, with any anti-intervention resolution postponed until the next session, five more American destroyers were steaming toward the Nicaraguan shores, twelve hundred additional Marines were on their way there, and an air bombardment of El Chipote had blasted the mountain bare.

"During the sixteen days when we were under seige," Sandino wrote, "the pirates' air squadrons paid us daily visits. The first four planes would come in at 6:00 A.M. and start dropping bombs. Naturally we shot back at them, and several of their steel birds were mortally wounded. After four hours of bombing, another squadron would appear, bomb for four hours, and then be replaced by another—they kept this up till nightfall.

"The bombs did little damage to our men because we were well protected, but we lost some two hundred cavalry mounts and cattle for our table. The situation was serious because the animals' decaying bodies made the camp insupportable. The air was full of vultures for days. They did us a service in wrecking visibility for the planes . . . but life there was getting tough and we decided to clear out."

For several weeks after his stronghold was smashed, Sandino was reputed to have been killed in the bombardment. He claimed later to have staged his own funeral to aid in the deception, but when he reappeared near the town of Jinotega, alarm bells went off in Washington. Col. Charles A. Lindbergh made a barnstorming tour of Central America on behalf of the Coolidge administration; he was showered with rose petals on Latin airstrips, but many back home wondered aloud whether he had attached his name to a bad issue.

More outraged Republican and Democratic voices asked why Coolidge had committed soldiers to slaughter in Central America without first obtaining the legislators' approval. Even Will Rogers, the revered cowboy philosopher, wondered why the country was getting involved in Nicaragua.

Diplomacy was rediscovered—it was, after all, an election year at home—and Latimer's successor, Adm. David F. Sellers, was ordered to open a dialogue with Sandino. The guerrilla responded with a demand for withdrawal of American soldiers and the proposal that Latin American nations, not the North Americans, should supervise and guarantee free elections. As this was not part of U.S. plans, the Americans and Sandino became engaged in one of the most peppery diplomatic exchanges ever recorded. An exasperated Sellers stiffly complained of the "insolence" of "bandit" Sandino's replies.

"Who are you, anyway?" Sandino wrote a Yankee officer. "How dare you threaten with death, and otherwise, the legitimate sons of my country? Do you think you are in the heart of Africa? Don't believe that I am afraid of you! If you are any kind of man come out and fight it out with me single-handed on neutral ground, whenever you want."

The unproductive correspondence continued despite the launching of a concerted drive to wipe out Sandino within two months. American forces were told to travel light and adopt the guerrillas' tactics. "If you want to eat," the soldiers were told, "catch a bandit and take his beans from him."

Dispatches and official releases took on a pronounced tone of confidence in the spring of 1928, but the war was as savage and hard as all guerrilla wars. Both sides traded charges of atrocities, which, as our melancholy experience in such conflicts has shown, were at least in part accurate.

As 5,480 Marines and 2,000 National Guardsmen pursued the rebels, the first American journalist managed to find his way to Sandino's camp. In a widely publicized series of articles and interviews, Carleton Beals, writing for *The Nation*, portrayed Sandino as a dedicated nationalist, politically sophisticated, capable of humor and confident. Sandino was indignant when people called him a communist or a bandit, and he was also, Beals wrote, "a bit flamboyant and boastful and with a tendency to exaggerate his successes."

"My record is absolutely clean," Sandino told Beals. "Any man can examine every step I have ever taken. He will never find that Sandino his life long has ever taken anything that has not belonged to him, that he has ever broken a promise, that he has ever left any place owing any man a cent." A few minutes later the guerrilla showed Beals his ledger of army expenditures. "Everything we take in and spend is faithfully recorded here," Sandino explained. "Today, for instance, I gave Colonel Colindres fifteen dollars, all I had at the moment, to buy clothes for five of his soldiers who escorted you from El Remango and who came in dirty and ragged. I suggested to him that he tell the shopkeeper we are poor and that he make the money go as far as possible, and if it didn't quite stretch to send the bill to President Coolidge, who is to blame for this violation of my country."

From his command post in the hills, Sandino appealed on the eve of the American-supervised election in 1928 to the leaders of fifteen Latin American nations. He urged them to protest diplomatically or with arms "the uncounted crimes being committed by the Government of the White House, in cold blood, in our unhappy Nicaragua." His agents had tried to convince Indians in remote hamlets that Americans ate babies—causing prospective voters to flee into the jungle when Marines rode in to conduct registration and balloting. Such campaign dirty tricks, however, had little lasting effect.

Despite the election of General Moncada (as expected), Sandino's popularity was growing in the cities as well as in the mountains, and the new Nicaraguan president feared that the Marines would be withdrawn by the new administration of Herbert Hoover in Washington, leaving him with no support for his regime. He tried to organize a private army but was told by the Marine commander to concentrate on nonmilitary measures such as public works if he wanted to win over the people. The National Guard, supposedly a nonpartisan police force, would eventually have its American officer corps replaced by Nicaraguans; Moncada was told to forget about armies until that time.

Sandino, who had opinions on everyone and everything, released his estimation of the new president in 1929. Moncada, he said, "is surely the most dismal and dangerous of the men who are now astride of our people, with his fakery about public works, prosperity, and grandeur—as false as it is ridiculous . . . the income from customs and other taxes loaded on the people goes to pay a National Guard in which bad Nicaraguans take orders from Yankee officers. . . . Everything [Moncada] does smells of sadness, disaster, and death."

These words paled before Sandino's opinion of Hoover. "Like a rabid but impotent beast, Herbert Clark Hoover, the Yankee president, hurls abuse at the head of the army that is liberating Nicaragua," Sandino wrote. "He and Stimson are the modern assassins . . . who have earned the eternal curses of parents, sons, and brothers of the Marines fallen on Segovian battlefields."

His words were brave, but the years of guerrilla warfare were beginning to take their toll on Sandino. In July 1929 he turned over command of his forces to a subordinate and traveled to Mexico. Despite his youth Sandino appeared, according to one reporter, "greatly enfeebled by ill health and the rigor of his campaign." He planned to stay in Mexico for a brief time to recover his energy and, he hoped, to raise money in the name of Latin American brotherhood. In August, however, he wrote: "As we haven't so far found even half a centavo divided in half, nor a pistol bullet for the cause of liberty in Nicaragua, I must wait a bit." The Mexican government was not entirely cordial to its guest and saw to it that Sandino stayed in the Yucatán instead of in Mexico City, where he might prove an embarrassment.

One group that responded to his fund-raising efforts was the local communist organization, but they stipulated that Sandino lend his name to their cause. Sandino balked; the communists got furious. They spread a rumor that Sandino had taken a fifty-thousand-dollar bribe to leave Nicaragua—which he hotly denied "with many picturesque Spanish adjectives," a journalist reported—and that when Sandino returned home he would "sell out to the highest bidder."

Sandino came back to Nicaragua bearing only two submachine guns (declared for Honduran customs as "carpentry tools"), which represented all of the arsenal he was able to raise in Mexico. The subordinate he had left in command, Gen. Pedro Altamirano, had kept their enemy at bay in a year of skirmishes, but the character of warfare had changed. The Hoover administration had come to believe that all its Marine might could not defeat a popular guerrilla movement. The American troops had begun to be rotated home, and those remaining had been withdrawn to the larger towns because of the danger of ambush. Instead of ground troops, the Marines backed the national constabulary with an air force that had grown from thirty to seventy warplanes—a commitment unprecedented in the world at that time. Latin American journalists protested to Hoover in July that the planes were dropping "asphyxiating gases" on rural Nicaragua. The Navy did not rebut the charge.

The size of the Nicaraguan National Guard had risen to five thousand, swollen by a large officer corps, all of them graduates of a hastily established and expensive national military academy. The Guard existed independently of the national government; it had its own postal and telegraph systems and had absolutely no accountability to the government for expenditures. The Americans had created a new military caste.

In the mountains the National Guard, still led by Americans, had adopted guerrilla tactics. They employed espionage and they avoided towns and well-traveled routes. By the time Sandino resumed command, both sides had dispensed with the formalities of taking prisoners.

A Central American journalist who visited Sandino's encampment gave this description of a rebel detachment coming back from a clash in the forest: "men of the most varied aspects, dried and hardened by weather and privations; some, the fewest, white-skinned and even blond; others with the light brown complexion of the local *mestizo*; many Indians of the mountain region with their air of abstraction; and even a black man, corpulent and with tight curly hair. Many of them wore virtual rags, their bronze skin showing through their tattered shirts or pants. Their *sombreros*, some of felt and others of straw, all bore the classic red and black ribbon. Less than half of them had Springfield rifles of the sort taken from the North Americans; the rest had pistol and machete or just a machete. . . . Behind came the mounted men, comprising about a third of the whole, riding the small tough mules of the region and a few wretched horses past their time for the slaughterhouse. . . . The cavalrymen ranged from graying old-sters with bent backs to boys who were really infants, twelve- and fourteen-year-olds who followed the column like seasoned veterans."

Sandino boasted that his army was "the most disciplined, devoted, and disinterested in the entire world because it is conscious of its lofty historical role." Certainly it was hard to defeat. Although slightly wounded in June of 1930, Sandino led his irregulars in at least nineteen skirmishes during the closing months of that year.

By then the Americans had decided to get out of Nicaragua entirely before the 1932 election. As Americans continued to get killed, the Marines were told to stay out of the nation's interior, and civilians were warned that they could be protected only in the coastal towns. The original justification for America's role in the war—protecting American people and property in Nicaragua— was in effect rescinded, after four years of a conflict that had cost the lives of two hundred Marines and countless Nicaraguans.

In a Washington press conference in April 1931, Hoover's anger at the situation he had inherited was evident. He called Sandino a "cold-blooded bandit outside the civilized pale." There was no revolutionary movement in Nicaragua, Hoover asserted, merely "sporadic disorders fomented by a murderous band." The President was confident that Sandino would be brought to justice.

But a series of mountain and jungle battles that wore on well into 1932 further consolidated the rebels' positions. In April, after issuing a string of announcements of an impending attack upon Managua, Sandino mounted a "victory drive" against the southern cities. Not until the end of June did the Marine-led National Guard repulse his army.

General Moncada was not only in military trouble but he found himself politically outmaneuvered. A cabal of Liberal politicians made it impossible for him to run for a second term. The less abrasive Dr. Sacasa was brought back from a sulky self-imposed exile to head the ticket.

Progressives in both the Liberal and Conservative parties indicated a willingness to sit down with Sandino after the elections, but this did not satisfy Sandino's goal of getting the North Americans out of Nicaragua. Newspapers reported skirmishes every few days in the months preceding the American-supervised election. Sandino proclaimed a national boycott, saying that anyone going to "polling stations sentineled by Yankees will only pay lamentable homage to foreign bayonets." A third of Nicaragua's voting list of one hundred and fifty thousand stayed away on voting day.

Barely a thousand Marines were left in the country by the time the election was over, and Dr. Sacasa had finally attained the position he had claimed back in 1926. He turned out, however, to be a poor president and was easily overshadowed by the husband of his own niece, whom he appointed—at the Americans' insistence—as the first Nicaraguan chief of the National Guard. The man was Anastasio Somoza García.

Born in 1896 only a few miles from Sandino's birthplace, Anastasio Somoza was the son of a politician and coffee grower. He was a difficult child, and when, at nineteen, he got the family maid pregnant, relatives packed him off to Philadelphia to learn a trade. He studied bookkeeping and advertising at the Pierce Business School, but the talents he learned that would change his life—and Nicaraguan history—were a command of American culture and an expert grasp of colloquial English.

Back in Nicaragua in 1919, Somoza changed his politics to Liberal so he could marry the daughter of a wealthy surgeon; if he had his eyes on the family money he was disappointed, for they offered no aid, and his attempts at making a living were dismal. A car dealership failed because there were few Nicaraguan roads; he picked up a pittance refereeing boxing matches, worked as an electric meter reader, and inspected privies for the Rockefeller Foundation's Sanitation Mission to Nicaragua. He even tried his hand at counterfeiting and avoided prison only through a wealthy relative's intercession.

His political and military skills were equally dreary, as the Liberals learned when he joined their side in the 1926 civil war. He presided over a few small defeats before attaching himself to Moncada's staff. There he found a niche, for his smooth manner and fluent English made him a favorite with the Americans. Henry Stimson made him his translator in 1927; eighteen months later President Moncada appointed him as his personal aide, and before the end of that term the president appointed him an undersecretary for foreign affairs. During all of the years of trouble besetting Nicaragua, Somoza busied himself cementing his relationship with the Americans.

It seemed to be a natural choice to make Somoza—whose Americanized patter, salted with jokes and baseball statistics, put Marines at ease—the head of the National Guard, though he possessed no military training. Under his guidance, according to a Somoza biographer, the army would come to be known as the "best-armed, best-drilled, worst-conceived, most vicious little army in Central America."

News of Somoza's appointment on November 16, 1932, alarmed Sandino. From afar he had watched the career of the *Yanquista*, as Somoza was called. Though he habitually derided him, Sandino's disdain camouflaged real fear. In December he warned through his spokesman that Somoza would overpower the government if the National Guard was not taken away from him and reorganized, and that President-elect Sacasa's only chance lay in making peace with the guerrillas.

The last American Marines departed on January 2, 1933, taking their planes with them. Thus, with Sandino's main goal realized, barriers between himself and traditional politicos seemed surmountable. Therefore, when he received word from Sacasa that it was time to discuss a settlement, Sandino agreed. The peace parley ended on January 25, and Sandino announced he would fly to Managua to demonstrate his sincerity. After signing a truce, he slept in the presidential palace. And in a beneficent mood, he declared: "I have nothing against North Americans. Let them come to Nicaragua—as workers, not as bosses." Even American newspapers that had equated him with a highwayman allowed in editorials that he was a "patriot."

Granted amnesty, eighteen hundred guerrillas surrendered one-fourth of their arms and were given preference in public work projects and land along the Coco River for a communal enterprise. Sandino refused any compensation but retained a personal guard of one hundred men. As if to show that everything was now settled, Somoza had a photographer snap a picture of him in a back-thumping embrace with the rebel leader.

The following year was an uneasy one; Sandino learned that the absence of Americans did not automatically usher in social change. National Guardsmen made life hard for the disarmed *Sandinistas*; President Sacasa, concerned only with his own stability, played Somoza off against Sandino, keeping them both edgy. And though Sandino drew satisfaction from having expelled the American Army, and from the belief that his moral stance was unimpeachable, he felt a sense of impending doom.

In February 1934, when Sandino's complaints of Guard cruelties to his men could be ignored no longer, Sacasa invited the former rebel to come down out of the highlands to Managua. A presidential envoy, Sonfonías Salvatierra, assured Sandino that Sacasa was planning no perfidy.

At 5:00 P.M. on February 21, Sandino and his father dined at the presidential palace. Concurrently, a council of war convened at the home of Anastasio Somoza, who told the sixteen assembled officers some astonishing news, the veracity of which has never been proved. Somoza claimed he had just come from the American Embassy, where Ambassador Arthur Bliss Lane assured him that the Washington government supported and recommended the elimination of Augusto César Sandino as a threat to Nicaraguan peace. All present signed a document committing them to the pact, which rapidly took shape.

At 10:00 P.M. Sandino, his father, two *Sandinista* generals, and the Sacasa aide Salvatierra said good-night, boarded a limousine, and left the palace grounds. Several hundred yards down the road their passage was blocked by an apparently stalled truck attended by Guardsmen. A sergeant toting a Thompson machine gun ordered the Sandino party out of the car. Sandino told the men not to resist, because of the presence of his father and Salvatierra. A civilian who saw what was happening hurried back to the palace to inform Sacasa, who immediately tried to phone Somoza. There was no answer. Sandino remonstrated with the guards. "Why do this, if we're all brothers?" he asked. "All I've done is fight for Nicaragua's liberty." He persuaded a major to call Somoza, but the officer returned a few minutes later to say he could not find him.

Sandino climbed into the truck, saying that it was obviously a military order, and "that is obeyed immediately." His two generals followed. Don Gregorio and Salvatierra (who provided this account) were allowed their freedom.

After a short ride the three condemned men were taken to a remote place, allowed to sit on a rock, and shot. Sandino's last words, according to the firing squad, were: "My political leaders have played jokes with me."

Augusto's brother Sócrates was also killed that night. Meanwhile in the remote community of Wiwilí on the Coco River, National Guardsmen crept up on Sandino's disarmed followers and slaughtered three hundred men, women, and children.

"It was pure patriotism to kill Sandino," exulted the retired Moncada from Granada. General Somoza, present at the same celebratory banquet, said the death was inevitable, as Sandino had been planning to overthrow the government. At another banquet, this one at the American Embassy, a drunken Somoza boasted openly of having ordered the assassination. To lend legality to the murder, the National Guard began releasing "evidence" of a longstanding Sandinist plot.

President Sacasa, a virtual prisoner in his own palace, was finally ousted in a coup in 1936, succeeded by a Somoza henchman. In November of that year, Anastasio Somoza was elected president, thus beginning a brutal political dynasty that, inherited in 1956 by his son, ruled Nicaragua with American acquiescence until revolution deposed it in 1979. It is one of history's ironies that finds Nicaragua today with rebels again in the Segovian highlands, and a shaky regime trying to survive in Managua. But many of the guerrillas are former *Somozista* National Guardsmen, and the government, which enshrined Sandino's memory by appropriating his name, is Marxist, a philosophy the nationalist leader never believed in.

# II. U.S. POLICY IN THE 1980S: SUPPORT FOR THE COUNTERREVOLUTION

## EDITOR'S INTRODUCTION

From the time of Ronald Reagan's assumption of the presidency early in 1981, the U.S. administration's policy toward the Sandinista government has been deeply and unrelentingly hostile. The articles comprising the second part of this book examine the present official U.S. attitude toward Nicaragua and the complex and emotional arguments surrounding the centerpiece of U.S. Nicaraguan policy: financial support for the Contras, the Nicaraguan counterrevolutionaries who militarily oppose the Sandinistas on Nicaraguan soil.

The first article, by William M. LeoGrande, excerpted from the book *Nicaragua: The First Five Years,* closely examines particular aspects of the Reagan administration's antagonistic attitude, including the ongoing dispute with Congress over the overt and covert means employed in the struggle against the Sandinistas. Secretary of State George P. Shultz, in the second (*Department of State Bulletin*) article, offers an overall justification for U.S. policy from the administration's point of view; then two U.S. senators, the late John P. East and Edward M. Kennedy, present Congressional arguments, reprinted from *Congressional Digest,* for and against the administration's initiatives.

The case for the Contras is summarized in the fifth article, by the editors of the *New Republic.* Robert Leiken, who has written widely on Nicaragua during the 1980s, then offers, in another *New Republic* article, measured support for the Contras' aims coupled with an expression of considerable dismay at their methods and organization. Edgar Chamorro, a Contra leader from 1982 to 1984, presents in the seventh article, also reprinted from *New Republic,* an inside analysis of the activities of the U.S. Central Intelligence Agency in masterminding the Nicaraguan insurgency. Finally, Eldon Kenworthy, writing in *Current History,* offers a detailed account of the failings of U.S. policy in Central America.

## THE UNITED STATES AND NICARAGUA[1]

As the insurrection against Somoza gathered momentum in 1978 and early 1979, the clear objective of U.S. policy was to prevent the FSLN from gaining a predominant position in a post-Somoza regime. Washington bent every effort to this end, with the sole exception of restoring large-scale military assistance to the National Guard—an option so at odds with the human rights emphasis of the Carter Administration's foreign policy that it was ruled out.

When the dynasty collapsed on July 17, 1979, U.S. policy shifted 180 degrees from an attitude of outright hostility toward the FSLN to one of cautious cordiality. The change was no less stark for having been forced by circumstances, since it carried with it the implication that even radical social and political change in Nicaragua did not necessarily endanger the vital interests of the United States.

Nevertheless, considerable tension born of mistrust lay below the surface of this peculiar friendship. The long history of U.S. support for the Somozas could not be wholly forgiven or forgotten by Nicaragua's new leaders, nor could they shake the fear and suspicion that Washington might yet concoct a counterrevolutionary scheme to rob them of their victory. In Washington, policymakers could not ignore the Marxist origin of many of the Sandinista leaders, even though Somoza's defeat had been engineered by a politically heterogeneous multiclass coalition. There was always the possibility that the guerrillas, having won power, would shed their moderate garb, dump their middle class allies, and steer the Revolution sharply to the left down the road of Cuban-style Marxism-Leninism.

Yet the interests of both Nicaragua and the United States lay in maintaining cordial relations if at all possible. Nicaragua was in desperate need of foreign assistance to rebuild an economy shattered by war. The United States had pledged to help in the recovery effort as part of the arrangements for Somoza's departure, but the maintenance of cordial relations was obviously a

[1]By William M. LeoGrande, associate professor of political science at American University. From *Nicaragua: The First Five Years* edited by Thomas W. Walker. Copyright © 1985 Praeger Publishers. Reprinted by permission of Praeger Publishers.

necessary condition for the fulfillment of that promise. Moreover, international assistance from Latin America, Western Europe, and the international financial community would tend to follow the lead of the United States. A deterioration of U.S.-Nicaraguan relations would therefore have economic ramifications far beyond the aid dollars from Washington alone.

For the United States, maintaining cordial relations was a means of salvaging something from the failure to keep the FSLN out of power. Although, from Washington's perspective, the insurrection had been "lost," perhaps Nicaragua itself need not be. Policymakers in the United States set out quite consciously to avoid repeating the errors of 1959–60 when U.S. hostility drove the Cuban Revolution into alliance with the Soviet Union.

The Carter Administration's objectives were realistically suited to circumstances in which the United States had limited leverage. Washington recognized that the revolutionary coalition was inherently unstable. Once the overriding objective of defeating Somoza had been accomplished, the coalition was bound to deteriorate as it confronted the issue of what postrevolutionary Nicaragua should look like. The Sandinistas' "logic of the majority" could be pursued only at the expense of their upper and middle class allies, and that would inevitably produce conflict. Washington's objective was not to prevent such conflict, but rather to keep it within reasonable bounds, preventing a radicalization of the Revolution that would eliminate the private sector and any vestige of political pluralism.

In foreign policy, it was clear that Nicaragua would have a strong and friendly relationship with Cuba, the only country that had consistently supported the FSLN in its struggle against Somoza. Washington had no illusion that it could block a close relationship between Cuba and Nicaragua, but it hoped to minimize it, particularly in the military field. There was little doubt that the Sandinistas would support the Salvadoran guerrillas, since they had supported the Sandinistas during the insurrection against Somoza. But Washington hoped to restrain Nicaraguan involvement so that it would not constitute a major factor in the Salvadoran war.

During the first year of revolutionary government in Nicaragua, none of the worst fears of either side was realized. Despite conflicts between the FSLN and the private sector, capitalism was not abolished and pluralism, though not robust, survived. On occasion, U.S. Ambassador Lawrence Pezzullo acted as mediator between the government and opposition to prevent their disputes from escalating into apocalyptic confrontation.

Nicaragua's relationship with Cuba blossomed quickly as Cuba sent several thousand teachers, hundreds of medical experts, and scores of technical advisors (including some military personnel) to help Nicaragua reconstruct. The Sandinistas preferred Cuban military advisors to Panamanians, but their numbers remained relatively small.

Finally, though there was evidence of arms flows from Nicaragua to El Salvador in early 1980, the amounts were not substantial. President Carter chose to interpret the intelligence findings generously, accepting the Nicaraguan government's assurances that any arms smuggling was being undertaken contrary to its policy. In September he certified to Congress, as required by law, that Nicaragua was not exporting violence to its neighbors and was therefore eligible to receive $75 million in economic assistance.

As the 1980 U.S. presidential election approached, the Carter Administration's efforts to moderate the Nicaraguan Revolution seemed reasonably successful. The Sandinistas understood the implicit "rules of the game" and generally abided by them. Nicaragua, Ambassador Pezzullo declared, was "an acceptable model" of revolution.

## The Reagan Transition

The architecture of Carter's whole Central America policy began to collapse as soon as Ronald Reagan was elected president. Throughout the region, political forces on both the right and left began acting in anticipation of what Reagan's policy would be. The Republican Party platform called for halting U.S. aid to "Marxist" Nicaragua and helping the Nicaraguan people "restore democracy." Key Reagan advisors were on record attacking the Carter Administration for "losing" Nicaragua to communism and urging less reticence in the use of military force abroad to resist Cuban-Soviet expansion. In December the report of Reagan's State Department transition team was leaked to the press; at the top of a "hit list" of ambassadors slated for immediate replacement were Robert White in El Salvador and Lawrence Pezzullo in Nicaragua.

In both Washington and Managua, virtually everyone expected the new administration to adopt a policy of hostility toward
Nicaragua and to vastly increase U.S. military aid to El Salvador.
The Salvadoran revolutionary movement sought to preempt
Reagan by mounting a "final offensive" to depose the Salvadoran
regime on the eve of Reagan's inauguration, thereby confronting
him with a fait accompli.

For the arms to mount such an offensive the Salvadoran guerrillas turned to Cuba, Nicaragua, and the Eastern bloc. For Managua, the request posed a difficult dilemma. The Sandinistas had
faced a similar supply problem prior to the final offensive against
Somoza, and Cuba had helped fill the breach. Yet the issue of
Nicaraguan aid to the Salvadoran insurgency was the most sensitive issue in Managua's relations with Washington. Though the
Sandinistas had turned a blind eye to the Salvadorans' use of Nicaragua as a way station in their own arms smuggling operations,
the Nicaraguans had refrained from making a major commitment to the guerrillas in order to maintain their relationship with
the United States.

The expectation that Reagan's policy toward Nicaragua
would be a hostile one regardless of how the Sandinistas behaved
diminished the incentive for moderation so carefully crafted by
the Carter Administration. In November and December 1980,
U.S. intelligence detected a major increase in the flow of arms
into El Salvador from Cuba and Nicaragua.

In its last few weeks in office, the Carter Administration was
forced to respond to the unraveling of its Nicaragua policy, even
though events had slipped beyond control through no fault of its
own. The September certification that Nicaragua was not exporting revolution had been the subject of intense controversy within
the administration, partly because the intelligence community
had evidence of some arms flows even then, and partly because
conservatives in the administration had hoped to block the certification until after the November election. In December 1980
and January 1981, as evidence of Nicaragua's complicity in the
arms smuggling became unequivocal, the pressure to "decertify"
became intense. In January the Carter Administration announced that it was suspending the $15 million in economic aid
not yet disbursed from the $75 million aid package on the
grounds that Nicaragua was shipping arms to the revolutionaries
in El Salvador. By suspending the aid rather than canceling it,

Washington held out the prospect that it might be restored if Nicaragua changed its behavior. That, however, would be a determination that would fall to President Reagan.

The Reagan Administration immediately seized upon Central America as a perfect issue with which to assert its new hard line foreign policy. Secretary of State Alexander Haig, anxious to establish himself as the "vicar" of foreign policy, declared the region to be a "test case" in the struggle with international communism. Haig's major concern was the defeat of the guerrilla insurgency in El Salvador; his metaphor of "drawing the line" against communism was apt, for Haig's policy was vintage containment.

The lesson Haig learned from Vietnam was that you must "go to the source" to defeat a guerrilla insurgency—that is, cut off external logistical support for the insurgents. But during the early weeks of the new administration, Haig was not irrevocably convinced that "going to the source" required military action; if external support for the Salvadoran Revolution could be ended by diplomatic means, that would do just as well.

Pezzullo was able to convince Haig that it was possible to reestablish the understanding between Nicaragua and the United States that had prevailed during the Carter Administration. With the proper mix of economic incentives and the specter of U.S. hostility, the Sandinistas could be persuaded to halt their material assistance to the Salvadoran guerrillas. Pezzullo was so convincing that in February he was able almost singlehandedly to defeat an effort by administration hard-liners to make the suspension of economic aid to Nicaragua permanent. Instead, the administration set a 30-day deadline for Nicaragua to end the arms flow into El Salvador.

From Managua's perspective, the Reagan Administration was not acting quite as anticipated. Pezzullo had not been fired; on the contrary, he was insisting that the old rules of the game, if reestablished, could still form the basis of a workable relationship. The Salvadorans' final offensive had failed so dismally it was clear that there would be no victory there in the foreseeable future, and the Sandinistas' irritation at having been misled by the Salvadorans about their strength made Nicaragua amenable to Pezzullo's proposal. Nicaragua assured Washington that it would refrain from further aid to the Salvadorans, closed a clandestine Salvadoran radio station operating on the outskirts of Managua, and began to curtail the flow of weapons. By mid-March, U.S. intelligence indicated that the flow was much reduced, and the administration's 30-day deadline was extended because of Nicaragua's efforts to comply.

At this point Pezzullo's efforts were derailed by administrative hard-liners whose objective was not simply to contain the insurgency in El Salvador but also to roll back "communism" in Nicaragua. In late March they launched a second effort to cut off economic aid. Pezzullo was not informed until the decision had already been made, and it was leaked to the press before he had an opportunity to notify the Nicaraguans. The announcement of the aid cutoff was made, appropriately enough, on April Fool's Day. A few months later Pezzullo resigned his ambassadorship and retired from the Foreign Service.

Relations between Nicaragua and the United States stagnated for the next few months, but Central America returned to the top of the Reagan Administration's agenda in June when the Salvadoran guerrillas launched a surprisingly strong offensive that destroyed Washington's hopes for a quick military victory there. Once again, Haig was intent upon "going to the source," initiating the first of several attempts to convince Reagan of the need to blockade Cuba.

With regard to Nicaragua, Thomas Enders, the newly installed Assistant Secretary of State for Inter-American Affairs, was prepared, like Pezzullo had been, to try to close the Nicaraguan arms channel by diplomatic means. He convinced a reluctant Haig to let him make the effort.

In August 1981 Enders traveled secretly to Managua to open discussions with the Sandinistas. He set forth two basic conditions for an improvement in bilateral relations: Nicaragua must halt its support for the Salvadoran guerrillas, which intelligence sources indicated was continuing, albeit at a level well below that of late 1980; and it must curtail its own military buildup, which had accelerated after the collapse of the Pezzullo initiative. In exchange, the administration would sign a nonaggression pact with Nicaragua under the terms of the Rio Treaty, make an effort to close exile paramilitary training camps in the United States, and ask Congress to restore economic aid to Nicaragua.

The Sandinistas, deeply skeptical of Washington's intentions after the fiasco of February–March, did not respond positively to Enders's proposals. They denied supplying arms to the Salvadoran guerrillas and rejected any constraint on their own military posture as a violation of their sovereignty. They also regarded Washington's promises as hollow. The Rio Treaty already obligated the United States to refrain from the threat or use of force against Nicaragua, and the U.S. Neutrality Act prohibited training camps of the sort operating in Florida and California. If the Reagan Administration was unwilling to comply with domestic and international laws already on the books, of what value would any additional pledge be? The idea that Congress would restore economic aid was particulary farfetched, since only the most strenuous efforts of the Carter Administration had managed to get congressional approval of the $75 million aid package in 1980.

Between August and October 1981, Nicaragua and the United States exchanged a number of communications on these issues. Within the Reagan Administration, the hardliners were able to insist that Washington's proposals be phrased in imperial language certain to irritate the nationalism of the Sandinista leadership. The only agreement that was reached was that each side would refrain from using incendiary public rhetoric against the other.

Even this thin thread was broken in October when the United States conducted an amphibious assault exercise with the Honduran Armed Forces as part of the Halcon Vista joint maneuvers. At the United Nations, Daniel Ortega denounced the exercises as a rehearsal for an attack on Nicaragua. Washington interpreted this as a violation of the agreement to suspend the war of words and on that basis broke off the diplomatic dialogue.

Two years later, with the wisdom of hindsight, the Sandinistas wished they had been more receptive to the Enders proposal since, despite the language in which it was posed, it was close to Pezzullo's offer. By allowing their distrust of Washington and their offense at the proposal's style to divert them from its substance, they allowed the hard-liners in the Reagan Administration to defeat those who sought a diplomatic concordat. With the failure of the Enders initiative, Washington turned to the more traditional means of dealing with renegade Latins—brute force.

*The Not-So-Secret War*

In early October 1981 the Salvadoran guerrillas launched a major offensive against the government, scoring successes far beyond anything anticipated in Washington. While their June offensive had produced serious concern within the administration, their fall offensive set off a panic. A full-scale review of U.S. policy in Central America was undertaken; some, including Secretary Haig, warned ominously of the collapse of El Salvador unless the United States acted decisively. True to form, Haig still looked to the source, recommending direct military action against both Cuba and Nicaragua, if not El Salvador itself.

Haig's call to war was opposed within the administration by the Joint Chiefs of Staff. The Joint Chiefs recommended against Haig's proposal to blockade Cuba on the grounds that it risked confrontation with the Soviet Union, would divert naval forces from more critical theaters around the globe, and would probably not achieve its professed objective of halting arms shipments to Central America. They also opposed direct involvement in El Salvador or Nicaragua, not wishing to enlist in a potentially unwinnable and politically unpopular ground war that could demolish the recently reconstituted congressional majority for a major strategic buildup.

In a series of National Security Council meetings in November, President Reagan approved a ten-point policy plan for Central America. Haig's proposals for direct military action were rejected; instead the United States would increase military aid to El Salvador and Honduras, expand the U.S. military presence throughout the Caribbean Basin by mounting large military exercises, expand the CIA's intelligence-gathering capacity in Central America, develop military contingency plans for the region, and initiate covert paramilitary operations against Nicaragua. In part, approval of covert operations against Nicaragua was a consolation prize for Haig, to ease the pain of his failure to convince Reagan of the need for direct military action.

During the November National Security Council meetings, the CIA proposed a variety of covert operations. The least controversial was to continue a program of financial aid to internal opponents of the Sandinistas begun by the Carter Administration and expanded when Reagan first came to office. Recipients of this largesse reportedly included opposition labor organizations, political parties, press, and the private sector. A second program, also approved without opposition, was to expand U.S. intelligence-gathering capabilities in Central America as a whole.

Among the paramilitary operations proposed, the most ambitious called for the CIA to assemble, train, and arm a commando force of 500 Latin Americans, mostly Cuban exiles, to conduct military operations against Nicaragua from base camps in Honduras. The primary mission of this force would be to attack Nicaragua's economic infrastructure in the hope that the resulting economic hardship would produce political destabilization. It was also suggested that such a force would enable the United States to take "paramilitary action against special Cuban targets" in Central America. The initial budget for this option was reportedly $19.95 million.

A second paramilitary option, proposed as a complement of rather than an alternative to the first, called for the United States to provide financial and logistical support for an Argentine effort, already underway, to train 1,000 Nicaraguan exiles for the purpose of overthrowing the Nicaraguan government.

A third more limited option involved funneling military aid, particularly small arms, through the Honduran Armed Forces to Nicaraguan exiles already operating along the Nicaraguan-Honduran border. This may have been simply an extension of a paramilitary operation approved in March 1981 to interdict arms flows from Nicaragua to guerrillas in El Salvador and Guatemala.

The CIA's paramilitary plans touched off a heated debate within the Reagan Administration over the goals of U.S. policy toward Nicaragua. Some officials argued that the program of covert operations should be aimed at overthrowing the Sandinista government. Others, including some officials from the State Department, the Defense Department, and even the CIA itself, argued that the objective of U.S. policy should be the more limited one of interdicting the flow of arms from Nicaragua to the Salvadoran guerrillas. This second group argued that efforts to overthrow the Sandinistas would inevitably entangle the United States in a partnership with the remnants of Somoza's National Guard—an association that would allow the Sandinistas to rally popular opinion in their favor. They also warned that efforts to depose the Sandinistas would spark a wider regional war, drawing the United States into direct military involvement.

After an extended debate within the administration, President Reagan signed National Security Decision Directive 17 as well as a December 2, 1981, Presidential Finding that granted the CIA broad authority to conduct covert political and paramilitary operations against Cuba and Cuban supply lines in Nicaragua and elsewhere in Central America, and to cooperate with other governments to accomplish this.

The CIA was authorized to proceed with the creation of the 500-man commando force, to assist Argentina in the creation of a larger army of Nicaraguan exiles, to establish direct liaison with exile groups based in Honduras, and to work toward the creation of a broad political opposition front to the Sandinistas. Those in the administration who sought to overthrow the Sandinistas won a victory; all the operations initially proposed were approved. Those who thought a program to overthrow the Sandinistas would be counterproductive managed to salvage something, though. The objective of the paramilitary programs approved by the president was defined as the limited one of interdicting arms flows, and it was to be implemented without giving direct assistance to the former National Guardsmen.

When the CIA's program of covert operations was presented to the Intelligence Committees of Congress, many members voiced concerns similar to those that had been debated within the administration. There was strong bipartisan opposition to creating the 500-man commando force to attack "special Cuban targets." As a result, this aspect of the operation was apparently dropped. In addition, the intelligence committees approved guidelines restricting the objective of the paramilitary operations to arms interdiction.

Like most policies that are arrived at through a process of bureaucratic bargaining and compromise, the elements of the CIA's covert operation against Nicaragua were not entirely consistent with one another. In order for the United States to avoid involvement with Somoza's Guardsmen, Argentina was slated to supervise the creation and operation of the exile army, and to act along with Honduras as a conduit for military supplies. It made little substantive difference, however, whether U.S. aid to the contras was provided directly or laundered through Honduras and Argentina. Moreover, while the United States was supposedly limited to interdicting arms, Argentina was explicitly creating an exile army in order to overthrow the Sandinistas, and the exiles themselves were, of course, dedicated to the same end. Finally, within the Reagan Administration itself, operational control over the covert war fell to people who had, from the outset, advocated getting rid of the Sandinistas rather than simply containing them.

The Falklands/Malvinas war brought these inherent problems to the surface. When Washington sided with Great Britain, Argentina began to withdraw from Central America. As Argentina withdrew, the United States gradually assumed control over the operations that Argentina had begun—providing arms, money, and training to the expanding exile army in Honduras. To stay within the original guidelines of the policy (which prohibited direct U.S. aid to the exiles) an elaborate system was constructed so that U.S. efforts could be handled through the Honduran Armed Forces. But this arrangement could not conceal the fact that the United States had assumed the central role in the covert war in the wake of Argentina's withdrawal.

The covert war was the most important element in the administration's policy of hostility toward the Sandinistas, but it was by no means the only one. As the exile army was being assembled, the administration mounted a campaign to cripple the Nicaraguan economy by cutting off external sources of financing. The Sandinistas inherited an economy devastated by war and bankrupted by Somoza's larceny. They faced a Herculean task of reconstruction at a time of global recession that, under the best of circumstances, would have meant hardship for an underdeveloped export economy like Nicaragua's. During the first two years of revolutionary government, the Sandinistas received crucial financial aid from international financial institutions, Latin America, Western Europe, and the United States.

The Reagan Administration halted bilateral aid to Nicaragua almost immediately. As the policy of hostility unfolded in late 1981 and early 1982, the administration moved to cut off other sources of bilateral and multilateral assistance as well. To discourage private businesses in the United States from investing in Nicaragua or trading with the Sandinista government, Nicaragua was excluded from the programs of the Export-Import Bank (which provides short-term credits to facilitate trade) and the Overseas Private Investment Corporation (which offers insurance for U.S. companies investing abroad). To discourage private banks from loaning to Nicaragua, the U.S. government's Inter-Agency Exposure Review Committee, which rates underdeveloped nations' creditworthiness, downgraded Nicaragua's rating in early 1983 from "substandard" to "doubtful"—despite the fact that Nicaragua was at that time on schedule with its repayment of the massive external debt inherited from Somoza.

From November 1981 onward, the United States voted against all loans to Nicaragua in both the World Bank and the Inter-American Development Bank on the dubious grounds that the macroeconomic situation in Nicaragua was so bad that development loans could not be used effectively. In general, the United States was outvoted when loans came up for review, but when serious objections to a loan are raised in these banks, the normal procedure is to defer consideration of it. The size of the U.S. contribution to the banks gives the U.S. representative considerable political leverage. The exercise of that leverage to block loans to Nicaragua caused sharp controversy within the banks, but the fact remains that loans to Nicaragua virtually ceased. In 1979 Nicaragua received $179 million from the Inter-American Development Bank and the World Bank; in 1983 it received only $30 million.

Following the model established by the CIA's successful destabilization of the Allende government in Chile, the Reagan Administration's credit blockade was combined with a program of economic sabotage. Beginning in mid-1982, the exile raids from Honduras targeted economic resources—farms, bridges, warehouses, and so one. In 1983 the CIA took direct control of major sabotage operations, carrying out the successful attack on the oil storage facilities at Corinto on October 11, and a series of speedboat attacks on shipping in Nicaraguan harbors. In January 1984 the CIA escalated its campaign to disrupt shipping by mining Nicaragua's major ports, but the mining operation brought forth such a firestorm of criticism from Latin America, Western Europe, the U.S. Congress, and the World Court that it was subsequently halted.

In addition to the covert war and the effort to strangle the Nicaraguan economy, the Reagan Administration's policy of hostility also included a major political offensive with several distinct elements: explicit threats of military action designed to intimidate the Sandinistas; vociferous denunciations of the Nicaraguan regime designed to build domestic political support for the administration's overall Central American policy; and diplomatic efforts to isolate Nicaragua from both its neighbors and potential friends in Western Europe.

In the last week of November 1981, both Haig and Presidential Counselor Edwin Meese warned that although Reagan had ruled out the use of U.S. troops in Central America, other military actions, including a naval blockade of Nicaragua, were still being considered. The rhetoric grew so intense that Mexican president José López-Portillo was moved to describe it as "verbal terrorism" and to warn that a U.S. attack on Nicaragua would be "a gigantic historical error."

At the Organization of American States (OAS) meeting in St. Lucia in December, Haig, invoking the Rio Treaty, called for joint hemispheric action to block Nicaraguan and Cuban subversion. He also repeated the warning that the United States would do whatever was "prudent and necessary" to prevent any nation in Central America from becoming a "platform for terror and war."

At home, the Reagan Administration launched a public relations campaign to portray Nicaragua as a Marxist-Leninist dictatorship guilty of gross human rights abuses, a pawn of Cuba and the Soviet Union, and the primary source of external support for the Salvadoran insurgency. United Nations Ambassador Jeane Kirkpatrick led the assault on Nicaragua's human rights record, characterizing the regime as a totalitarian dictatorship "even more repressive . . . than was the dictatorship of Somoza." Secretary Haig focused on Nicaragua's alleged assistance to the Salvadoran guerrillas. In March he charged that the Salvadoran insurgency was being run out of Managua.

By far the most impressive element of the administration's public relations campaign against the Sandinistas was a press briefing conducted jointly by the CIA and the Defense Intelligence Agency. The briefing was organized to convey the drama of the Cuban Missile Crisis. It was conducted by the same analyst, replete with aerial reconnaissance photographs labeled in the same way as the famous missile sites two decades earlier. The thrust of the briefing was that Nicaragua had undertaken a major military buildup with Cuban and Soviet assistance, a buildup so far beyond normal defense requirements that it must be intended for aggressive use against Nicaragua's neighbors.

The substance of the briefing was not very compelling. The most ubiquitous photographic evidence was "Cuban-style obstacle courses" at various Sandinista military bases. Absent from the briefing was any evidence that the Nicaraguans had introduced

major new weapons systems or that they were systematically channeling arms to the Salvadoran guerrillas. As the Nicaraguans
were quick to point out, they had never denied that they were
strengthening their military or that they were receiving military
aid from the socialist bloc; what did the United States expect, Sergio Ramírez asked, when Washington was fomenting counterrevolution?

The aerial briefing, for all its theatrics, was fundamentally
disingenuous. The administration was fully aware that the
Sandinistas had neither the capability nor the intention of invading their neighbors, and that their military buildup was, as they
claimed, defensive. Administration spokesmen, in a classified version of the aerial briefing given to the House Intelligence Committee, admitted as much.

The administration's public relations campaign collapsed a
few days later when the State Department arranged a press briefing to display a Nicaraguan soldier allegedly sent to command
guerrilla forces in El Salvador. The young Nicaraguan, captured
the previous year in El Salvador, recanted his story as soon as
briefing began. He claimed that he had gone to fight in El Salvador on his own accord, and that the story of his being ordered
there after training in Ethiopia was entirely fabricated—a product of torture at the hands of the Salvadoran armed forces. The
debacle produced an immediate suspension of the administration's campaign to rally domestic opinion.

On the diplomatic front, the administration sought to isolate
Nicaragua from its Central American neighbors and to reduce
West European support for the Sandinistas. In early 1982, France
announced that it had agreed to sell $16 million of military equip-
ment to Nicaragua. The administration was outraged. Under
U.S. pressure, France delayed shipment of the military supplies
and agreed not to make any additional sales. Similar pressures
were brought to bear on other West European countries, not only
to prevent arms shipments to Nicaragua but to reduce economic
support for the Sandinistas as well. This effort was only partially
successful. No further military equipment went to Nicaragua
from Europe, but significant amounts of economic assistance continued to flow.

In Central America, the United States organized the Central
American Democratic Community, composed of Costa Rica,
Honduras, and El Salvador. The explicit objective of the new or-

ganization was to seek joint measures to counter Nicaragua, but the whole enterprise was so transparently a creation of the United States that it faded quickly into oblivion after its initial meetings.

The administration combined these diplomatic moves with military actions designed to intimidate the Sandinistas. In addition to the constant drumbeat of rhetoric about Nicaraguan subversion and the willingness of the United States to counter it with force, the administration undertook a massive military buildup in Honduras. From fiscal year (FY) 1980 to FY 1984, U.S. military aid to Honduras rose from $3.9 million to $78.5; the number of U.S. military personnel stationed there (apart from troops participating in exercises) rose from 26 to 346; and the United States built or planned to build 11 military installations at a total cost of $87.85 million. All of this was justified to Congress as necessary to counter the threat of aggression from Nicaragua.

But the most dramatic efforts at intimidation were the U.S. military exercises mounted in Honduras and off Nicaragua's coasts. Beginning with the relatively small Halcon Vista joint maneuvers with Honduras in October 1981, the implicit or in some cases the explicit purpose of all the exercises was to "pressure" Nicaragua by demonstrating the ability of the United States to project military force into Central America. The exercises grew larger and longer in duration; by 1984 they had become virtually continuous, leading some congressional critics to conclude that the exercises were a façade for the permanent stationing of U.S. forces in the region.

### The Search for Peace

As the U.S. policy of hostility toward Nicaragua unfolded, Mexico became increasingly fearful that the conflict in Central America might spiral out of control, leading to direct U.S. intervention. To avert such a catastrophe, President López-Portillo on several occasions offered Mexico's good offices as an intermediary between Nicaragua and the United States. In December 1981 Haig traveled to Mexico City to confer with López-Portillo, and the Mexicans agreed to convey the Reagan Administration's concerns to Nicaragua.

Mexico's mediation led to a meeting between Haig and Nicaraguan Foreign Minister Miguel D'Escoto in St. Lucía just prior to the OAS General Assembly. Haig raised the two issues that had been discussed by Enders in the August–October exchanges— Nicaragua's arms buildup and its aid to the Salvadoran guerrillas—but he also added a new issue: U.S. concern over the decline of political freedom inside Nicaragua. D'Escoto repeated earlier Nicaraguan denials that it was aiding the Salvadorans or that it had any intention of acquiring MIG fighter aircraft—a charge that had been made repeatedly by administration spokesmen. Little more than a restatement of positions on both sides, the meeting had no salutary effect.

The Mexicans, however, were not prepared to give up. Having failed in their attempt at quiet diplomacy, they launched a more public effort. Speaking in Managua in late February, López-Portillo warned of the "three knots of tension" in Central America: the conflict in El Salvador, the hostility between the United States and Nicaragua, and the hostility between the United States and Cuba. He offered Mexico as mediator to help launch negotiations around each of these issues.

Nicaragua, Cuba, and the Salvadoran opposition quickly accepted the López-Portillo initiative. The United States was less interested. President Reagan, in a major address to the OAS given the week after López-Portillo's proposal, made no reference to the Mexican plan. Administration spokesmen told the press that no improvement in relations with Nicaragua were possible until the Sandinistas stopped aiding the Salvadoran guerrillas.

Congress, however, responded positively to the Mexican initiative; 106 members of the House of Representatives signed a letter to Reagan urging him to accept the Mexican plan. The administration was forced at least to pronounce its receptivity to the initiative, lest it appear to be the major obstacle to peace in the region. After a series of meetings between U.S. and Mexican officials, the administration finally agreed to allow Mexico to convey the U.S. position to Nicaragua. The agenda of U.S. concerns was essentially the same as what Haig had presented to D'Escoto in December. Nicaragua responded immediately that it was willing to discuss all the issues raised by the United States and set forth an agenda of its own as well. The United States, however, was not prepared to begin discussions until after the Salvadoran election in late March.

The Salvadoran election was a benchmark for U.S. policy in Central America. With the war in El Salvador going badly, the administration had wagered a great deal on the outcome of the elections. They would, it was hoped, convince the Congress to continue its support of administration policy. In that regard at least, the election proved to be a great success. In their wake, the administration's attitude toward Nicaragua hardened perceptibly. U.S. officials told reporters that the administration would not open direct discussions with Nicaragua until it halted its aid to the Salvadoran guerrillas, regardless of the Mexican proposals. Yet even this position was something of a façade. One official explained the administration's attitude toward the López-Portillo initiative: "We were cool to the initiative from the beginning, but we were effectively ambushed by Congress and public opinion. We had to agree to negotiate or appear unreasonable."

In fact, the administration had no interest in negotiating with Nicaragua. The text of a National Security Council planning document written during this period summarizes U.S. policy as stepping up pressure on Nicaragua, isolating Mexico, and "coopt[ing] the negotiations issue." No mention is even made of the López-Portillo initiative.

Contacts between Nicaragua and the United States under the auspices of the López-Portillo plan limped along until August 1982, with Nicaragua constantly urging that negotiations be started and the United States refusing. Finally, in August the administration abandoned even this pretext; Nicaragua's diplomatic note of August never received a reply.

During July and August 1982, Nicaraguan exiles launched a series of major attacks against Nicaragua from their base camps in Honduras. As rumors of war between Nicaragua and Honduras swept the region, President Herrera Campins of Venezuela and López-Portillo appealed to Nicaragua, Honduras, and the United States to take swift diplomatic action to avert the outbreak of war. It was the first joint Mexican-Venezuelan initiative on Central America and marked a change from Venezuela's previous support of U.S. policy.

The Mexican-Venezuelan letter proposed measures to reduce the border tensions between Nicaragua and Honduras and urged the United States to upgrade its diplomatic contacts with Nicaragua. Once again, congressional support for the initiative was strong. President Reagan's response, however, was noncommittal. In his reply to Herrera Campins and López-Portillo, he reiterated U.S. policy and the proposals made a few weeks earlier at a

meeting of the Central American Forum for Peace and Democracy—a successor to the Central American Democratic Community
and, like its predecessor, a creation of U.S. diplomatic efforts to
isolate Nicaragua. Without the support of the United States,
nothing came of the Mexican-Venezuelan initiative.

## Congress and the Covert War

The covert war against Nicaragua changed in several important ways during the summer and fall of 1982, and these changes
produced a growing concern in Congress about the ultimate intent of U.S. policy. As Argentina gradually withdrew from the
region in the wake of the Falklands/Malvinas war, the CIA assumed control over the exile army that Argentina had been con-
structing. The military assistance provided by the United States
transformed the exile force from a ragtag collection of small, independent groups numbering fewer than 1,000 men in total into
a well-equipped and professionally trained army of some 4,500 by
July 1982. Calling itself the Nicaraguan Democratic Force
(FDN), it increased the size and frequency of its forays into Nicaragua during the summer of 1982.

Most of the attacks came across the eastern and central por-
tions of the Nicaraguan-Honduran border, far from the purport-
ed arms-smuggling routes in the west. This, combined with the
contras' disclaimer that they were trying to interdict arms, made
it difficult for the Reagan Administration to keep up the fiction
that the purpose of the covert war was to interdict arms flowing
from Nicaragua to the Salvadoran guerrillas. In the fall of 1982
the administration changed the basic rationale for the covert war,
at least as it was presented to Congress. Direct arms interdiction
was replaced by the stated objective of harassing and punishing
Nicaragua in order to convince the Sandinistas to end their support for the Salvadoran insurgency. As one administration official explained, "it became clear that cutting the roads from
Nicaragua was not enough. It was necessary to raise the cost to
the Sandinistas and the Cubans of meddling in El Salvador."

In practice, harassment meant exile attacks on border towns,
economic targets, and Nicaraguan army posts—exactly the sorts
of operations originally proposed by the CIA in November 1981
to overthrow the Nicaraguan government, and rejected for that
reason. With this change in U.S. strategy, the line between ha-

rassing Nicaragua to get the Sandinistas to behave and trying to overthrow them became difficult to discern since the operations being mounted served either purpose equally well. In practice, the line disappeared completely since both the U.S. officials running the operations and the contra commanders carrying them out were dedicated to deposing the Nicaraguan regime. By the fall of 1982, the contra army in Honduras was already three times the size of the CIA invasion force at the Bay of Pigs. By mid-1984 it would be almost ten times as large.

As the covert war widened, both the House and Senate Intelligence Committees began to worry that the operation was spiraling out of control. In an effort to hold the CIA to its original objective of arms interdiction, the committees added language to the Classified Annex of the 1983 Intelligence Authorization Act prohibiting U.S. aid to paramilitary groups " for the purpose of overthrowing the Government of Nicaragua or provoking a military exchange between Nicaragua and Honduras."

This language, signed into law in August 1982, was not designed to bring the covert operation to a halt. On the contrary, it was intentionally crafted to register the Intelligence Committees' unease while at the same time allowing the covert war to continue. The Reagan Administration was able to interpret it as allowing support for the contras so long as the purpose of the United States was not among those proscribed by the law. The administration continued to assert that its purpose was merely to halt the flow of arms, so even though the recipients of the CIA's largesse were trying to overthrow the Sandinistas, the law did not make them ineligible for assistance.

This mild restriction remained a secret until December when Representative Tom Harkin (D-Iowa) offered an amendment to the Defense Appropriations Bill (which included appropriations for intelligence activities) to prohibit U.S. assistance to any group involved in paramilitary actions against Nicaragua. Representative Edward Boland (D-Massachusetts), Chairman of the House Intelligence Committee, offered as a substitute for Harkin's amendment the language that had earlier been included in the Intelligence Authorization Act. The Republican leadership, seeking to avoid a vote on the Harkin amendment, supported Boland's substitute, which passed 411-0 and was eventually signed into law.

The administration continued to expand the covert war during the early months of 1983, and the issue returned to the top of the congressional agenda as the war escalated. In March, 1,500 exile troops invaded Nicaragua. Though they were thrown back to Honduras, the new attacks prompted a series of stories in the U.S. press documenting the continued U.S. involvement in training, financing, arming, and advising the exiles.

The new revelations convinced several members of Congress that the administration's real intention was to overthrow the Sandinistas, in violation of the Boland amendment. Daniel Patrick Moynihan (D-New York), Vice-Chairman of the Senate Intelligence Committee, reported that a number of his colleagues on the Committee shared that suspicion. Senator Patrick Leahy (D-Vermont) traveled to Central America on behalf of the Intelligence Committee to investigate U.S. operations and upon his return said that it appeared to him the administration was ignoring the intent of Congress. Representative Wyche Fowler (D-Georgia) conducted a similar investigation for the House Intelligence Committee and returned with the same conclusion. Finally, Boland himself declared that the evidence was "very strong" that the administration was violating the amendment bearing his name.

The pervasive and growing congressional suspicion of the administration's conduct of the covert war led the House Intelligence and Foreign Affairs Committees to propose the Boland-Zablocki amendment to the 1984 Intelligence Authorization Act, an amendment that effectively cut off all funds for the covert war against Nicaragua. On July 28, after several days of bitter debate, the House of Representatives passed the Boland-Zablocki amendment by a vote of 228-195.

The Republican majority in the Senate, however, was not prepared to halt the war. Eventually, the House and Senate reached a compromise whereby the administration received $24 million (about half its initial request) to keep the covert war going from October 1983 to June 1984. In June the administration returned to Congress seeking an additional $21 million, which the Senate again approved. The House, however, was willing to compromise no further; the administration was unable to secure additional funds for the war during 1984. A final congressional review of the issue was slated for March 1985.

The congressional rebellion against the covert war was rooted in a variety of issues: the ineffectiveness of the operation in achieving its stated goals, its counterproductive effects, its tenuous legality, and, perhaps most important, the apparent contempt in which the administration held congressional prerogatives.

The ineffectiveness of the covert war in actually interdicting arms shipments from Nicaragua to El Salvador was apparent early on—no significant amount of arms was ever captured. Virtually no one even within the administration was willing to argue that the operation could actually overthrow the Sandinistas. Moreover, the operation seemed counterproductive in a number of ways. It tended to polarize the internal political situation in Nicaragua, contributing to a reduction of political freedom for the opposition while at the same time rallying the population in support of the Sandinistas. Internal economic difficulties could be, and were, rationalized as the fault of the United States and its Somocista allies. In effect, all the warnings articulated by people within the Reagan Administration who had initially opposed a major commitment to the covert war came true.

Internationally, the covert war angered U.S. allies in Latin America and Europe, and raised the danger of open warfare between Nicaragua and Honduras—a war the Honduran economy was in no shape to sustain. Moreover, the covert war was such an obvious violation of U.S. treaty obligations under the OAS charter, the Rio Treaty, and the United Nations Charter that the standing of the United States in the international community as a whole suffered considerably as the war intensified.

But the issue that ultimately led the House of Representatives to repudiate the war was one of institutional prerogatives. The quality of the administration's reporting to the Intelligence Committees was so poor that members simply stopped believing what they were told. Their efforts to restrain the operation were ignored or circumvented by convoluted interpretations of the law, until they felt there was no alternative but to bring the whole operation to a halt.

### Preparing for War

By early 1983, the Reagan Administration's Central American policy was in crisis. The war in El Salvador was slowly but surely being lost to the guerrillas, the contras had made no military progress against the Sandinistas, and the U.S. Congress was growing restive at the ever-escalating cost of a policy that had yet to show any signs of success. This crisis produced a showdown inside the administration between the relative moderates in the State Department, led by Enders, and the hard-liners in the White House, led by National Security Advisor William Clark and U.N. Ambassador Jeane Kirkpatrick. Various tactical and strategic policy differences divided the two factions, but perhaps the most fundamental issue was whether the United States could prevail in Central America through a strategy of containment (that is, winning the war in El Salvador and containing Nicaragua), or whether the United States would have to roll back "communism" in Nicaragua by removing the Sandinista regime. The hard-liners won, Enders was fired, and the State Department lost control over policy in Central America to the National Security Council, the CIA, and the Department of Defense.

The practical effect of the hard-liners' victory was quickly apparent. In August, just after the House of Representatives voted to halt the covert war, the United States launched Big Pine II, the largest and longest military exercise in Central American history. It lasted seven months and at its height, two carrier battle groups stood off the shores of Nicaragua. The Pentagon also announced a series of further exercises that, taken together, meant virtually continuous maneuvers through 1988. Displaying a sardonic sense of humor, the administration dubbed the exercises after Big Pine II as Granadaro I, no doubt to remind the Sandinistas that the invasion of Grenada began as a naval "exercise."

The newly ascendant hard-liners moved to step up the covert war as well. The CIA was authorized to expand the contra forces to 15,000 men—an army larger than the National Guard the Sandinistas defeated in 1979. It was also at this point that CIA operatives took direct control of sabotage operations against Nicaraguan ports and oil storage facilities.

The intensification of the war was accompanied by an intensification by other countries of the search for peace. In January 1983, Mexico and Venezuela joined with Panama and Colombia to form the Contadora group (named for the Panamanian island where it first met). Fearful that the United States was moving inexorably toward direct military intervention, the four nations hoped their joint efforts might succeed at finding a diplomatic solution for the Central American crisis. In a number of meetings with the foreign ministers of the five Central American nations, the Contadora states made some modest progress. In September the Central American nations, meeting under the auspices of Contadora, reached agreement on 21 objectives in the areas of security, economic cooperation, and politics. In January 1984 these principles were spelled out in greater detail, and working groups were formed to draw up formal accords for implementing them.

In the area of security, where agreement was most difficult to achieve, the basic objectives of Contadora were to remove Central America as much as possible from the East-West rivalry, and to begin to demilitarize the area. The 21 points called for a prohibition on foreign military bases and troops, a reduction of foreign military advisors, a halt to the regional arms race, and an end to external support for insurgencies.

Despite verbal support for the process, the posture of the Reagan administration was a major obstacle for Contadora. In the first place, the United States continued its military buildup in Honduras and El Salvador, as well as its support for the contras, despite the fact that these actions ran counter to the objectives espoused by Contadora. Moreover, the United States consistently held that any diplomatic agreement would have to be both multilateral and comprehensive—that is, all the Central American nations would have to agree on all issues before any agreement on any issue could be concluded.

Although the United States had no direct participation in Contadora, its influence in Honduras and El Salvador gave it the ability to effectively block any agreement that did not suit its policy. The Reagan Administration insisted that a necessary part of any agreement would be a verifiable pledge by the Sandinistas to hold free and fair elections that met Washington's definition of pluralism.

Until June 1984, the administration consistently refused to reply to Nicaraguan diplomatic initiatives, characterizing them as Sandinista efforts to subvert Contadora. In June, however, the United States suddenly reversed itself and agreed to begin bilateral talks with Nicaragua. Those talks lasted until early 1985, when they ware abruptly terminated by the United States.

As the United States entered its own 1984 election campaign, the policy of the Reagan Administration toward Nicaragua seemed to be consolidated and well-defined: to depose the

Sandinista government. Indeed, administration spokesmen, including the President himself, had come close to saying so explicitly on several occasions. Deputy Secretary of Defense Fred Ikle called repeatedly for "military victory" for the "forces of democracy" in Central America, and he warned that the continued existence of the Sandinistas would require a partitioning of Central America analogous to the partitioning of Europe. President Reagan referred to the contras as "freedom fighters" at every opportunity and announced his doubt that peace could be restored to the region as long as the Sandinista government survived. Finally, the Kissinger Commission, which offered the most complete rationale for Reagan's Central American policy, concluded that a policy of "static containment" toward Nicaragua was unacceptable, that the Sandinistas would remain a permanent threat to peace in the region unless the charter of the Nicaraguan regime were changed. The Commission held out the vague hope that the Sandinistas might somehow agree in negotiations to remove themselves from power but, failing that, it noted that force would remain the "ultimate recourse" for achieving U.S. objectives.

The Reagan Administration's dilemma, however, was how to implement this policy. The covert war, under growing attack in the Congress, had not succeeded in posing any serious military threat to the Sandinistas. The economic embargo had damaged the Nicaraguan economy but had not brought it to collapse. The other nations of Central America showed little interest in reviving the Central American Defense Council as an instrument for use against the Sandinistas. In short, Reagan's policy of hostility seemed incapable of achieving its goal. By late 1984 it seemed clear that the second Reagan Administration would have to face the choice of tolerating the Nicaraguan Revolution or intervening directly and massively to exterminate it.

## NICARAGUA AND THE FUTURE
## OF CENTRAL AMERICA[2]

In recent years, around the world, we have seen the yearning for freedom take extraordinary forms. Last week, the world watched as the people of the Philippines rose up to claim their democratic rights and recapture their democratic heritage.

We saw in the Philippines a government increasingly at odds with its own people. We saw a Catholic Church, a middle class, moderate opposition parties, the business community, the media, and other segments of society increasingly disaffected from their government. We saw an election in which the government was shaken by the vigor of the opposition's campaign and sought by fraud to perpetuate itself in power. We can be thankful that as his moral authority slipped away, President Marcos had the wisdom and courage to step down peacefully.

Today, we see similar phenomena in a country much closer to home—Nicaragua. But with a striking difference: it's *far worse* in Nicaragua. There, opposition parties have been systematically harassed and intimidated, including by violence or threat of violence; independent media are not merely hampered but censored or shut down; the Catholic Church has been stifled or abused for being a voice of democratic conscience. The secret police have rounded up leaders of private sector, labor, and church organizations, subjecting them to interrogations and threats. A massive military buildup by the Soviet Union and Cuba threatens not only the regime's internal opponents but all neighboring countries as well. And the regime—after a manipulated election over a year ago—is clearly determined to maintain itself in power by whatever brute force is necessary.

In the Philippines, the forces of democracy were able to rally, organize, compete for and, eventually, win power peacefully, despite the flawed election, because it was, at bottom, a pluralist democratic political system. In Nicaragua, once the communist regime consolidates its power, the forces of democracy will have no such hope. A Leninist regime seeks a monopoly of power and

[2]An address by Secretary of State George P. Shultz before the Veterans of Foreign Wars, Washington, D.C., March 3, 1986. Reprinted from *Department of State Bulletin*, 86:37–40, May, 1986.

the strangulation of all independent institutions. The church, the independent media, the business community, the middle class, and democratic parties are all severely beleaguered and struggling for their very survival. Thousands of the regime's opponents—estimated at as many as 20,000—have been driven to take up arms to resist the communist attempt to consolidate a totalitarian system.

For historical, moral, and strategic reasons, the United States took a direct interest in the progress of Filipino democracy. For similar reasons, we are deeply concerned with the hopes for democracy in Nicaragua. After 6½ years, it is clear that, without our help in strengthening the Nicaraguan democratic opposition, hope for democracy in Nicaragua is doomed and progress elsewhere in Central America could be undone.

*Subversion Abroad*

Despite our efforts to coexist with, and even aid, the revolutionary leadership that overthrew the dictator Somoza in 1979, the strategic threat posed by the Nicaraguan communists has grown steadily. Today, the country is home to some 200 Soviet advisers, some 7,500 Cubans, and assorted personnel from East Germany, Bulgaria, Libya, and the Palestine Liberation Organization (PLO). You can see who its friends are.

Nicaragua's military machine has no parallel in the history of Central America. Since 1981, the country has received more than half a billion dollars in Soviet arms shipments, including tanks and other heavy armaments that, in the context of Central America, are clearly not defensive. By the end of 1980, Nicaragua's Armed Forces were twice as large as the Somoza National Guard at its height. By the end of 1982, the army of the Nicaraguan communists had doubled again. Today, Nicaragua has some 60,000 troops on active duty and 60,000 more in reserves. Honduras, by contrast, has 21,000 troops; Costa Rica, the oldest democracy in Latin America, has no army. No other country in Central America has as many tanks and armored vehicles as Nicaragua. Only Nicaragua has one of the most sophisticated attack helicopters in the world, the Soviet-built Mi-24 HIND.

Why such a formidable buildup? [Interior Minister] Tomas Borge gave the answer in 1981. "This revolution," he said, "goes beyond our borders."

What do these words mean? Look at the record. Almost immediately, the communists in Nicaragua joined with Salvadoran communists to prevent democratic reforms in El Salvador. They armed guerrillas who maintained their central headquarters in Managua until late 1983. (Incidentally, they moved not long after our liberation of Grenada.) And they still maintain radio transmitters, training facilities, R&R camps, and major logistics support facilities in Nicaragua.

But for the Nicaraguan communists, subverting El Salvador has not been enough. Nicaragua has also been equipping, training, organizing, and infiltrating guerrillas and agents into Honduras. It has launched direct attacks into that country using its regular armed forces.

Costa Rica is another target. The Nicaraguan communists have used their diplomatic presence in Costa Rica to conduct bombings and assassinations; they have financed, equipped, and trained Costa Ricans for subversive activities; and they have conducted cross-border incursions almost at will.

They are also involved in Colombia. Many of the arms with which the M-19 terrorists attacked the National Palace of Justice have been traced to Nicaragua. And what were the M-19 terrorists after? Just those Justices trying drug traffickers. It should be no surprise to find that the Nicaraguan communists are involved in this criminal activity.

Think about the pattern that emerges from this record. It is violent. It is indiscriminate, aimed at democracies and even Contadora peacemakers. And it is intimately tied to Cuba and Soviet military power. These efforts at subversion and infiltration are facilitated by the regime's close relations with terrorists from across the globe. It has issued Nicaraguan passports to radicals and terrorists from the Middle East, Latin America, and Europe. Groups with a known presence in Nicaragua include the Basque ETA terrorists, the German Baader-Meinhof gang, the Italian Red Brigades, and the Argentine Montoneros. Alvaro Baldizon, a high-ranking Sandinista who defected in 1985, reported that Interior Minister Borge is personally involved in cocaine smuggling from Colombia to the United States. Videotapes by a DEA [Drug Enforcement Administration] informer on the ground in Nicaragua show at least one other regime official personally supervising the loading of a narcotics shipment for the United States.

Agents of the PLO working in Central America and Panama use Nicaragua as their base of operations. Their ties to the PLO are particularly strong. Some were trained in PLO camps in the 1960s and 1970s. Some have even participated in PLO hijackings.

The Nicaraguan communists have another benefactor in the Middle East: Libya. By the time they took power in 1979, they had developed a direct relationship with Qadhafi. And Qadhafi has obligingly sent them arms. One shipment labeled "medicines" was intercepted by accident in Brazil in April 1983; authorities found about 84 tons of arms, explosives, and other military equipment.

*Repression at Home*

By betraying their promises of pluralism, the Nicaraguan communists have forced the citizens of Nicaragua to take up arms once again. Like Somoza, they don't seem to listen to anyone who isn't armed. And, like Somoza, they seek to blame outside forces for the resistance of their own people to their policies.

The Nicaraguan communists like to say that covert U.S. support created the resistance; that their opponents are all agents of the CIA [Central Intelligence Agency] and heirs of Somoza. This is nonsense. It was their repression that in 1979, 1980, and 1981 destroyed the coalition that overthrew Somoza and sparked the resistance. In 1979, 1980, and 1981, the United States was providing aid to the Government of Nicaragua, not to the resistance.

From mid-1984 until late in 1985—well over a year—the U.S. Government provided no aid to Nicaraguan resistance forces. During that time, the resistance grew by 50%, roughly from 10,000 to 15,000. So much for the theory that the resistance is a creature of U.S. cash.

Who are these Nicaraguans who are willing to risk their lives against the communist security apparatus? The resistance fighters are overwhelmingly rural youths. Most are between 18 and 22 years old. They are fighting to defend their small plots of land, their churches and, in some cases, their indigenous cultures. Some joined the resistance rather than be forced by the Nicaraguan communists to fight against their friends and neighbors. In defending their families and communities, these young Nicaraguans are fighting for self-determination above all else.

Their leaders are more likely to come from urban areas and have more diverse occupations and backgrounds. They include both former National Guardsmen and former Sandinista fighters, but most are civilians from the very groups the communists claim to represent: peasants, small farmers, urban professionals, and students. One was a primary school teacher; another, an evangelical pastor.

An analysis of the backgrounds of the 153 most senior military leaders of the largest resistance group last November shows that 53% were civilians, 27% served in the National Guard, and a full 20% were former comrades-in-arms of the communists themselves.

The evidence irrefutably confirms that the Nicaraguan resistance is the product of a popular, pervasive, and democratic revolt.

*A Tide of Democracy*

Historians will detect an irony in the changing course of Latin American tyranny throughout these years. While Nicaragua was trading one dictatorship for another, strongmen elsewhere in the region were falling in rapid succession. In the past decade, elected civilian governments have replaced authoritarian regimes in Argentina, Bolivia, Brazil, Ecuador, El Salvador, Grenada, Guatemala, Honduras, Peru, and Uruguay. Over 90% of the people of Latin America now enjoy self-government, as opposed to less than one-third 10 years ago.

The contrast between communist rule in Nicaragua and the political trend in the rest of Latin America could not be more dramatic. After centuries of struggle, self-government has taken root. Now, Nicaragua is not only the odd man out; its policies of militarism and subversion place all the region's hopes for democracy at risk.

No one is more aware of that risk than the leaders of Latin America. For years, they have been searching for a way of defusing the threat from Nicaragua. Indeed, the central purpose of the Contadora negotiations is to ensure that military tensions created by the Nicaraguan regime's behavior can be overcome peacefully and democratically without the widening conflict the Nicaraguan communists seem bent on provoking.

Not surprisingly, the communists have consistently torpe-doed these negotiations. In 1984, the United States pursued di-rect negotiations with Managua in an attempt to help the Contadora nations negotiate a settlement. Nine rounds of talks were held over 5 months. But the Nicaraguan communists proved mainly interested in manipulating the bilateral talks to short-circuit the Contadora process.

They have also refused the proposal of the country's Roman Catholic bishops, made in their 1984 Good Friday pastoral letter, to negotiate with all Nicaraguans—armed and unarmed, inside Nicaragua and outside of it. The democratic resistance called for a cease-fire and agreed to negotiations mediated by the Catholic Church. The regime refused. So the dialogue that counts the most—the internal dialogue between the regime and its oppo-nents—is stymied by the regime's intransigence. The commu-nists know what they want and have no intention of changing.

Nicaragua's neighbors are well aware of the regime's inten-tions. So are we. And we are profoundly concerned with the threat Nicaragua poses to the security and well-being of other Latin American nations. We have been deeply involved with en-couraging democracy throughout Central and South America, supporting free elections and giving moral and economic support to democratic governments and democratic forces. And like our democratic neighbors, we don't want to see these gains rolled back by Nicaraguan subversion.

Just 2 weeks ago, I met with representatives from the eight nations involved in the Contadora negotiations. They are com-mitted, as we are, to political solutions. But there is no mistaking their grave concern about Soviet and Cuban support for Nicara-gua's attempts to undermine regional stability.

### U.S. Policy

Our objectives in Nicaragua, and the objectives of our friends and allies, are straightforward. We want the Nicaraguan regime to reverse its military buildup, to send its foreign advisers home, and to stop oppressing its citizens and subverting its neighbors. We want it to keep the promises of the coalition government that followed Somoza's fall: democratic pluralism at home and peace-ful relations abroad.

The United States and its friends have sought these objectives through diplomacy. We continue to believe that a negotiated settlement represents the ultimate hope for peaceful change in Nicaragua. But all serious efforts at negotiation have been blocked by the Nicaraguan communists. They believe that they can continue their domestic oppression and foreign aggression with impunity, and they continue to regard their military might as their guarantee of success. The United States has the power to help Nicaraguan freedom fighters convince the communists that their course is disastrous. We must give them help before it is too late. And when we do that, we increase our leverage in support of our diplomatic objectives.

Our goals are limited and reasonable. They are also essential for our values and our security and those of our neighbors. We must consider many options. Some are so stern that we hope never to resort to them. The United States does not want its own military directly involved in Nicaragua. So far, we have not had to consider this option, because we know there is another way of discouraging the regime from its destructive course. That is why we support the democratic resistance.

Military help for the democratic resistance will give the Nicaraguan communists an incentive to negotiate seriously—something they have yet to do. They did not negotiate with the Carter Administration when the United States was Nicaragua's largest supplier of aid. And they did not negotiate seriously either with us or with their neighbors when the Congress suspended all aid to the resistance 2 years ago. On the contrary, in the fall of 1984, instead of bringing their political opponents back into the political process through competitive elections, they imported assault helicopters from the Soviet Union.

The resistance finds itself at a critical juncture. They have proven themselves by their extraordinary growth and by the desperate measures to which the regime has been driven to combat them. But the Soviet, Cuban, and Eastern-bloc military buildup confronts them with unfair odds. If *we* fail to help the forces of democracy, these forces will suffer severely—not because their cause lacks merit but because the communists will have shown more determination than we.

A strengthened democratic resistance is the only way to force the Nicaraguan communists to halt subversion in this hemisphere; it is the only way to counter their stifling tyranny at home.

Power and diplomacy must go hand in hand. That is a lesson we should have learned by now. Diplomacy without leverage is impotent. Whether in arms control negotiations with the Soviet Union or in the resolution of regional conflicts, diplomacy works best when our opponents realize they cannot win military victory or unilateral advantage. Sometimes we have forgotten that lesson and paid the price.

That is the lesson we are seeking to apply in Nicaragua today: we are trying to convince the communist regime that a military option does not exist. Only stout internal resistance by the Nicaraguan people can pressure the regime into seeking national reconciliation and fulfilling the democratic promise of 1979.

### Consequences of Inaction

If we do not strengthen the resistance, our worry in the future will be a very different one—a far more serious one. Our worry will then be a Soviet and Cuban base on the mainland of Latin America, a regime whose consolidated power will allow it to spread subversion and terrorism throughout the hemisphere.

Nor is that all. If the Nicaraguan communists succeed in consolidating their power and in destroying the democratic resistance, their victory would immediately boost radical forces everywhere that rely on violence, militarism, and terrorism to achieve their ends—particularly in Latin America. Radicalism will seem irresistible; the forces of moderation and democracy will be disheartened. *All* the countries in Latin America, who *all* face serious internal economic problems, will see radical forces emboldened to exploit these problems for their own destructive ends.

A communist victory in Nicaragua would also have global repercussions for U.S. policy. It would severely damage our credibility with adversaries who would test our mettle and with those around the world who rely on us for support in their battles against tyranny. If democratic aspiration is snuffed out in Nicaragua, then where can we claim to nurture it or protect it? If an armed aggressor on our own doorstep is allowed to have its way, despite enormous opposition inside the country and out, then how can our reputation for deterring aggression be credible in places farther removed?

The bipartisan Kissinger commission put it starkly in its 1984 report, listing the possible consequences of a failure to contain the present conflict in Central America. The consequences included:

- A series of developments which might require us to devote large resources to defend the southern approaches to the United States, thus reducing our capacity to defend our interests elsewhere. . . .
- A proliferation of Marxist-Leninist states that would increase violence, dislocation, and political repression in the region.
- The erosion of our power to influence events worldwide that would flow from the perception that we were unable to influence vital events close to home.

## Whose Vision?

This brings me to my final point. In the long run, the debate over military aid to the Nicaraguan resistance is no partisan affair. It is a debate over what moral and political principles shall inspire the future of this hemisphere, over whose vision will be allowed to prevail. One vision—the vision of democrats throughout the Americas—calls for economic progress, free institutions, and the rule of law. The other is a vision of two, three, many Nicaraguas—a hemisphere of burning churches, suppressed newspapers, and crushed opposition.

The Nicaraguan dictatorship may soon have the power to dog the resistance to its death. The United States *now* has the power to prevent that tragic outcome. Will we allow this hemisphere to be taken hostage by totalitarians? That is the question that the Congress faces. For the security of our own country and of the young democracies who turn to us for support, we should give the Nicaraguan people what they need to struggle for the freedoms that were denied them by Somoza and then snatched from them by an armed communist minority.

## IS THE REAGAN ADMINISTRATION POLICY
## TOWARD NICARAGUA SOUND? (Pro)[3]

I speak in opposition to this amendment which I think is ill-conceived and would be counterproductive to the very thing which its proponents seek to avoid in Central America—namely, a greater broadening of the conflict.

Former Secretary of State Henry Kissinger has indicated that in order to accomplish the very ends that the supporters of this amendment seek—namely a more equitable social and economic system—that in order to build that infrastructure, there must be a shield, if you will, a military shield, in view of Soviet-Cuban military intervention in the area, behind which this process can take place. If you eliminate the military option completely, you certainly telegraph to the enemy the idea that they are free to pursue a military solution.

I recall that when President Duarte was here—at that time, President-elect—he said it is a very complex situation. It is military, it is social, and it is economic. But his point was that if you have one army on one side and one army on the other and one is armed and the other is not armed, the armed army will win and you, in fact, will have a military solution.

If, in fact, we say and we telegraph to the people in this area and to the world that the United States, under no circumstances, would give sufficient latitude to the President to utilize our conventional military capability, I think you bring about what President Duarte was talking about—namely, that there will be a military solution, and it will be imposed by the Soviet Union and Cuba and those military forces it is backing in that area.

I think it is simply impossible in our time to micromanage American foreign policy, let alone defense decisions, from the floor of the U.S. Senate. To do so will greatly imperil the effectiveness of this country to meet the very serious challenge it meets today from the Soviet Union and her surrogates in every continent in the world.

[3]By Senator John P. East (Republican) of North Carolina. From the debate of June 18, 1984, on the floor of the U.S. Senate. Reprinted from *Congressional Digest* 63:266+, November, 1984.

Let me put it another way: If we do fail in Central America, if the Marxists take control of the military solution, who will be held accountable? Yes, the President will be. I say that if we are going to hold him, as Commander in Chief, and his principal spokesman and formulator for American foreign policy responsible, we had better give him enough elbow room to do that which is necessary in order for his policies to succeed.

But if we try to micromanage every move he makes, we cannot hold him responsible. I think our policy will fail, and you will see, yes, a military solution in Central America, and it will be dictated by Moscow, Havana, and Managua. That is what is going on currently.

Invariably, in a debate of this kind, I often find it interesting that our most honorable and patriotic opponents say there must be a political solution, in citing Vietnam. Of course, as Duarte has pointed out, if you do not have the military shield, you will not have a political solution; you will have a military solution, and it will be imposed by the superior military forces, which in this case, again, would be those forces in the area backed by the Soviet Union and by Cuba.

The current struggle in the world today, going on right now in the underdeveloped world, is of a guerrilla type. It does not candidly lend itself to formal declarations. It does not lend itself to micromanagement from the floor of the U.S. Senate. Guerrilla warfare is the key to military success in our time.

Alexander Solzhenitsyn remarked one time, "You need not worry about nuclear war in your time." Why? "Because," he said, "they are taking you with their bare hands," and they are. They are doing it in every part of the world. Solzhenitsyn said he did not think the West had read the Communist Manifesto. He did not think they had read the works of Lenin.

The point was that you would take the soft underbelly of the world, the underdeveloped continents of Asia, Latin America, and Central America. You would do it militarily. Yes, you would do it through guerrilla warfare. Those are the realities of warfare in our time. They cannot be denied. Solzhenitsyn is correct: We are losing. We lost in Southeast Asia. Cam Ranh Bay, which used to be a military base, is now a Soviet base. Yes, we were told we were looking for a political solution. What did we get? A military solution, Soviet and Vietnamese imposed. Then they moved into Cambodia, and so it continues.

The same scenario is being repeated in Central America. The same problem exists in Africa. It would exist in the Middle East, were it not for the strength of Israel. Syria and the PLO, backed by the Soviet Union, would impose a military solution in Lebanon—indeed, throughout the entire Middle East. Would it make sense to say to the Israelis, for example, "Disarm"? Or, should we say that we would never, ever, under any circumstances, intervene? That simply telegraphs to the Soviet Union and her surrogates that military solutions are possible. It rules out the potential for political solution. It rules out the shield to which Henry Kissinger has referred.

How are you going to build the infrastructure for social and economic justice and social and economic growth and development where the enemy, the opposition, is free to shoot its way to power, as President Duarte put it?

Recently we adopted overwhelmingly, as I recall, an amendment supporting the Monroe Doctrine concept of 1823, which stated that the United States would not accept foreign intervention and military presence in the New World from the Old. This is precisely what we are allowing to happen now in Central America. The Soviet Union and Cuba are intervening in Central America. They are supplying the armed support to Nicaragua, all out of proportion to the needs of Nicaragua to defend itself.

If you tie the hands of the President of the United States publicly in the Senate and the House and say that under no circumstances can he do this without formal declarations or authorizations, and so forth, it simply telegraphs to Managua, to Havana, and to Moscow: "Gentlemen, full steam ahead." And what will we get? A military solution—the very thing that the proponents, the very honorable proponents, of this amendment hope to avoid.

Let me end on this thought in terms of the reality of international relations of our time. There is no question about it. It has been spelled out carefully that the Marxist-Leninist solution is through military guerrilla operation to take the soft underdeveloped parts of the world and ultimately, as Marx and Lenin stated it, "You surround the urban industrial continents of Europe, of North America, including ultimately now Japan, and they in time will fall like ripe fruit."

We have to develop the acumen, the astuteness, the alertness, the ability to respond to that military challenge and it is of a guerrilla warfare nature, and hence we must allow the President the latitude, because we will hold him accountable now, will we not? We will not bear the burden, we will not accept responsibility if the military solution is imposed. We will point down Pennsylvania Avenue to the White House and say they failed, he failed.

I leave us with this thought: Has the United States no area in the world where we have self-interest to assert?

We were told during the Vietnam conflict that was distant, far away, and it was none of our concern. We were told in the Middle East that that perhaps is distant and far away and none of our concern. We are told that Africa is distant and far away and none of our concern.

And now, we are in our own hemisphere. We are in Central America. We see the Monroe Doctrine repudiated de facto, and once again it seems to me the thrust of what the proponents of this amendment are saying again is we have no self-interest.

I ask you this: Where do we, as one of the two great superpowers in the world, have a self-interest?

The Soviet Union moves with impunity into Afghanistan. It sends its surrogates, such as Syria, into Central America. It sends its surrogates into Africa in the form of Cuban troops and into Ethiopia, Angola, and Mozambique. It sends the PLO into Central America. It sends the Eastern European forces into Central America. It sends Cuban forces into Central America. In the Far East it takes over again Southeast Asia, uses Cam Ranh Bay, our former base, as its own base of operation. It gives the moral, logistic support to Vietnam to take over Cambodia, to threaten Thailand, and to broaden and expand its power in that whole part of the world.

Apparently, we have no self-interests in either we are told.

Now, here we are right in our own hemisphere and, again, it seems to me it is the old refrain: So we have no self-interests there. It makes no difference.

But is has been pointed out repeatedly if you allow Nicaragua to become the model in Central America, El Salvador will fall, Costa Rica will fall, Honduras will fall, Guatemala will fall, and Belize will fall. The pressure will be on Mexico and it ultimately will have no option except to itself to succumb to what? Yes, a military solution imposed by Moscow, Havana, and Managua.

Now, as has been pointed out repeatedly between the Rio Grande and the Panama Canal are 100 million people. We have heard this before, but let me say it. I think it is worth repeating. We have learned from past experience that at least 10 percent of the population invariably flees when the Communists take over. All the voting is one way. Where they can vote with their feet, they come here.

Look at the poor pathetic boat people who went out and drifted in the South China Sea, just waiting for any vessel to come along and pick them up. Is it not curious where people have a choice, they leave? They leave the Communist system. We have to build up walls to keep them out. They have to build up walls to keep them in.

Now, I ask this, and in this case they would not even have to get into boats, they would simply walk. If they take over that area between the Rio Grande and the Panama Canal, of 100 million people, 10 million people will move northward across the Rio Grande. How will you stop it? Will you machinegun them down? Of course you will not.

It will create enormous economic and social disruption in our country and it poses an enormous geopolitical threat to the peace and the freedom and the security and the well-being of this country. It jeopardizes not only your freedom and mine in our time, but that of our children and our grandchildren.

This amendment is a part of that whole fabric of thinking that seems to operate on the assumption that nothing is going on in the world today of consequence. I put it this way: We fiddle while Rome burns. We are excused by two facts. We do not know, first, that we fiddle and, second, we do not know that Rome burns. But Rome is burning in Central America and if you do not allow the President of the United States, who has the responsibility as the Commander in Chief under the separation of power, who has the principal responsibility for the conduct of foreign policy and for the protection of this country, the latitude to do what must be done in this area, I think that what you are going to see is all Central America fall under Soviet and Cuban control and domination and the whole Caribbean basin will simply become a dominant sphere of Soviet influence, military influence.

That I find totally unacceptable. Totally unacceptable from whose standpoint? From not only those people in that part of the world who must fall under this tyranny, but from the standpoint of the security, the freedom, and the well-being of this country.

So, I urge my colleagues to reflect very seriously on this. The stakes are high in Central America. They are in our own hemisphere, and if we will not defend our friends, our democratic friends, such as Duarte, in our own hemisphere, I simply question, gentlemen, who will we help? Who will we defend?

It is an eminently fair question to ask where would you draw the line—anywhere? Apparently not.

And that would be the great tragedy of our time and World War III has been subtly lost and it has been lost to Moscow. It has been lost to the Marxist-Leninist world vision. And it is over with a whimper.

And I suspect in due course, as Marx and Lenin predicted, the industrial urban continents of North America, Europe, and Japan will eventually have to succumb to the realities of power in their time. Solzhenitsyn has said the world is finite in geography. At some point the balance tips against you.

I do not know if it has occurred or not. He said psychologically it occurred in Vietnam. Perhaps it has. But it will have occurred, as a matter of reality, if we tie the hands of the President of the United States and allow the Soviet Union and Cuba and her surrogates such as in Managua to take over that area.

It is a very heavy question we face; I think the most serious facing this Congress and this country at this point in our history. And I vigorously disassociate myself from this amendment. I vigorously oppose it. And I hope my colleagues would reflect long and hard and repudiate it, vote it down.

---

## IS THE REAGAN ADMINISTRATION POLICY TOWARD NICARAGUA SOUND? (Con)[4]

---

The Administration has embarked on a major effort to construct a vast military infrastructure that could support the deployment of American forces in a contingency. By the end of the present exercise underway in Honduras, the United States will have built or improved eight airfields in Honduras, with the two

[4]By Senator Edward M. Kennedy (Democrat) of Massachusetts. From the debate of June 18, 1984, on the floor of the U.S. Senate. Reprinted from *Congressional Digest* 63:267+, November, 1984.

most recent additions within 25 miles of the Salvadoran and Nicaraguan borders. Two radar stations were established and manned by Americans. The administration sought $8 million to construct a prestock ammunition depot and an airplane hangar plus living quarters at Palmerola Airbase and a prestock ammunition depot at San Lorenzo, supposedly a temporary facility.

The administration has staged repeated, largescale, almost continuous military exercises in the region. Big Pine II last year involved up to 5,000 American troops over an 8-month period. Grenadero I, now underway, involved several thousand American forces. Such exercises, the administration has stated, "were conducted to demonstrate U.S. resolve and willingness to support our regional friends."

The American military presence in the region has increased. According to Defense Department figures, there are now 111 U.S. military personnel in El Salvador. The number of U.S. military in Honduras even when exercises are not underway has jumped to over 1,000.

U.S. military personnel in U.S. military aircraft over El Salvador are providing real-time intelligence for combat activities by Salvadoran forces on the ground.

U.S. military personnel in El Salvador have been in areas that came under hostile fire three times since November 1983.

And since we last debated Central America, we have learned about increased involvement of U.S. personnel in the hostilities in Nicaragua. Let me give you some examples:

We learned that, 3 months before the mining of the harbors in Nicaragua, U.S. personnel directed a sabotage raid against the Nicaraguan port of Corinto, destroying 3.2 million gallons of fuel and forcing the townspeople to evacuate.

We learned that, with respect to the mining of the harbors, the involvement of U.S. personnel was much, much more direct than anyone had ever believed. U.S. personnel were operating a ship in the Pacific—called the mothership—from which the mining activities were supervised and directed.

We also learned that U.S. personnel directed two air strikes against Nicaragua in February. The planes and bombs used in the February attacks—and in other raids—were provided by the CIA. The attacks were planned and supervised in Honduras and El Salvador, and the people in charge of the operations were Americans.

We also know that U.S. financial commitments in Honduras and El Salvador have been steadily and dramatically rising.

In 1980, 1 year before Ronald Reagan became President, the United States sent $8.5 million worth of military supplies to El Salvador, Honduras, and Costa Rica. Last year, the United States agreed to send $170 million, 20 times as much. This year, if Congress approves the administration's request, we will be signing contracts to send more than $580 million in military equipment, 70 times as much as we spent in 1980.

This last figure does not include the money for training—$22 million—nor the tens of millions of dollars that have been used for constructing airstrips, radar sites, and other facilities. Nor does this $580 million figure include the covert aid.

How is this assistance being used? What has been the involvement of U.S. personnel?

The answer is clear. In the course of the last 3 years, Central America has become an armed camp. Honduras is bristling with weapons and warriors. El Salvador has tripled the size of its military, and we are now paying for 12,000 Contras in Nicaragua.

And as for U.S. forces, on land, sea, and air, our people have become more and more directly involved in the conflict, and we are moving closer and closer to the fighting.

Do these activities sound like an administration with no intention of involving American forces in combat?

Do these sound like the activities of an administration seeking to promote a negotiated settlement in the region?

Or does this sound like an administration getting ready to pick a fight and commit American forces?

The conclusion is unmistakable: The Reagan Administration is systematically placing U.S. ships, planes, and personnel in harm's way, by injecting them into situations where, directly or indirectly, they are becoming increasingly involved in hostilities in violation of the War Powers Act.

In Central America we need to give diplomacy a chance to work before the President of the United States takes the Nation any closer to combat in that region.

For this reason, I offer an amendment that prohibits the introduction of U.S. Armed Forces into or over El Salvador and Nicaragua for the purposes of combat. This amendment reflects the deep and growing concern of the American people that the administration is taking us to war in Central America. Congress must not permit the President to go to war without the consent of the American people.

The amendment I offer today is straightforward. It bars the use of any funds in this bill to send U.S. Armed Forces into combat in or over El Salvador or Nicaragua.

As stated in the amendment, the word "combat" means "the introduction of U.S. Armed Forces for the purpose of delivering weapons fire upon an enemy." U.S. Armed Forces are not precluded from conducting military training in El Salvador. Nor does the amendment limit flights by American military aircraft in the region carrying out reconnaissance activities. Only the introduction of U.S. Armed Forces for the purpose of delivering weapons fire upon an enemy is prohibited.

The amendment does not apply in all circumstances. The exceptions are clearly stated:

This prohibition does not apply if Congress has declared war or enacted specific authorization for such introduction.

The amendment does not apply when such introduction is necessary to meet a clear and present danger of hostile attack upon the United States, its territories or possessions.

The prohibition does not apply when such introduction is necessary to meet a clear and present danger to, and to provide necessary protection for, the U.S. Embassy.

The prohibition does not apply when such introduction is necessary to meet a clear and present danger to, and to provide necessary protection for and to evacuate, U.S. Government personnel or U.S. citizens.

The amendment leaves to the President the determination of when force is necessary under the three circumstances I have just listed. The amendment thereby preserves the President's authority to respond to threats to the United States, its embassies, personnel, and citizens.

Some may say this amendment usurps the War Powers Resolution. I would reply that the War Powers Resolution is not enough for this President under these circumstances. We need to protect the right of Congress to exercise its constitutional responsibilities. We do not want to wake up one morning to find American troops fighting and dying in Central America without the consent of the American people.

A number of my colleagues have expressed concern about how this would basically change the War Powers Resolution. We know at the current time that if the President of the United States decides to send American troops into combat in Nicaragua or in El Salvador, he would be free to do so and would only have to notify the Congress under the procedures of the War Powers Act. He would then be able to maintain those troops for a period of 60 days. What this particular amendment provides is that, prior to the involvement of American combat troops in combat, as defined in the amendment, the President would simply have to obtain approval, positive approval, by the Congress of the United States before sending those troops. We are simply asking that the Congress be permitted to act prospectively, not after the fact.

It does seem to me that this is not an unusual precedent. There is a precedent for what we are proposing in our amendment in the action that was taken by the Congress on a resolution involving American troops in Lebanon. That was in response to the serious concern in this body about the application of the War Powers Act. We acted in this body to modify the War Powers Act in that particular country and on that particular resolution. I did not support it, but nonetheless the Senate did act in that fashion.

I believe that given the factual situation—the escalation of American involvement in El Salvador and in Nicaragua, with more military personnel in that area and with the kind of activities that I mentioned earlier in my statement, that it is important that we, the Congress, play some role in the decision before American combat troops are sent to these two countries "for the purpose of delivering weapons fire upon an enemy."

But the War Powers Act would still apply and be in effect. We have tried to make that clear, and I believe we have made it clear in the amendment itself.

President Reagan has stated that he has no intention of introducing U.S. Armed Forces in Central America for combat. This amendment simply takes the President at his word and puts into law what has been stated as the administration's official position.

We just want to make sure that the deeds will match the words. The stage has now been set for the United States suddenly, massively, and without warning to intervene with U.S. troops. I do not think we should go to war in Central America—nor should we send American combat troops to El Salvador or Nicaragua—unless the Congress has been consulted, and unless the

Congress has given its consent. That is why I urge the Members of the Senate to support this legislation.

At this time, to complete my presentation, I want to mention a few things that this amendment will not do. It will not affect the activities of the current military advisors assigned to El Salvador, nor their role in assisting in the training of the Salvadoran military. It will not limit the current reconnaissance flights by U.S. military aircraft in the region. It will not limit the ability of the U.S. Naval or Air Forces in the high seas or in the air to monitor Soviet or other naval activities of concern to our Armed Forces.

It will not inhibit any duly authorized military operations currently under way in Central America or elsewhere in the Caribbean. It will in no way limit our treaty obligations in the regions, or in the hemisphere. It will allow the President to carry out his constitutional responsibilities to protect the United States from aggression, or to protect the U.S. citizens. And it will allow the President to use U.S. combat forces to eliminate any threat he deems is a clear and present danger to the United States, its territory or its possessions. The judgment is up to him; and under this legislation he would be justified in using U.S. combat forces in a preemptive strike against any missiles that might be introduced in Central America by the Soviet Union.

It will allow the President to use U.S. combat forces to protect American lives, if he deems that there is a clear and present danger to their safety. Again the judgment is up to him. Under this legislation, he would have been justified in using the U.S. combat forces to intervene in Grenada.

This legislation will require the President to seek authorization from Congress to invade Nicaragua with U.S. combat troops in the absence of any of the exceptions set forth in the legislation. It will require the President to seek the consent of Congress to send combat troops to El Salvador in the absence of any of the exceptions set forth in the legislation.

The President is recognized as the Commander in Chief, but the ability to declare war is retained in the Congress of the United States. It is a balanced responsibility. That is what our Founding Fathers intended. And it seems to me that, given the particular fact situation that we find ourselves in El Salvador and in Nicaragua, and given the type of activities that have been taking place, and given the increasing involvement of the American military personnel in that region, and given the dramatic escalation of the reliance upon military solution—it seems to me that it is appropriate for us in this body to make a determination and a judgment that before combat troops are going to be used in this particular area we ought to have some ability to express ourselves.

## THE CASE FOR THE CONTRAS[5]

The upcoming vote in Congress on military aid to the Nicaraguan *contras* is one of the most important foreign policy votes of the decade. The future of Central America hinges on its outcome.

The position of the *contras* is precarious. They certainly have people: anywhere from 14,000 to 20,000, depending on whom you believe. That represents about twice the number of guerrillas in El Salvador, a country with about twice the population of Nicaragua. And about three times the number of Sandinista troops at the time of the overthrow of Somoza.

They also have people on the home front. Not even the most anti-*contra*-aid congressman denies that the Sandinistas have become extremely unpopular. Among those strongly opposed to Sandinista rule is the Church, the most popular institution in Nicaraguan society. The pope's divisions are not the only disaffected. These now include ordinary people deprived of the necessities of life in a wrecked economy; the business and middle classes, which have been denied the promises of freedom; and many intellectuals, some in exile, who don't relish life as functionaries of the estate. The *contras*, a peasant army, themselves represent the deep resentment in the countryside at Sandinista offenses to tradition and religion. Add to that the general uprising of the Miskitos against Sandinista colonialism, and you have a vast popular opposition. These are the people whose hopes would be betrayed by the liquidation of the armed resistance and the consolidation of Sandinista rule, which will be the inevitable result of an American denial of military aid to the *contras*.

[5]By the editors of the *New Republic*. Reprinted from *New Republic*, March 24, 1986, pp. 7–9. Copyright 1986 The New Republic Inc. Reprinted with permission.

But if they are so many, why haven't they already won? For the same reason Solidarity, ten million strong, lost in Poland. Under Leninist regimes, Philippine-style "people power" does not do terribly well. Nor do vastly out-gunned, out-trained guerrilla armies do well against Cuban-Soviet-style military machines.

The Soviets have poured something on the order of $500 million in arms into Nicaragua in the last five years. Since 1984 the U.S. has been prevented from sending the *contras* a penny's worth of arms. The recent delivery of helicopter gunships to the Sandinistas, reportedly piloted in combat by Cubans, has been decisive. It has made it extremely difficult for the *contras* to move and to resupply. In the absence of antiaircraft weaponry, they are quite defenseless.

As a result, *contras* advances and successes in the past several years are being reversed. In the last six months, particularly since the introduction of the MI-24 gunships, all but between 3,000 and 6,000 *contras* have been driven from Nicaragua. The rest are in Honduran camps waiting for arms. The civil wars numbers alone can't determine the outcome, particularly if one's side is barely armed.

And also barely trained. Again out of congressional scrupulousness, the U.S. military has been prohibited from training and professionalizing the *contra* forces, as it has done in El Salvador with a resulting marked improvement in the country's human rights record. It is somewhat paradoxical to argue that we shouldn't be training the *contras* because they are so undisciplined when one of the major reasons this peasant army remains undisciplined is that the U.S. military is prohibited from training it.

Thus the upcoming vote will be critical. Without military aid, the *contras* will fight and bleed perhaps for some time longer, but without hope. First to wither will be the armed resistance, overcome by vastly superior Soviet-supplied firepower. Then, just as certainly, the unarmed resistance, demoralized and abandoned, will follow, leaving the Sandinistas in total, permanent control of Nicaragua.

What's so bad about that? What, after all, does the resistance hope to achieve? Sandinista defense minister Humberto Ortega explained it well when, in 1981, he denounced former Sandinista junta member Alfonso Robelo as an enemy of the revolution. "The democracy that Robelo asks," charged Ortega, "is . . . that they [the bourgeoisie, presumably] have the army, the power, and that we Sandinistas be what the left is in Costa Rica, a sector, an organization that is free to move about, that publishes its newspaper." In other words, Robelo wants, for Nicaragua, Costa Rican–style democracy, where all political tendencies, including the left, are free to compete for (rotating) power. For Humberto Ortega, such a program amounts to political criminality. It is what made the Sandinistas push Robelo out of the junta, crush his party, and drive him to exile and resistance. Robelo is now one of the three leaders of the *contra* political leadership, the United Nicaraguan Opposition, known as UNO.

What is at stake in the civil war is any hope for a democratic Nicaragua. The end of the *contras* means the end of that hope. And a ban on military aid will likely mean, sooner or later, the end of the *contras*.

One would think that House Democrats, who for years have been urging, pushing, encouraging, threatening, and finally celebrating the return of democracy in the Philippines, would be equally eager to see democracy returned to Nicaragua. But they are not. Why? They put up a case that we find, for an issue of this gravity, stunningly weak.

*By what right does the U.S. try to bring democracy to a place where it enforced dictatorship for so long?* This is the "because of our tainted history we have no moral standing" argument. It is mystifying. The United States stood by the dictatorship in Haiti for at least three decades. Does that mean that we should therefore have ruled ourselves morally ineligible to assist in the transition to democracy? The United States ruled the Phillippines as a colony for nearly five decades, then stood by a dictator for the last two. Does that mean that the United States should have disqualified itself from aiding the restoration of democracy?

Certainly the U.S. has a very blemished history in Nicaragua. It is equally certain that our aims now are different than they were 60, even 20, years ago. As in Guatemala and El Salvador, as in the Philippines and Haiti and other places where our history is stained, in Nicaragua the relevant question is American intentions today, not Teddy Roosevelt's at the time of the building of the Panama Canal.

*We have no right to try to impose democracy on another country.* After the Philippines and Haiti, and the general self-congratulatory jubilation of liberals and conservatives alike over two triumphs of

American diplomacy, this argument stands exposed as a camouflage. Those who advocate dramatic American intervention in pro-American dictatorships should not be suddenly stricken with scrupulousness about the sanctity of sovereignty when intervention is proposed in states ruled by pro-Soviet Leninists.

*But one situation involves peaceful change; the other, war.* If in Nicaragua transition to democracy were possible without war, we too would oppose any fighting. But that option does not exist. Does anyone believe that the Sandinistas will ever peacefully transfer power or permit a free allocation of power by election?

*The* contras *can't win.* This argument is invariably heard from those who vote again and again to cut off aid to the *contras.* Yes, unarmed they can't win. Maybe House Democrats expect Nicaraguan democrats to win by lying down in front of Sandinista tanks, Philippines style.

Can the *contras* win the way the North Vietnamese won in South Vietnam? No, but they can win in the way the Sandinistas won in Managua. They could win not by rolling over the Sandinista army, but by controlling the countryside, which would in turn help undermine what little urban support the Sandinistas have. A Leninist regime with a conscript army on the defensive, losing the countryside and undermined in the city, would ultimately find its situation untenable.

*The* contras *are not democrats but Somocistas.* It is true that some top commanders are ex-Guardia. But even the most conservative (and powerful) of the three political leaders, Adolfo Calero, was a longtime opponent of Somoza and jailed for his efforts. The other UNO leader Arturo Cruz, an impeccable democrat, says the *contras* represent "the revolt of Nicaraguans against oppression by other Nicaraguans." One doen't raise an army of 15,000 peasants with promises of restoring a universally despised dictatorship.

*We should try diplomacy, not force.* The United States should be working out with the Sandinistas some kind of diplomatic arrangement under the umbrella of Contadora. This imagined solution of Sandinista regional power and ambitions is a parchment barrier: the Sandinistas are given free rein within their borders, and in return, they promise not to trespass on anyone else's. Certainly we can expect the Sandinistas to adhere initially to such a nonaggression or revolution-with-frontiers agreement. Time enough for the *contras* to wither away and be repatriated in Miami. At which point the Sandinistas will be secure in the knowledge that no future opponents are ever going to risk their lives in a second insurgency, having seen the first one sold out. With a free hand, does anyone imagine that they will adhere to their agreements any more than, say, the Vietnamese adhered to theirs? We have experience with Sandinista parchment. In 1979 they pledged to the Organization of American States to establish an open, democratic, and pluralistic society.

It takes willful blindness to imagine that some kind of paper agreement with the Sandinistas that allows them to consolidate their power will ensure stability in Central America. In fact, the opposite is almost certainly the case. A highly militarized, highly disciplined country with by far the largest army in Central America, with ideological ambitions stretching far beyond its borders, and supported by Cuba and the Soviet Union, is bound to be a source of constant instability in a region of weak and fledgling democracies.

*The neighboring countries seem to want a Contadora solution.* What does one expect from, say, Costa Rica, a country with no army facing a 50,000-man military across its border? It sees a starved insurgency, an isolationist U.S. Congress, and a rising military power in Managua. Does one expect Costa Rica publicly to come out in support of overthrowing its neighbor, given the odds now that its neighbor will be in power permanently? Of course such countries will make muted public statements. But as many of the leaders of these weak democracies told the Kissinger Commission and others since, they are desperate to see the United States get rid of the Sandinistas for them.

What is the government of Colombia, one of the original Contadora countries, to say? It publicly denies but privately knows that an assault on its Palace of Justice and the massacre of its Supreme Court was carried out by M-19 guerrillas with weapons of Nicaraguan origin. It knows that Sandinista *comandante* Thomas Borges attended a mass, complete with an M-19 flag draped over the altar, for the guerrillas killed in that raid. The reach of the Sandinistas is impressive. Latin American governments, many of which face left-wing insurgencies, are hardly likely to make themselves more of a target by public calls for the Yankees to save them from communists.

*The* contra *policy is driving the Sandinistas into the hands of the Soviets.* It is hard for Americans to believe that some people act out of ideological conviction. Look, therefore, at what the Sandinistas did long before there was a Reagan, long before there were *contras*. In one year the Carter administration gave them in aid the equivalent of half of what Somoza received in 16 years, and during that time they systematically eliminated their democratic allies and aligned themselves with the Soviets.

On June 23, 1981, Humberto Ortega said to the Sandinista army and militia officers: "We are saying that Marxism-Leninism is the scientific doctrine that guides our revolution, the instrument of analysis of our Vanguard for understanding [the revolution's] historic process and for carrying out the revolution. . . . " He then asserted that the FSLN had made the pact with the moderate opposition only for the purposes of getting rid of Somoza, holding off U.S. intervention, and keeping the economy in place.

It is remarkable that for House Democrats Sandinista ideological commitment requires constant theatrical demonstration. It took Daniel Ortega's flight to Moscow a few days after a *contra* vote last year to dramatize Managua's connection with Moscow. You can be sure that this time Ortega's handlers will take away his American Express card until after the vote. Don't expect to see him visiting New York for eye wear or Moscow for hardware until the coast is clear.

*The Cubans and Soviets will match our escalation.* This is the counsel of pure defeatism. It cedes to the Soviets the power to set the level of violence and superpower commitment on the North American continent. It is, in effect, to say that the Soviet will to annex Nicaragua exceeds that of the United States to prevent it from happening. The prophecy is, of course, self-fulfilling.

*The* contras *will draw the United States into war.* Probably the root argument, certainly the one on which Tip O'Neill hangs his hat. Its origin is the fear of another Vietnam and the isolationist hope that if we only will stay out of this fight no harm will come to us.

But nothing is more likely to force American military intervention than the consolidation of an aggressive, highly militarized, pro-Soviet regime in the area. The *contras* want to do their own fighting. Cut them off, and the only body in the hemisphere able to restrain the Sandinistas will be the U.S. Army. Of course, American military involvement can never be ruled out. But destroying the only indigenous armed opposition to the Nicaraguans hardly seems the way to prevent it.

And what will be more likely to bring about American military involvement? Even Democrats argue that the United States has a vital interest in preventing the establishment of a Soviet base in Nicaragua. Even Democrats would call for American military action in that situation. Walter Mondale, for example, suggested a quarantine. When tried in October 1962, that idea brought us closer to World War III than any other moment in postwar history. A democratic Nicaragua is the only guarantee that the threat will not materialize.

The consolidation of the Sandinistas will lead to a second Cuba on the mainland, or more precisely, to an enlarged first Cuba. As Robelo recalls, during his days in the ruling junta no important decision was ever made without the assent of the Cuban invariably present at the meeting. Even those who think it sentimental for the United States to concern itself with the state of pluralism and democracy in other countries must recognize what a strategic defeat the establishment of a Soviet satellite in Central America would constitute for the United States.

We do not have any illusions about the tragedy that is civil war and the suffering it causes. Guerrilla war is of necessity nasty, brutish, and long. And this peasant army, ill-trained and ill-equipped, is hardly a perfect model for insurgency. But our choice is this model—which could be vastly improved in combat effectiveness and discipline if given sufficient American aid and training—or none.

We believe that preventing the establishment of a Leninist dictatorship in Nicaragua is a goal worthy of American support, and that those willing to fight for this cause are deserving of American assistance. A decision to support one side in a civil war is not one to be taken lightly. We come to it in the full realization that, whatever tragedy it brings, the liquidation of the democratic side of Nicaraguan civil war will bring infinitely more tragedy to Nicaragua, to Central America, and ultimately to the rest of the hemisphere.

## REFORM THE CONTRAS[6]

Congress faces an excruciating dilemma in its vote on aid to the Nicaraguan rebels. Should it approve President Reagan's proposal for military aid and underwrite a mainly reactionary leadership unable to gain the full support of the Nicaraguan or the American people? Or should it vote down military aid and face the inevitable consequences—both for Nicaragua and eventually for Central America, Mexico, and the United States—of a consolidated, Soviet-backed expansionist Sandinista regime?

In recent weeks the Sandinistas have launched a major diplomatic and public relations campaign aimed at convincing the world that they are David fighting the U.S. Goliath, and that they will be responsive and fair to their people just as soon as the gringo guns are lowered. But few are still naive enough to believe Sandinista promises.

On October 15 President Daniel Ortega announced "emergency measures" that virtually suspended all civil liberties, including the rights of speech, assembly, personal security, freedom of the press, movement, to form labor organizations, and to strike. Ortega blamed "U.S. imperialism" and rebel "sabotage and political destabilization" for the new crackdown. The real target of this latest crackdown is Nicaragua's political opposition, independent press, labor unions, and above all, its religious organizations.

From February 8 to 15, I participated as an observer on a mission to Nicaragua of the International League for Human Rights. There was overwhelming evidence of an intensifying campaign of intimidation, harassment, and coercion. According to Monsignor Bosco Vivas, auxiliary bishop of Managua, more than 100 Catholic lay and religious workers and 50 priests have been detained and interrogated since October. Evangelical ministers and lay workers have been subjected to the same treatment. The Sandinistas have prohibited open-air Masses, shut down the Catholic radio station, suppressed its newspaper, confiscated its printing press, seized its social welfare office, prevented the establishment of a human rights office, illegally drafted seminarians into military service, and imprisoned and deported priests.

[6]Reprint of an article by Robert Leiken, a senior associate at the Carnegie Endowment for International Peace. *New Republic*. Mr. 31, '86. pp. 18–20. Copyright 1986 The New Republic Inc. Reprinted with permission.

Opposition political parties and labor unions have also been singled out. Two Social Christian Party activists were brutally murdered in November. The International League for Human Rights has a list of 57 members of PLI (Independent Liberal Party) from Condega in Esteli province who are under detention. The Sandinista attacks and intimidation have focused on less visible opposition activists in outlying provinces. But the campaign has been sweeping—virtually all political parties have felt its effect, including not only the right wing and the center, but also the Communists, Socialists, Social Christians, and Social Democratic parties. In response, a broad civil anti-Sandinista front is slowly emerging. The once-enormous popular support for the Sandinistas has virtually vanished, and their power now depends on a military and security apparatus built by Moscow and Havana.

After talking to many professionals, and to union, party, and religious leaders and activists, it was clear that there is a major Sandinista effort to infiltrate opposition groups and to coerce members into collaborating with Sandinista-created "internal fronts" of the FDN (Nicaraguan Democratic Force). Later these activists are pressured to denounce fellow members as FDN agents to justify repression against their organizations.

We also talked to scores of political prisoners and their families. The International League for Human Rights estimates that there are now between 3,500 and 7,000 political prisoners in Nicaragua, not including the 2,500 National Guardsmen. It is impossible to be more precise because of the secrecy of Nicaragua's prisons and its state security system, which controls the clandestine state security prisons. Political prisoners are subject to solitary confinement in subterranean cells without sanitation facilities. They are denied food and water for as long as four days at a time. We heard of cases of simulated executions, threats to family members of prisoners, including their pregnant wives, and a gamut of psychological torments known in Nicaragua as "white torture." We also spoke to individuals who had suffered physical torture.

In the remote Indian communities of the Atlantic coast, Sandinista repression is less discreet. The Sandinistas are waging an air war involving bombing and strafing of villages and noncombatants. On February 8, 1986, *New York Times* correspondent Steven Kinzer described "craters made by rockets and 500-pound bombs" dropped by government planes on Indian villages while pursuing Miskito leader Brooklyn Rivera. Rivera succeeded in escaping through the remarkable cooperative efforts of Miskito villagers. Rivera's Misurasata group receives no support of any kind from the U.S. government. In fact, the U.S.-backed FDN (with U.S. government and Honduran government compliance) has prevented Rivera from entering Honduras to meet with Indian refugees and leaders there. Misurasata had met several times with the Sandinista government in an effort to reach a peaceful settlement recognizing Indian rights. Despite their promises of peace and reconciliation, Sandinista troops carried out this recent search-and-destroy operation with the full knowledge of the government in Managua.

Leaders of Nicaragua's internal civilian opposition believe that the Sandinistas are out to destroy them, and that the rebels are at the very least a necessary evil. One left-of-center leader told me that if there is any chance for negotiations now with the Sandinistas, the U.S. would be "foolish" to remove the one instrument of pressure that has a real effect on the Sandinistas: the armed resistance.

The problem confronting Congress and the American people is with the "instrument of pressure" designed to moderate or to remove the Sandinistas. The Nicaraguan armed opposition has been divided into as many as six different groups, with varying ideological orientations, political bases, and military potential. The United States has by and large supported the FDN, formally under the umbrella organization UNO, United Nicaraguan Opposition.

The FDN was created by Argentine military and security agents and by the CIA. Strong ties of loyalty, or fealty, have developed between CIA officials, acting as imperial patrons, and their colonial adjutants in the FDN. Most of the FDN High Command was drawn from the National Guard. These officers are intensely loyal to Commander in Chief Enrique Bermudez, and have the allegiance of some of the field commanders. However, Bermudez—along with Aldolfo Calero, who was installed as the political leader of the FDN by the CIA, and Aristides Sanchez, a former landowner—forms part of a cabal closely linked to a shadowy network of expropriated landowners, businessmen, former associates of Somoza, and U.S. right-wing donors. These exiles influence the FDN leadership through family ties or as former or current employers.

These leaders have been reluctant to unite with the other resistance organizations and are in turn distrusted by them. They have resisted efforts to democratize the FDN and UNO apparatus, and thus have often stood in the way of the effort to create a unified, democratic national resistance to the Sandinistas. Above all, the struggle in Nicaragua is a national struggle, yet to date it has been led by a small ideological sector of prerevolutionary Nicaragua.

This is true even though the popular base of the resistance has grown enormously. There are some 20,000 armed insurgents in a Nicaraguan population of three million, of which the FDN makes up some 12,000. The FDN claims that 40 percent of its troops are former Sandinista soldiers and fewer than two percent are former National Guardsmen. Among the rebel groups there is much unhappiness with the current CIA-imposed leadership. *Comandantes* in the field often share their troops' resentment of the FDN's leadership. A former associate of rebel leader Eden Pastora has described these field commanders as "a mixed bag of Zapatas and Pancho Villas," i.e., troops' peasant revolutionaries and rebel brigands.

Recently the FDN has suffered serious military reverses. These have been due to the intensive Soviet-Cuban training of the Sandinista forces, to their acquisition of Soviet helicopters, and to the introduction of Soviet heavy artillery. The FDN troops are poorly trained and suffer from a lack not only of equipment but of combat officers. The ratio of officers to troops is about one to 200. This means that the FDN cannot break down into small units in the face of Sandinista bombardments and artillery, and it has lacked the trained organizers necessary to create a political and military infrastructure.

Nonetheless, the FDN receives information and aid from local residents and is enjoying substantial and growing support among Nicaragua's small farmers and campesinos. FDN fighters are peasants with deep economic, political, and ideological grievances against the regime. They have maintained high morale despite a lack of military equipment and training—and sometimes boots and food. The FDN, in short, is a movement with a peasant base, populist middle-echelon officers, and a mostly reactionary leadership imposed and maintained by the United States.

The most important groups outside of UNO are BOS (Southern Opposition Bloc), led by Alfredo Cesar and Eden Pastora, and

Misurasata. The political tendencies of these groups is social democratic. They have also enjoyed strong local support and fight on without U.S. funding. Only the unity of all anti-Sandinista forces and the establishment of strong southern and Atlantic coast fronts will turn the armed resistance into a militarily viable enterprise.

The disunity of Nicaraguan resistance forces and their failure to develop a democratic leadership have helped to isolate internationally our Central American policy. The administration's own policy and rhetoric have contributed to this isolation. The national and democratic character of the Nicaraguan civilian and armed struggle has often been drowned in a torrent of administration invective that has conveyed both impotent rage and hegemonic presumption. This rhetoric buttresses those among the Nicaraguan civilian and armed resistance who prefer to wait passively for an imagined U.S. invasion. And it has offended the dignity of Latin American governments, which are sensitive to U.S. bullying and mired in debt to U.S. banks.

One must hope that the bipartisan policy that helped oust dictators in the Philippines and Haiti will open a new chapter for Nicaragua as well. The United States needs a policy that has a political, diplomatic, and organizational dimension as well as a military one. Our goal should be to promote a broad national movement for a democratic solution to the Nicaraguan crisis. This solution could come about if the Sandinista government accepts the February 6 proposal of the six Nicaraguan political parties (ranging from the left to the center to the right) for a ceasefire, amnesty, lifting of the state of siege, and a new election schedule. It could also come from direct dialogue between the Sandinistas and the armed and civilian opposition, or as UNO leader Arturo Cruz has recently suggested, with the civilian opposition tacitly representing the armed resistance as well.

These offers—along with Salvadoran president José Napoleón Duarte's March 4 proposal to Daniel Ortega for parallel government-guerrilla negotiations in the two countries—provide a framework for a viable regional peace settlement. In the face of imminent U.S. military aid and increased diplomatic pressure, the Sandinistas may choose to follow the course of the Guatemalan military, permitting real elections while seeking to retain control of the army for the long haul.

But for any of this to happen, the United States must reform its policy. It must support the creation of a broad internal and external united front against the Sandinistas. It should encourage efforts of the political opposition from the Communist and Socialist parties on the left, through the Social Democratic, Social Christian, PLI, and Conservative Democratic parties in the center, and the Conservative parties on the right to unite their efforts for political reform inside Nicaragua. At the same time it should support efforts to create a coalition of the resistance forces, including BOS and Misurasata, which would then receive U.S. military aid. In this respect the Nicaraguan opposition must take a leaf from the Sandinistas. Only a broad unity movement with an armed component was capable of forcing out Somoza. Only a broad unity movement will force the Sandinistas to hold elections, or to negotiate, or to relinquish power—whichever they choose.

At the same time, UNO must reform if it is to become an effective political, ideological, diplomatic, and military force. The administration must abandon its special relationship with Calero and Sanchez, allowing UNO to become a democratic institution. Only under the leadership of true democrats united with other anti-Sandinista groups can UNO-FDN become an organization capable of gaining the sympathy of America.

This means that UNO must have control of all public and private funds it receives. It must have the right, upon the recommendation of the recently created UNO Human Rights Office, to punish officers and troops found guilty of human rights violations. Although UNO should not be involved in the day-to-day conduct of the war, it should have final control over military appropriations, strategy, and general policy and organization. These reforms, as Senator Nancy Kassebaum recently stated, are up to "the *contras* themselves," but Congress should vote no military aid until they are undertaken.

However, sufficient military aid to a united and democratic resistance is needed desperately. Once firm steps are taken to strengthen the social, political, and ideological character of the resistance, the resistance will have a real chance of success.

It is no secret that there is an atmosphere of bad faith between the administration and Congress on the Nicaraguan issue. Many Democrats have been reluctant to recognize the true situation in Nicaragua because in addition to their fear of direct U.S. military involvement, they fear vindicating the president. They have preferred to assail him because they feel he is weak on this issue. At the same time the administration has itself often sought to exploit Nicaragua for narrow domestic gains, most recently through blatant Red-baiting by senior White House official Pat Buchanan. Some in the administration seem more interested in fighting the Democrats than in effectively opposing the Sandinistas.

Last June the president wrote a letter to Representative Dave McCurdy that seemed a move toward ending this debilitating and self-destructive quarrel. In it he promised not to "seek the military overthrow of the Sandinista government or to put in its place a government based on supporters of the old Somoza regime," and committed himself to urge rebel leaders to investigate human rights abuses and take action to prevent further abuses. Many members of Congress feel that the administration has not fulfilled these promises. This time promises will not be enough.

Commenting on the president's promises, House Speaker Thomas P. O'Neill vowed that the Democrats would "hold him to his new position." Yet Congress has done nothing to accomplish that end. Some Democrats who continue to cherish illusions that the Sandinistas can be reformed by diplomacy argue that reforming the rebels is too difficult. In fact, they are amenable to reform, especially now. Their movement now rests on a popular rebellion with new field commanders who are more responsive to pressure, both from within and without. Guerrilla armies are not created overnight. The Salvadoran FMLN has been in the field for nearly 15 years. The Vietnamese and Chinese fought for more than a decade before creating effective guerrilla armies. The American people and Congress and the administration should be aware that armed resistance to the Sandinistas must necessarily take the form of a protracted struggle. This will require a sustained bipartisan U.S. policy of support.

To establish and sustain such a policy, the administration must make a good-faith effort to give Contadora a chance. Contadora's efforts at achieving peace and national reconciliation will not be successful without military pressure. But the administration should agree to delay arms deliveries so as to permit Contadora and the Central American countries to reach a settlement. The delay, however, should not be so long as to allow the Sandinistas to repress rebel civilian supporters in contested areas while it pretends to negotiate.

We have seen in Afghanistan and in the Philippines that the American people are willing to support national and democratic movements in the Third World. They will not support a U.S. invasion of Nicaragua. They would back a national movement for democracy. They would support a true national resistance movement but not a proxy army. The administration and Congress must put aside narrow partisan interests to forge a national policy toward Nicaragua.

## CONFESSIONS OF A 'CONTRA'[7]

*Miami*

On December 7, 1982, I met with five Nicaraguans and two Americans in an executive suite at the Four Ambassadors Hotel in downtown Miami to rehearse for a press conference we would be holding the next day. The Nicaraguans were prominent (and in my case not so prominent) opponents of the Somoza and Sandinista regimes who were to be introduced as directors of the Nicaraguan Democratic Force (FDN), that is, the *contras*. The Americans were CIA agents. The one in charge, known to us as Tony Feldman, was accompanied by Thomas Castillo, one of his several assistants. They wanted to make sure we said the right things in our first joint public appearance.

Feldman introduced two lawyers from Washington who briefed us on the Neutrality Act, the American law prohibiting private citizens from waging war on another country from U.S. territory. Feldman was worried we were going to tell the press that we were trying to overthrow the Sandinistas, which, of course, is exactly what we wanted to do. He emphasized that we should say instead that we were trying to "create conditions for democracy." After the briefing we asked each other the questions we were likely to face in the morning.

"Where have you been getting money?" someone asked.

"Say your sources want to remain confidential," Feldman advised—a truthful and very clever answer.

"Have you had any contact with U.S. government officials?"

[7]Reprint of an article by Edgar Chamorro, director of the anti-Sandinista rebel organization, the Nicaraguan Democratic Force, from 1982 to 1984, with Jefferson Morley. *New Republic.* Ag. 5, '85. p. 18+. Copyright 1985 by The New Republic Inc. Reprinted with permission.

The CIA men agreed there was no way to finesse this one. We simply had to lie and say, "No." We practiced like this for three hours.

The press conference, held in Fort Lauderdale to avoid the risk of demonstrations in Miami, was all very solemn and pompous. We filed into the Hilton Conference Center one at a time, as if we were a government taking power, the one thing missing was the music. Then I read our statement of principles and goals.

"We the Directorate of the Nicaraguan Democratic Force," I declared, "commit ourselves to guide and support this effort of the Nicaraguan people to salvage our sacred patriotic honor, offering for this purpose all-out industry, dedication, and if necessary, our very lives." I felt some remorse reciting these words. Our original text had made no such offer, but the CIA men had thrown that version out. A young man named George (I never learned his last name) had been called in from Washington to rewrite our statement, and it was he who bravely offered up our lives.

The seven of us who later took questions from reporters had never worked together. Previously, the *contras* had been primarily a military movement, led by former Somoza National Guardsmen, that skirmished with the Sandinista army on the Nicaraguan-Honduran border. These forces were trained and advised by Argentine military officers. We civilians had been active in anti-Sandinista activities in the U.S., but had no formal connection to the military commanders. The CIA had brought the groups together with money and unequivocal promises of support.

I hadn't even met Enrique Bermudez, the former National Guardsman who commanded the *contra* troops in Honduras, until the rehearsal the day before. Alfonso Callejas, a former vice president of Nicaragua who broke with Somoza in 1972 and who lived in Texas, had only arrived that morning. He came to the press conference straight from the airport. We told him, "You weren't at the rehearsal, so don't say anything." He spoke anyway, but we managed to keep his answers short, and he didn't do much damage.

There were some unavoidable contradictions in our answers. On the one hand, we were careful to say that we had great admiration for, but no formal connection with, the freedom fighters battling the Sandinista army on the Honduran border. On the other hand, we claimed that the directorate would put the *contra* forces under civilian control. But overall we thought we made a good impression, and when I met Thomas Castillo again that night, he said he was pleased. We returned to Miami, and I began my two years as a *contra*.

I came to Nicaraguan politics late, especially considering my background. After Somoza, my family name is perhaps the best known in Nicaragua; four Chamorros served as president of Nicaragua in the 19th and early 20th centuries. My family led the Conservative Party, for decades the major opposition to Somoza's Liberal Party. My father, like many of my relatives, was persecuted and jailed several times by Somoza. I, however, preferred education to politics, joining the Jesuits in 1950 at age 19. I went on to become a priest and a teacher, studying at different times at the Catholic University in Ecuador, at St. Louis University, and at Marquette, and later becoming a full professor and dean of the School of Humanities at the University of Central America. Even after leaving the priesthood in 1969, I continued studying, earning a master's degree from Harvard University in 1972.

For me the Sandinista revolution began with the earthquake that devastated Managua in 1972. We learned that large buildings, thought to be indestructible, could become rubble in minutes. Still, I was not very involved in politics. In Managua I founded my own advertising agency, Creative Publicity, and handled accounts for businesses owned by people in my family, including the local General Motors and Toyota dealers, and Toña, Nicaragua's most popular beer. My only political venture was to accept a one-year appointment in 1977 to the Nicaraguan Mission to the United Nations. (Under Somoza, members of the opposition Conservative Party, to which I nominally belonged, were given non-essential government posts.) The most political thing I did there was secretly pass a message from Sandinista friends to U.S. Ambassador Andrew Young in October 1977 asking him to denounce Somoza. He never did.

As the insurrection against Samoza grew in 1978, I helped out in other small ways. When my close friend Sergio Ramirez, now Daniel Ortega's vice president, was being hunted by the National Guard, I hid him in my children's bedroom. But in 1979 the growing chaos in Managua made me fear for my family's safety. Somoza's planes were bombing the barrios near my house and desperate National Guardsmen were shooting innocent people on the street. On June 17, a month before Somoza was overthrown, my wife and I and our two children came to Miami.

I returned in September 1979 to see if things had calmed down enough for us to return. I traveled to the south to visit an uncle and to attend a ceremony in which the Sandinista national leadership turned over power to local authorities. Many of the leaders of the revolution were there: Daniel Ortega, Ramirez, Violeta Chamorro, the widow of my distant cousin Pedro Joaquin Chamorro, the anti-Somoza editor of *La Prensa* who was assassinated in 1978. Talking with people at the big picnic held after the ceremony, I could see that Castro was in control of the revolution—not as a manipulator but as the only available role model. Even the less fanatic people like Violeta were outspoken that day. "On to El Salvador!" she cried. I didn't want to oppose them. I believed the spirit behind the revolution was authentic and true. But I knew if I joined them my life would be in the hands of the culture of the revolution. I wished them well. Perhaps if I had been younger and single, I would have joined their cause.

Back in Miami, I continued meeting informally every two weeks or so with other Nicaraguan exiles. Most of them, like me, were from the Conservative Party, and favored social change without going so far as the revolutionary transformation favored by the Sandinistas.

Our group became more formal in late 1980 when Francisco Cardenal, an engineer who had been a high-ranking Sandinista, left Nicaragua and joined us in Miami. We named ourselves the *Union Democratica Nicaraguense,* but we limited ourselves to activities such as writing letters to members of Congress urging them to cut off aid to the Sandinistas. By this time Cardenal was receiving money from the CIA. He often traveled to Washington to meet with people from the Agency and the State Department, and to Honduras to establish contact with the former National Guardsmen.

As the Sandinistas grew more repressive in 1980, many of us became convinced that they had to be replaced, and that only armed opposition could do it. The Sandinistas had gone too far in imitating Cuba, in chanting slogans that had no bearing on the situation in Nicaragua. Finally, the assassination of Jorge Salazar in November 1980 made it clear that the Sandinistas would not tolerate any serious political opposition. Salazar had been a popular spokesman and a brave leader, organizing coffee and cattle producers into independent cooperatives. We had not wanted to believe they would be so dictatorial as to kill him.

In August 1981 our group sent a representative to an important meeting in Guatemala with U.S. officials, the National Guardsmen, and their Argentine military advisers. Did we want to merge our efforts? The question sparked long debates in the exile community in Miami. I remember arguing long into the night that we should accept this alliance. I said—mistakenly, it turned out—that the Somoza National Guardsmen were professional soldiers and not necessarily bad guys. Besides, I pointed out, we didn't have the capacity to train a fighting force, and we had to work with people who did. The others responded by telling stories of being unfairly arrested, beaten, or robbed by the National Guard. They insisted that anyone associated with the National Guard had done so much damage to Nicaragua that we should never, never work with them. Despite these objections, we joined our efforts with those of the *contras* in Honduras.

Cardenal, along with another civilian and Enrique Bermudez, became the directorate of the *contras.* Cardenal immediately clashed with the military commanders. He was very nationalistic, very strong-minded, and he had a tremendous dislike for the National Guard. He expected civilians to be in charge, and he prematurely tried to control the military leadership. For his efforts, he was expelled from Honduras by Bermudez in September 1982.

Plotting against the Sandinistas was not a full-time job for me. In November 1982 I was working as a commodities broker for Cargill when I received a totally unexpected phone call from an American who called himself Steve Davis. "I am speaking in the name of the goverment of the United States," he said in a voice accustomed to giving orders. He asked to see me that day. Over lunch at a restaurant near my house in Key Biscayne, Davis told me that Cardenal had been fighting too much with National Guardsmen, and that the United States wanted to increase the size of the *contras'* political leadership.

I told him that I favored creating something like a *contra* congress, composed of perhaps 21 leading Nicaraguans. This would have several advantages, I explained. First, it could create more debate, allow more participation by civilians, and possibly open avenues to the Sandinistas. Second, it could include representatives from the other rebel groups such as the one led by former Sandinista hero Eden Pastora, who shunned any contact with National Guardsmen. Third, one military commander could not defy or challenge 20 other important people. Fourth, and most important, I wanted to establish the supremacy of laws, not leaders, within the Nicaraguan opposition. I wanted to have a written constitution and formal procedures that would prevent us from succumbing to the perennial Latin American weakness for the caudillo.

Davis liked my proposal. But even at this first meeting I noticed a distinctive trait of CIA agents: they immediately reinforce what you have to say. "Well, yes," they respond, "we completely agree." Davis knew my views, and knew he had to sound liberal. "We don't want anybody in the directorate who is Somocista, who has robbed money from Nicaragua, who has committed crimes," he claimed. He was overdoing it.

As Davis said good-bye, he told me that I wouldn't always see him, that sometimes others would call or visit me on his behalf. And in the days that followed other men did come. Their activities were somewhat mysterious. All of them were getting ready for the arrival of someone from Washington who wanted me to be a part of something and to share in the administration's plans with respect to Nicaragua.

Finally, in late November 1982, Davis asked me to have dinner in his suite at the Holiday Inn in downtown Miami. There I met the man who came from Washington—Tony Feldman. He was about 40 years old, alert and good-looking. He had thinning hair, a long face, an easy smile, and a gentleman's manner. He would have made a superb car salesman. He asked me to serve on a seven-member directorate of the FDN (anything larger would be unmanageable, they had decided). He promised this directorate would have the full backing of the United States government and that we would march into Managua by July 1983. When I said that struck me as very little time, he conceded that the victory might take until the end of the year.

I was glad to see that the Americans were committed enough to our cause to be taking such an active role, and I was flattered

as well. I said yes. Over the next several days Feldman took control of the operation and moved the headquarters two blocks
down to the less fancy Four Ambassadors, where we met constantly. The men from Washington wanted at all costs to have a
woman on the directorate. What did I think of Lucia Salazar, Jorge Salazar's widow? I agreed that appointing her would be a good
idea. They ran down the general qualities required for all the directors: must have been anti-Somocista; must have a reputation
for honesty and not too much fondness for money; must be willing to move to Honduras and devote all their time to politics.
They suggested names quickly, as if spontaneously. But I sensed
that they had already decided whom they wanted. It was clear
they didn't want Cardenal because he didn't get along with Bermudez. When Cardenal was not named to the new directorate,
he quit politics altogether. He now sells life insurance in Miami.

Along the way my friends and I tried to raise the substantive
issues that had concerned us all along. Knowing that Bermudez
had forced Cardenal out of Honduras, we wanted assurances that
we civilians would have authority over the military officers. Feldman and his assistants told me they wanted to dilute Bermudez's
power with a larger directorate, to kick him upstairs. I also wanted Nicaraguans to approve the budget and control the money.
Feldman agreed to this in principle, but said we would work out
the details later. I also asked for a clear definition of what our
goals were and what the Americans' goals were. This I never received.

We didn't discuss these things in great detail. The most important thing Feldman said repeatedly was that the CIA had to
put together a group of Nicaraguans—non-Somocistas—before
Congress voted on the Boland Amendment prohibiting U.S. aid
to forces fighting to overthrow the Sandinistas. He emphasized
that we had to go public quickly in order to get Congress to ease
its position.

So we moved on to cosmetic issues. Some other Nicaraguan
exiles working with me wrote the statement for the press conference. It was mostly about the right to private property, and it was
very anticommunist. Thomas Castillo was sitting at the conference table in the suite at the Four Ambassadors when he read it.
"Shit, who wrote this?" he said, shaking his head. "It sounds like
all you want is to get back what you lost. You have to write something more progressive, more political. We'll get someone from

Washington to help you." That's when George was called in. My friends who worked with him told me later that he insisted they rewrite everything to make it more socialistic. The Americans, I began to realize, liked to make all the crucial decisions.

My doubts, though, were still relatively minor. I was convinced the Sandinistas had to be thrown out. All along I had said we had to see how serious the Americans were about helping us, and the only way to do that was to play by their rules. So I quit my job at Cargill and devoted myself full-time to the FDN. The CIA promised me a salary of $2,000 a month plus expenses and I was put in charge of public relations.

We wanted to set up highly visible headquarters in a shopping center or office building, but the CIA didn't like the idea. They said it would become a target for demonstrations or violence. They insisted that we take an elegant suite at the David Williams Hotel in Coral Gables, which they paid for. The directors met there to draw up work plans. The CIA men sat by, with their yellow legal pads, writing down whatever we said we needed.

The FDN's first public relations coup was not my doing. It originated, I think, with Feldman's superiors in Washington. The idea was to put out a 12-point peace initiative—a move I thought was premature given the fact that we had launched our war initiative only a month before. But on January 13, 1983, we released the initiative, which essentially demanded the surrender of the Sandinista government. I asked why we were doing all this.

"This is 90 percent propaganda," Castillo explained. He suggested I write a letter to the Socialist International asking to be invited to explain the initiative at its upcoming annual meeting. "There's no way they will invite you, but it will give the FDN lots of publicity. It'll be news." So I signed the letters to the Socialist International.

In March 1983, while Bermudez and I were in Honduras, the other five directors spent a month presenting the case for the *contras* to politicians and reporters in Europe. Adolfo Calero, a former Coco-Cola distributor in Managua and increasingly the most powerful civilian on the directorate, and Indalecio Rodriguez, a former rector of the University of Central America, did a good job of winning support in Germany and Spain.

Unfortunately the other three directors mostly enjoyed the $5,000 in expense money that the CIA had given each of them.

Lucia Salazar, Alfonso Callejas, and Marco Zeledon, a prominent Nicaraguan businessman, sometimes treated the trip as a free vacation, courtesy of the American taxpayer. Zeledon, Salazar, and Callejas missed their planes and appointments. The CIA man began to suspect hanky-panky. "Is Zeledon screwing Lucia?" one of them asked me one day after their return. "I don't know if he's screwing her," I told him, "but he's screwing you."

I moved to Tegucigalpa, the capital of Honduras, to run the *contras'* public relations office. With CIA money I hired several writers, reporters, and technicians to prepare a monthly bulletin called *"Comandos,"* to run our radio station, and to write press releases. My friend George had been made deputy to the CIA station chief in Tegucigalpa, and he worked with me in our headquarters in a safe house.

Bermudez stayed in Honduras to command the *contra* troops, and Indalecio Rodriguez stayed to work with refugees fleeing Nicaragua. The other four directors worked out of Miami or Washington, mainly to lobby Congress. I sat in on meetings where the CIA men advised them how to win votes for continued CIA funding. The CIA men didn't have much respect for Congress. They said we could change how representatives voted as long as we knew how to "sell" our case and place them in a position of looking soft on communism. They suggested members whom we should lobby and gave us the names of big shots we should contact in their home districts.

I continued to press for some clear definiton of what we were hoping to achieve and how specifically we were going to achieve it. Once we arrived in Honduras, Feldman's promise that we would be in Managua before the end of the year seemed to recede. The CIA station chief in Tegucigalpa spoke only of holding territory in the Isabelia mountain range, and pestering the Sandinista army so as to weaken it. I knew the CIA was talking with other anti-Sandinista groups in Miami and Central America, but they never put us together. And I don't think it was just political differences among the groups that blocked unification. If Bermudez and other National Guardsmen were the obstacle, the CIA could get rid of them. But I realized the CIA wanted to keep us apart. That way they didn't have to commit themselves to anyone. They were using us for their own purposes. Whatever their bigger plan was—defending the Monroe Doctrine or practicing "containment" or whatever—they were hiding it from us.

I slowly got a sense of what the CIA's plans did not include as I attempted to improve the *contras'* image. Especially in my first year, it was standard *contra* practice to kill Sandinista prisoners and collaborators. In talking with officers in the *contra* camps along the Honduran borders, I frequently heard offhand remarks like, "Oh, I cut his throat." It was like stomping on a cockroach to them. So I admitted to the press that there had been executions. I said that they were not part of our policy, and that we had to train our men better. The CIA and Bermudez didn't like my candor, but in the long run it won credibility with the press, and I believe it had a positive influence in the conduct of the war.

I also established a program of political education for the soldiers. I printed up a little manual called the *Blue and White Book* that talked about the meaning of democracy, social justice, and so on. The soldiers could carry it with them at all times and educate themselves about what they were fighting for. The military commanders liked it but never understood the importance of it. I doubt if Bermudez ever read it.

The political dimension of the struggle meant nothing to the commanders. They all had the simplistic belief that Somoza lost because he had his hands tied by Jimmy Carter and that if he hadn't he could have killed a lot of people and won. The Argentine officers who trained them had told them, "We're the only people in Latin America who've beaten the communists in a war. The way to win is to fight a 'dirty war' like we did in the 1970s." I became convinced that the combination of Argentine training and National Guard mentality was one of the major obstacles to putting the *contra* movement on a truly democratic path.

Bermudez's best friend was Ricardo "Chino" Lau, who was one of the most notorious and brutal National Guardsmen under Somoza. Even months after Calero announced that Lau had resigned from the FDN, Lau was still the last person to talk to Bermudez at night and the first person to talk to him in the morning. Bermudez was even feared by his own officers. At one meeting of the directorate three of our top intelligence officers said they each suspected that Bermudez and Lau were plotting to kill them, and they asked us what we were going to do. There was nothing we could do. Bermudez, of course, denied it. But Bermudez demanded total loyalty and intimidated physically those who didn't provide it. Along with Calero and Calero's top aide, a civilian Somocista named Aristides Sanches, Bermudez was unchallengeable. Privately, we referred to this threesome as the "Bermudez triangle."

Needless to say, the civilian directors of the *contras* did not gain control of the military. Despite Feldman's promise, we didn't even get complete control of the budget. It took six months just to get a Nicaraguan keeping the books. (One of the Argentines had been doing them up till then.) And even then we could only approve the budgets for troop supplies, for logistical goods such as gasoline and rented trucks, and for political efforts. We were never given the right to decide either how much we would spend on weapons or what kinds of weapons we wanted. I'm not sure the CIA even let Bermudez in on those decisions. And the civilians never had any say in military strategy. There was simply no mechanism for consultation. When I tried to raise the matter of civilian control with the CIA people, I was politely brushed aside. Their attitude was we were at the war stage of the struggle. Politics would come later.

The only time all seven *contra* directors came to Honduras was whenever Dewey Maroni, the chief of the project for the CIA, flew in. We first met with Maroni at one of our safe houses in Tegucigalpa in July 1983. He was a powerfully built man with a barrel chest and a Bronx accent. He smoked cigars and spoke with authority. As he sat among us, he reminded me of a proconsul come to tell his subjects what to do and how to do it. I have never witnessed such arrogance while working with a foreigner.

During his next visit in October 1983, Maroni proposed appointing a chairman of the directorate, an idea I favored. He started saying that this chairman should be able to work in Washington, not be Somocista, be known in Washington, and so on. It became obvious he was describing Calero. Calero was a politician who worked 15 hours a day and regarded the CIA as his constituency. We directors went into another room to vote. It was as easy as picking the color of Napoleon's white horse. When we came back in the room, Maroni shook Calero's hand. "Congratulations, Mr. President," he said. We had elected a chairman, and Maroni, in an unusual demonstration of the popular will, had immediately promoted him to president.

At 2 a.m. on January 5, 1984, George woke me up at my safe house in Tegucigalpa and handed me a press release in excellent Spanish. I was surprised to read that we—the *contras*—were taking credit for having mined several Nicaraguan harbors. George told me to rush to our clandestine radio station and read this announcement before the Sandinistas broke the news. Of course, we played no role in the mining of the harbors. This was not unusual. The CIA often gave us credit (or perhaps blame) for operations that we knew nothing about. The CIA employed its team of "Latino assets" to bomb the Sandinistas' petroleum tanks at Punto Corinto in October 1983. When I protested to George, asking why the CIA didn't simply give us the money and let patriotic Nicaraguans do the job, he sighed, "This is the way they want us to do it in Washington."

Meanwhile our own operations were getting inadequate support. We had doubled the number of volunteers in our forces from 3,500 to 7,000 in 1983. But we had too few machine guns and airplanes, and too little logistical support when we operated inside Nicaraguan territory. Finally, in the summer we received two C-47 planes that the CIA had been promising for months. They had poor avionics and poor defense systems. They were practically flying coffins. I remember meeting with the CIA people at the Marriott Hotel in Rosslyn, Virginia, around this time. One director told me the CIA had prepared a "nice treat" for his visit to Washington: a tour of museums and restaurants. I said, "Don't forget to go to the Smithsonian, where you'll see a C-47 as old as the one that these gentlemen will give us someday."

I got the feeling the CIA didn't want to let us in. I thought we should try to capture a town, but the CIA said it was impossible. In a way they were right. People in Nicaragua still half believed that the Sandinistas were getting better. They weren't ready for another change. Our troops took the town of Ocotal once for a few hours, but the people didn't rejoice to see us. They just said, "Good, you killed the brutal Sandinista guy." They didn't speak out for the FDN, and our soldiers didn't know how to talk to them. This was the price we paid for not emphasizing democratic goals and not working as a constitutional movement. The Americans wanted an army they could control. They didn't want to risk an insurrection that was not under their control.

My position in the FDN was getting more precarious. The chain of events that ultimately led me to leave began around this time. In the fall of 1983 a CIA man known as John Kirkpatrick arrived in Honduras. Kirkpatrick was a character out of a Graham Greene novel. He was very critical of the top brass of the FDN and loved the lowest and poorest soldiers. He drank too much and cried all the time. He was excited by my political education work with our troops, and wanted to prepare a psychological warfare manual as well.

We worked a few hours a day for a week or two, then Kirkpatrick finished the manuscript with my secretary. When the manual came back from the printer, I discovered two passages that I thought were immoral and dangerous. One recommended hiring professional criminals. The other advocated killing our fellow *contras* to create martyrs for the cause. I didn't particularly want to be martyred by the CIA in its struggle against international communism. Besides, the assassination of Pedro Joacquin Chamorro and the terrible consequences of changing the destiny of a nation through political killing was fresh in my memory. I locked up all the copies of the manual and hired two youths to cut out the offending pages and glue in expurgated pages. I thought that was the end of the matter.

I saw Dewey Maroni for the last time on June 14, 1984, and found his views had changed. A year before he had praised Eden Pastora for his ability to inspire the peasantry. Now he said he had given up on Pastora, and he addressed himself fondly to Bermudez; "Well done, Colonel. Keep it up. Your boys are doing fine." I realized that it was all over for those of us who wanted to make the *contras* a democratic political movement. Shortly after that Calero told me I could no long work in Honduras. I returned to Miami to work with the local FDN committe, but I learned that Calero had told FDN people not to invite me to any FDN functions.

In October 1984 a *New York Times* reporter obtained a copy of the original version of the psychological warfare manual, and the CIA and the Reagan administration were embarrassed by repugnant passages. Calero immediately concluded that I had told the *Times* about it (I hasn't't) in order to defeat Reagan in the presidential election. We met one last time in Miami a week after the election. He called me a traitor and I called him a dictator. On November 20, 1984, I received a letter saying that the FDN directorate had unanimously agreed to relieve me of my duties.

I now believe that a political dialogue in Nicaragua should be the United States's top priority. We have tried military pressure, and it hasn't worked. It hasn't created the conditions for democracy and it hasn't forced the Sandinistas to negotiate. The first step toward national reconciliation must be abolition of the *contra* army. By urging the rebels to lay down their guns, the United States would strengthen the moderates and weaken the extremists on both sides. President Reagan should also lower his inflammatory rhetoric and give more than lip service to the Contadora peace initiative sponsored by Mexico, Colombia, Venezuela, and Panama. Contadora still offers the best chance for achieving a lasting political solution.

When I joined the *contras* in December 1982, I thought the United States and the CIA wanted to restore the promise of the Sandinista revolution. Now I think they are very pro-counterrevolution. The idealistic young people who actually fought against the Sandinista army have real grievances. Their land has been confiscated or they have been persecuted for their religious views or they have resisted the Sandinista draft. But they are being used as an instrument of U.S. foreign policy by the CIA and the Reagan administration. And they are being used by the National Guardsmen and Somocista politicians who simply want to go back to Nicaragua to get back the money and the power they lost in 1979. If the *contras* ever took power, they would simply replace the communists with a law-and-order regime and no one would be any better off. What's more, many of the civilian *contra* leaders have children in their teens or 20s, and yet they do not send them to fight the war they favor so much. They expect the *campesinos* to continue to die while they live in Miami and wait for their dream to come true. I am now convinced that the *contra* cause for which I gave up two years of my life offers Nicaragua nothing but a return to the past.

UNITED STATES POLICY IN CENTRAL AMERICA:
A CHOICE DENIED[8]

Perhaps the most accurate statement to be made about United States policy toward Central America is that there is no coher-
ent United States policy toward the region. If each Central
American nation elicited its own considered, consistent response
from Washington, a regional policy might not be missed. But current policy is less tailored than torn. Not only do the President
and Congress not see eye to eye but the Executive—the dominant
force in foreign affairs—is of two minds, neither of which can
convince the other. As one State Department official recently put
it, "The two main alternatives to current policy—outright military intervention or a political solution—are both unacceptable,
but there's no agreement on what else to do."

The United States government is spending more money on
Central America, shipping more arms, cataloging its problems
more thoroughly, and intervening in elections more deeply—all
without a clear course set by the President, his Cabinet and his
aides. Each of the alternatives—"outright military intervention
or a political solution"—have their proponents in high office. But
each of these strategies carries a cost that, so far, the President
and his inner circle have been unwilling to accept, although the
White House has been unable to find a third alternative.

However, lack of agreement has not put United States action
on hold. Each Washington faction has its troops and pursues its
own vision. The State Department and Congress have explored
possible political solutions. "Special envoys" and congressional
delegations have talked with all parties to the Central American
conflict, including those the administration opposes—the
Sandinista government of Nicaragua and the Farabundo Martí
National Liberation Front and its political affiliate, the Democratic Revolutionary Front (FMLN-FDR) in El Salvador.

Many Latin American and West European observers believe
that a negotiated solution remains the best hope and a real possibility for ending the conflict. Since 1981, Mexico—joined the fol-

[8]Reprint of an article by Eldon Kenworthy, professor of government, Cornell University. *Current History*. Mr.
'85. p. 97+. Copyright 1985 Current History, Inc. Reprinted with permission.

lowing year by other countries bordering Central America
(Venezuela, Colombia and Panama)—has presided over many
meetings of the Central American states, trying to find common
ground. These negotiations by the Contadora group (named for
the Panamanian island on which the four countries first met in
1982) have produced a series of draft agreements, each one reducing the number of unresolved issues until a supposedly final
Contadora treaty emerged in September, 1984.

Hope for a political solution has also sprung from negotiations between the Sandinistas and the Democratic Coordination
Alliance (the regime's most influential opponents, which includes
politicians, businessmen and union leaders), and between the
Sandinistas and one of the two Indian groups that have taken up
arms against them. With the Archbishop acting as intermediary,
discussions between the Salvadoran government of President
José Napoleón Duarte and the FMLN-FDR have also been initiated. In most observers' eyes, the keystone of a political solution remains the Contadora process which enjoys the backing of most
Latin American and West European governments and is seen as
a Latin American solution to a Latin American problem.

The nearer Contadora has come to fruition, however, the
more obstacles Washington has placed in its path, principally by
influencing its clients—the governments of El Salvador, Honduras and Costa Rica—to raise new objections. When the Sandinistas accepted the treaty in its supposedly final form in
September, 1984, Washington pronounced the document
"unsatisfactory," although it had never before publicly criticized
its evolution. In its final version, the Contadora treaty addresses
all the issues the Reagan administration said should be addressed,
including democratic elections, and does so in ways that apparently accommodate legitimate United States national interests.
Thus Washington's newly found dissatisfaction with the treaty's
"verification mechanisms" seems contrived. United States surveil-
lance in Managua is extensive and sophisticated; it is hard to believe that verification presents a genuine obstacle for the Reagan
administration.

A leaked National Security Council (NSC) directive, signed by
the President in April, 1983, described administration strategy as
an effort "to coopt [the] negotiations issue to avoid congressional-
ly mandated negotiations. More recently, in another leaked NSC
briefing paper, the administration congratulated itself for having

"effectively blocked" the latest Contadora initiative. Given the financial and/or military dependence of several Central American governments on Washington and the reality of United States power in the region, the Contadora process cannot succeed if the Reagan administration continues to undercut it.

Thus, while Secretary of State George Shultz is described in the Washington press as interested in a political solution, either his views do not prevail or the solution he has in mind differs greatly from that painstakingly worked out by the Contadora countries, who are democratic allies of the United States. No doubt special United States envoys will continue to travel and talk but, lacking the President's commitment, the "political solution" will be more "used" than made use of.

Nonetheless, the Contadora treaty would seem to provide the answer to Washington's dilemmas. If implemented, it would dampen conflict by isolating one country's civil war from another's and by reducing the inflow of foreign arms; it would also prevent the Soviet Union or the Cubans from establishing a military presence in the area through bases or advisers. The fear the administration most frequently voices regarding leftists in power in Nicaragua—"a faraway totalitarian power . . . turning Central America into a string of anti-American, Soviet-styled dictatorships"—would seem to be effectively answered by Contadora. This is an agreement, moreover, that regional powers like Mexico and Venezuela have a stake in enforcing. In effect, in the Contadora treaty Latin America would acknowledge Washington's international role in Central America in exchange for clearer restraints on United States and Soviet and Cuban involvement in the internal affairs of this region.

Why, then, is this solution sabotaged by an administration that has its hands full in the Middle East and, more recently, in arms negotiations with the Soviet Union? Two answers point in the same direction. First, the United States refuses to legitimize the Sandinista government by endorsing an agreement shaped and signed by the Sandinistas. Second, Washington relies on a double standard in its dealings with Central America. The provisions in Contadora that limit Soviet-Cuban military influence in Nicaragua would also limit United States military influence in El Salvador. If Managua cannot supply leftist insurgents in El Salvador, then Washington cannot supply rightist insurgents in Nicaragua. There is no way that Mexico, Venezuela, Colombia and

Panama could lend their good offices to an arrangement that merely cloaks imperialism. Nor could Nicaragua, Costa Rica and Guatemala sign such an agreement.

### The Military Option

As in the case of the "political solution," preparations for a "military solution" have proceeded apace. Indeed, they have proceeded at a pace so rapid as to cause many observers to conclude that this is the United States policy. In this instance, as in the case of the political/diplomatic approach, officials near but not quite at the top of the decision-making apparatus have acted as if they had the green light, only to find their efforts checked. But far greater resources have been devoted to a military than to a political solution. It is the "unchosen" option with the greatest momentum.

By April, 1984, *The New York Times* found the Defense Department "now in a position to assume a combat role in Central America should President Reagan give the order." By that time, nearly 2,000 United States military personnel were on continuous duty in Honduras and El Salvador, compared to 200 a year earlier. Military maneuvers—begun in 1982 and projected into 1988—frequently boost this total to 20,000 or 30,000, including sailors and marines on ships nearby. A half dozen airfields have been constructed in Honduras, which borders both El Salvador and Nicaragua, and Honduras has been filled with military supplies. Sophisticated reconnaissance grids are now in place and links have been laid for coordinating United States commands with those of allied armies.

"Perhaps more remarkable than the buildup's pace," notes the *Washington Post*, "is the way it has unfolded, frequently overtaking administration pronouncements about the U.S. role and largely without the public authorizations that normally accompany foreign commitments. Congress has been continually surprised to discover how the restraints it placed on United States military involvement in this region have been stretched beyond the limits of language and law. "Military advisers" did not include "trainers," airfields were only "temporary," drawing combat pay did not mean soldiers were in danger, to cite only some statements from the Defense Department. Half the United States military aid sent to El Salvador has not been approved through the usual congressional channels.

The Central Intelligence Agency (CIA) has flouted the Boland Amendment, which prohibits the use of United States funds
"for the purpose of overthrowing the Nicaraguan government,"
and has withheld information from congressional oversight committees; for this reason, in October 1984, Congress took the unprecedented step of freezing all funding for CIA paramilitary
actions aimed at Nicaragua. This does not spell the end of United
States involvement, only the privatization of its role in dealing
with Nicaragua's contras. (Contras are anti-Sandinista Nicaraguans, operating primarily out of Honduras.) The CIA is currently facilitating support for the contras from private United States
citizens and organizations and from other governments, despite
the ban on such activity in the United States Criminal Code.

Not only has there been a fivefold increase in CIA operations
since Jimmy Carter left the presidency, half of them in Central
America, but there has been a significant growth in the uni-
formed services' "special operations" as well. Since both are secret, the extent to which United States personnel are now
engaged in combat missions can only be surmised. Sixteen of the
35 "accidental" fatalities reported by the United States Army in
1983 occurred in one battalion that ferries commandos to and
from clandestine missions. Pledged to secrecy, many of these helicopter pilots told their families they were "going south" before
being reported killed in accidents caused by "mechanical failure"
in United States waters.

Disguising the real role of United States soldiers reportedly
killed in the line of duty, along with the doublespeak disguising
the extent of military and CIA operations, point to the cost of any
military solution. Opinion polls consistently show the American
public to be wary of deeper involvement in Central America, primarily because Americans fear the loss of American lives. Rarely
has President Reagan received a higher than 30 percent approval
rating for his Central American policy. On few other issues does
this popular President meet such consistent skepticism and resistance. The United States invasion of Grenada was popular because it fulfilled the public's desire to see its country "stand tall"
at little cost. Inasmuch as administration-manipulated images of
the invasion cast it as a "rescue operation," this intervention also
flattered Americans' image of their role in the world.

But the administration has not been able to repeat this public
relations success in Central America. President Reagan delivers

a solemn speech to a joint session of Congress invoking duty and honor; there is a trumped-up charge that Soviet MiG's are being secretly delivered to Nicaragua; Central America has been a prime-time drama whose theme is Soviet penetration of the hemisphere. Yet, for whatever reason, according to pollster Barry Sussman, "on foreign policy Reagan has seldom been able to move the country toward his thinking."

Thus there is a paradox: every move toward a military solution in Central America is presented to the American people as a way to avoid sending troops there. Whenever the administration seeks more funding for the Central American armies it supports (including the anti-Sandinista contras) or for its own military maneuvers, constructions and operations, the White House presents its request as the only way to end the conflict in Central America without using American troops. According to National Security Adviser Robert McFarlane, the "gray area" of covert actions, accompanied by generous supplies to the Salvadoran and Honduran militaries, ensures that the United States will not face the agonizing choice of losing these conflicts or losing its soldiers. Funding is presented as the prudent middle choice.

This is no doubt the preferred policy: a military solution at minimal cost, especially in United States lives. The political solution inevitably confers a rough equality on all participants, like them or not, and at least means accepting the equal status of those sitting at the same bargaining table. The military solution avoids the need for compromise. Although the administration claims that its strong military posture promotes diplomacy, that claim rings hollow. In fact, the overwhelming military advantage enjoyed by Washington, and the use of that advantage to intimidate (massing warships off Nicaragua's shore, cracking sonic booms with illegal overflights) suggest the kind of "diplomacy" that leaves opponents only the option of capitulation. Certainly the Nicaraguans cannot negotiate away their very identity as Marxist reformers, which is what Washington seems to want.

*Fighting by Proxy*

To get one's way without compromise and without paying the cost that force usually entails means finding someone else to fight. In El Salvador—a nation the size of New Jersey, half of whose five million people are peasants—the United States has spent nearly half a billion dollars on the military, training four of its battalions, providing the technological edge (helicopter gunships) and setting military strategy. While the tide of battle shifts with the seasons and the offensives, who would say that the guerrillas are fewer in number, or control less terrain and population, today than before Washington's massive military transfusion began?

In Nicaragua, military solution by proxy fares worse. There one finds a similar pattern, with the CIA filling in for the Defense Department. Contra soldiers have been organized, trained, supplied and directed by United States personnel. As with the Salvadoran military, their numbers have ballooned but their capacity to achieve even modest victories has not been strengthened. Despite widespread criticism within Nicaragua of the Sandinista leadership, the contra support has not broadened beyond a small upper class and some Indian groups.

One problem with the cheap military solution is that client militaries in Central America have ingrained patterns of abusing their people. No serious student of El Salvador accepts the administration's contention that the Salvadoran death squads are independent of the military or that a month's training at Fort Benning can cancel a decades-old pattern of relying on brutality to silence protest. Most of those commanding the Nicaraguan contras in the field (in contrast to their political leaders who speak to the press) are ex-Somocista National Guardsmen with a similar tradition of abusing their citizens.

To compensate for their individual weaknesses and to gain for the military solution the mantle of "inter-American" legitimacy, the Reagan administration has tried to revive CONDECA, the Central American Defense Council, excluding Nicaragua, one of its three original members. A Defense Department suggestion would have the rightist governments of Central America and Washington recognize the contras who have established a toehold on Nicaraguan soil as Nicaragua's government. This government could then appeal to CONDECA for action against the Sandinistas. General Paul Gorman, the head of the Defense Department's Southern Command, has crisscrossed Central America, calling meetings and pressuring officials in pursuit of this objective. According to the *Washington Post*, Gorman has become a "virtual proconsul in the area, frequently overshadowing senior diplomats and at times overruling them."

In Washington, similar solutions have allegedly been promoted by Fred Iklé, the Swiss-born strategist on United States–Soviet affairs who, as the Undersecretary of Defense for Policy, runs the "little State Department" in the Department of Defense. In promoting a hard line Iklé is joined by Nestor Sanchez, Deputy Assistant Secretary of Defense for Inter-American Affairs, and by Constantine Menges, the National Security Council's senior adviser on Latin America. Sanchez and Menges have close ties to the CIA's upper echelons through prior employment there. All three have a close ally in CIA Director William Casey and, at the State Department, in J. William Middendorf 2d, the United States representative to the Organization of American States.

As the President turns his attention to negotiations with the Soviet Union with an eye to an entry in the history books, he must placate right-wing supporters who see agreement with the Kremlin as unsound, immoral or both. It is possible that some administration officials would allow hard-line right-wingers to determine Central American policy if the right-wingers allow the White House to bargain with the Soviet Union. In early 1985, those who advocate a military solution in Central America—for that is what refusing to accept the Sandinista government's existence means—occupy key roles. On this issue, the "ideologues" have not given way to the "pragmatists."

Attempts to revive CONDECA have run afoul of historic rivalries within the region and a growing reluctance, on the part of Hondurans and Guatemalans, to do Washington's bidding. The fig leaf of an inter-American action, which covered the United States invasion of Santo Domingo two decades ago, requires the approval of two-thirds of the members of the Organization of American States (OAS). Inasmuch as the majority of OAS members, including the influential four (Brazil, Mexico, Argentina, and Venezula), oppose a military solution in Central America, it is unlikely that Washington can muster the votes.

Civilian hard-liners may dream of "Central Americanizing" the conflict and United States officers in the field may try to make that happen. Gorman is described by associates as "not the sort to sit back and let events take their course." Nonetheless, one senses the caution of the Joint Chiefs of Staff behind Secretary of Defense Caspar Weinberger's assurance that United States military forces will not "creep—or be drawn gradually—into a combat role in Central America."

The Joint Chiefs are not represented, however, at the National Security Planning Group meetings the President instituted so that decisions on covert actions could be made by a few trusted principals without leaks and without undue staff influence. A *New York Times* description of these meetings merits quoting at length:

As a general rule, officials said those at the meetings were given no advance notification that proposed covert operations were to be discussed at a meeting. They said papers normally prepared by the CIA were passed out at the meeting itself and then collected at the end of the meeting. Mr. Reagan usually makes his decision at the table. Thus, according to the sources, those who attend are often without the benefit of staff advice before or during the meeting.

There is no cheap military way out of the United States dilemma. Military aid to El Salvador in fiscal year 1984 equaled that of the previous three years combined. Pressures are growing to increase the number of American military advisers there and to expand their roles. United States economic assistance sluices through the country in quantities no one can keep track of; two-thirds of the aid is underwriting trade in an attempt to dull the war's impact on the urban classes.

To most critics of administration policy, the costs of even flirting with a military solution outweigh the costs of a political solution, and critics doubt that a political solution can be fashioned while emphasizing the military. The foregoing analysis obviously identifies the author as a critic. In large measure this analysis is shared by students of Central America, be they scholars or professional diplomats. Resolutions on United States policy adopted by the Latin American Studies Association—the most inclusive organization of United States scholars involved with the region— mirror the recommendations of the Inter-American Dialogue sponsored by the Smithsonian Institute's Woodrow Wilson Center, comprised of recent Latin American Foreign Ministers, ex–United States Cabinet members, and other notables. They support Contadora.

## Credibility

The ultimate test for any analyst is to account for the opposing point of view. Why is it that the political solution that seems so promising to scholars appears so dangerous to policymakers? To answer this question one must confront the policymakers' charge that the "credibility" of United States global leadership is on the line in Central America, and then try to plumb the unvoiced fears that may lie behind this assertion. The Reagan administration came to power determined to reverse what it perceived as its predecessor's weakness in dealing with "communism" and "terrorism" abroad, especially in the third world. Central America seemed to offer the first and safest opportunity for the new administration to demonstrate to the world that the United States was back and standing tall. "Mr. President, this is one you can win," Alexander Haig, the incoming Secretary of State, told the new President. Haig had El Salvador in mind.

Haig also talked of "going to the source" of our troubles in Central America, meaning Cuba. Since the 1962 missile crisis, however, Cuba has had explicit Soviet protection; it is the Soviet Union's West Berlin. Nicaraguan and Salvadoran leftists do not enjoy comparable protection. Enough of the populations of these Central American countries oppose United States intervention, however, to threaten another Vietnam should Washington reestablish its credibility at their expense. In any case, credibility is a difficult god to appease. Does credibility require the removal of all Marxist regimes within the United States sphere of influence, whenever the United States is presumed capable of taking such action? Or is once enough? Where does Nicaragua stand, given Grenada?

From the beginning this administration has framed the debate over Central America in terms of United States credibility worldwide. "If the United States cannot respond to a threat near our own border," the President told a joint session of Congress convened in 1983 to sound the alarm on Central America,

why should Europeans and Asians believe we are seriously concerned about threats to them? If the Soviets can assume that nothing short of an actual attack on the United States will provoke an American response, which ally, which friend will trust us then? . . . Our credibility would collapse, our alliances would crumble.

The National Bipartisan Commission on Central America, created by the President to provide a rationale for United States policy, picked up the theme. Its report explains how United States credibility is undermined by *any* Marxist regime in the hemisphere, no matter how innocuous its behavior.

What are we to conclude? As with "domino theory," credibility deals in perceptions and worst-case possibilities, not in current events. Crudely or subtly, the Reagan administration tries to transfer fears rooted in the United States—Soviet nuclear stalemate—where a preoccupation with remote but extremely damaging possibilities is appropriate—to an arena where the United States confronts weak nonnuclear states to which Moscow has made no military commitment.

How did this moment arise for the United States in its relationship to Central America? Long the stated goal of United States policy toward that region, the actual "development" of strong states and politically conscious publics generated a dilemma. Abraham Lowenthal, a scholar writing on United States-Latin American relations out of considerable experience in Washington, sums up the situation this way:

The fundamental difficulty for the United States in Central America derives from the fact that our leadership is used to nearly absolute U.S. control. . . . The days of easy and total U.S. dominance are past.

While Nicaragua is the Central American nation that most clearly embodies the United States difficulty, the problem arises whenever a protest movement is popular enough to capture power, is Marxist/nationalist in orientation, and is in the backyard. There is every reason to believe more such combinations will arise in Central America and the Caribbean. Like it or not, dissent in this region uses the language of Marx more often than that of Jefferson, is nationalist more often than pan-American, and rarely trusts what President Reagan calls "the magic of the marketplace."

With the election of José Napoleón Duarte, El Salvador has been bent back into something Washington can recognize. There United States leaders can plausibly (if inaccurately) argue that the Marxist opposition is "unrepresentative" and can claim to support a process ("democracy"), not merely a client. The Nicaraguan election that ratified the "wrong" group, however, was no less fair than the Salvadoran. In Nicaragua, Washington discouraged opposition parties from participating in that election. In Nicaragua, the United States underwrites "freedom fighters" who, were they transplanted to El Salvador, would be condemned as "terrorists." In short, Nicaragua is—as the British found the fledgling United States in 1776—a world turned upside down.

Examining the pattern of United States policy toward Central America, critics notice behavior that can be termed reality avoidance. Such behavior includes the simultaneous pursuit of contradictory strategies, misnamings, retreats into rhetoric and fantasies rooted in the past. The so-called political solution seems promising to those not holding the reins of power but invokes fears in those who do, fears sometimes disguised as bluster à la Winston Churchill. On whose "watch," United States politicians ask, will Central America be "lost"?

What is threatening in the political solution is the potential reordering of relationships: away from the top-down control characteristic of spheres of influence toward the bargaining that recognizes the rights of all parties, including the right of each to know its own interest. The Panama Canal Treaties renegotiated by President Jimmy Carter embody this reordering. Is United States access to the canal now less secure? Most observers would claim the contrary. United States technological and economic superiority will not be lost if greater equality in diplomacy is accepted.

Sorting out a new relationship to Central America, in any case, means a discussion in Congress and among the public that has not yet been scheduled. The foreign relations committees of Congress have atrophied. The new leadership of the Ninety-ninth Congress has an opportunity to remedy that. The public has grown lazy, abetted by a long line of administrations that, under the rubric of "politics stops at the water's edge," have preached, "Don't question; trust us." This administration's frequent retreats behind secrecy have not helped. For example, it has withheld evidence it says it has of *massive* arms flows from Nicaragua to El Salvador, or what the President calls a "flood of weapons" (evidence most nongovernment specialists doubt exists). Neither is it helpful to dismiss as the "Vietnam syndrome" the instinctively intelligent public concern about deeper military involvement in Central America. For their part, the media moves from crisis to crisis without exploring long-term patterns. There is blame enough for everyone.

At the same time, the Central American crisis presents the United States with an opportunity. What relationship do Americans want with the small and impoverished societies that lie in North America's shadow? Is that relationship sustainable year in and year out, or is it a fantasy revived in moments of crisis after long lapses of indifference? The urge for control, to "stand tall" the way President Theodore Roosevelt (or John Wayne) did, is an anachronism, a turning away from this opportunity to go forward.

# III. THE NICARAGUAN RESPONSE: DEFIANCE AND WOUNDED NATIONAL PRIDE

## EDITOR'S INTRODUCTION

Virtually from its infancy, Nicaragua's revolutionary government has been in conflict with the U.S. The siege mentality created by this confrontation is analyzed in Forrest D. Colburn's article from *Current History*. The second article, reprinted from *America* magazine, is an interview with the Nicaraguan foreign minister, the Rev. Miguel d'Escoto Brockman, in which he describes the costly consequences for his country of the long antagonism with its northern neighbor and goes on to discuss such phenomena as the participation of elements of the Roman Catholic church in the government, as well as the suit brought by Nicaragua against the United States before the International Court of Justice, or World Court. The third article, by Saul Landau, is an assessment of the Sandinistas' consolidation of power reprinted from *The Progressive*. The following three articles, taken from the *U.N. Chronicle*, *Department of State Bulletin*, and the *American Journal of International Law* respectively, are responses to the suit before the World Court, in which Nicaragua tried to blunt U.S. antagonism by appealing to the world's only international legal tribunal.

In the seventh article, from the publication *Nicaragua under Siege*, Nicaragua's vice president, Sergio Ramírez Mercado, attempts to link the U.S. and Nicaraguan revolutions, maintaining that the latter is in many ways a completion and logical consequence of the former. This section concludes with the very disparate testimony of three Nicaraguans who have lived under the revolution from its beginnings: a successful Managua businessman, a former prostitute who is now a member of an agricultural cooperative, and a mother of four who works in a child care center in northern Nicaragua's war zone. These are all included in Alvin Levie's collection of interviews, *Nicaragua: The People Speak*.

## NICARAGUA UNDER SIEGE[1]

In the five years since President Anastasio Somoza Debayle took his last flight from Managua to Miami, the reigning Sandinista National Liberation Front (FSLN) has adroitly consolidated political power without the use of openly authoritarian tactics. The elections held on November 4, 1984, with great fanfare were only the pro forma institutionalization of an organizational drive that has extended the authority of the FSLN to even the smallest villages of rural Nicaragua. Special care has been given to train an army that "knows whose interests it is protecting and who the enemies of those interests are." Political strength and a consensus within the revolutionary leadership have enabled the new regime to begin a bold transformation of Nicaragua. The stated objective is to lift the country out of its backwardness and poverty.

Because of its initiative, the disarming concessions it offered, the absence of a well-organized alternative source of power, and its nature as the military vanguard of the revolution, the FSLN dictated the institutional structure of the new government and defined its authority and composition. The key to the FSLN's continued success has been its consistent practice of retaining final authority. The junta, the quasi-legislative Council of State, and the government ministries have always been subservient to the nine FSLN commanders who comprise the National Directorate. Concessions were made initially to other political actors, but they were all of the type that could be rescinded.

The appointment of moderates and conservatives to important government positions is not very consequential when they can be dismissed and replaced at any time. Final authority has enabled the FSLN to increase its authority incrementally, especially in the ministries that conduct most of the day-to-day affairs of the government. These incremental political changes have not been particularly significant individually, but in the aggregate they have had considerable impact.

The FSLN has tried to provide a support base for its consolidation of power at the highest levels of government. Parallel organizations have been established to weaken existing

[1]Reprint of an article by Forrest D. Colburn, assistant professor of political science, Florida International University. Current History. Mr. '85. p. 105+. Copyright 1985 Current History. Reprinted with permission.

organizations (ranging from newspapers to trade unions) that are
not necessarily tied to the FSLN. The most difficult and controversial attempt at undermining an established institution has
been the formation of a "popular church" to offset the strength
of the Catholic Church. Equally important, the FSLN has created
new institutions among the urban and rural poor. These new organizations are commonly called "mass organizations," and include everything from peasant organizations to block committees
(CDS's) modeled after Cuba's Committees for the Defense of the
Revolution (CDR's).

The FSLN-sponsored organizations have been developed and
strengthened through ongoing efforts at political suasion and by
channeling government services and goods through the organizations. For example, continued government employment is dependent on participation in government political organizations.
Ration cards are obtained from the neighborhood block committees. Peasants receiving credit from the government-controlled
banks are expected to affiliate with government organizations.
While outright coercion to affiliate with government organizations has been rare, there are economic costs for not participating. However, in the absence of coercion, the ability of the
government to maintain a relative degree of mobilization depends on its continued ability to channel goods and services to its
supporters.

State-sponsored organizations are strongest in urban areas
for a number of reasons. First, there is what the Mexican intellectual, Octavio Paz, has called the organic link between power and
cities. Labor unions, the church, economic associations, the media, and the government itself are all centered in urban areas.
Second, active support for the revolution has always been strongest in the cities (where the decisive battles were fought). Third,
apart from the counterrevolution, organized opposition is most
visible and strongest in urban areas, encouraging the FSLN to
concentrate its efforts in the principal cities. In contrast, rural organizations are fewer and less important politically.

The FSLN formalized its consolidation of power by winning
the elections held November 4. The validity of the elections has
been debated within Nicaragua and abroad, reflecting the larger
controversy over the leadership of the FSLN. Assessments range
from hagiology to character assassination. The central criticism
of the elections was the lack of participation by the most promi-

nent opposition group, Arturo Cruz's Coordinadora coalition. Another presidential candidate, Virgilio Goday, attempted to take his Independent Liberal party out of the election two weeks before election day, but the ballots had already been printed and distributed. Both candidates asserted that the conditions for meaningful elections did not exist.

International observers concluded that the actual voting was orderly and free from fraud. Many Nicaraguans were pressured to vote by local CDS's and other Sandinista organizations, but the actual casting of ballots was done in secrecy. The stated results of the election were a 91 percent voter turnout, with the FSLN receiving 67 percent of the vote. Three opposition parties to the right of the FSLN received 29 percent of the vote, while the three parties to the left of the FSLN captured less than 4 percent of the vote. The opposition parties together were awarded one-third of the seats in the new legislature. Six percent of the total votes cast were judged to be invalid. These included completely blank ballots and ballots improperly marked or defaced.

While the elections received a great deal of publicity and stimulated considerable debate, they were relatively unimportant. First, power will continue to be exercised not by the elected President, Daniel Ortega, but by the entire FSLN National Directorate (of which Daniel Ortega is a member). The National Directorate has managed to retain a remarkable degree of cohesion. Daniel's brother Humberto is held to be the most influential of the nine commanders, but they all have been steadfast in their commitment to rule by consensus and to keep their differences and ultimate intentions to themselves. Second, the elections did not alter the important configuration of international support or hostility for the regime. Allies were undeterred by criticism of the elections, and adversaries were not swayed by praise of the elections.

*An Economic Crisis*

The Nicaraguan economy is palsied. The FSLN's policies may be sound, but they have produced several economic problems that have threatened the welfare of all Nicaraguans. Nicaragua has fallen victim to the common dilemmas in the immediate, postrevolutionary periods of small third world countries. One set of policies leads to dislocations in productive sectors, resulting in reduced national output. Often this decrease in production is concentrated in the more remunerative export sector, because it tends to have been monopolized by elites—precisely because it was more remunerative. Valued production falls because of state expropriation, which gives an inexperienced bureaucracy an unmanageable responsibility (at least initially) and, equally important, expropriation depresses the private sector, which fears continued expropriations.

A complementary set of policies designed to aid impoverished sectors absorbs resources without a corresponding rise in output—at least in the short run—because the resources are used principally for consumption and not investment. Together the two sets of policies produce an economic crisis. In short, "supply" decreases and "demand" increases. Given the dependence of small developing countries on international trade, the focus of the crisis is usually the balance of payments and the availability of foreign exchange. Drawing down reserves and foreign assistance and borrowing can help cover the resulting imbalance, but ultimately these measures are likely to prove insufficient.

By all accounts, Nicaragua's key economic problem is its shortage of foreign exchange. Nicaragua is not industrialized and depends heavily on imports, so the lack of hard currency means that many products are scarce or unavailable. For the fourth consecutive year, the country is suffering a major trade deficit. The government projected export revenue to be $461 million in 1984. As a bare minimum, however, the government estimates that it needs to import $700 million in raw materials and spare parts annually to keep the economy functioning.

In addition to paying for needed imports, Nicaragua must make regular payments on a quickly growing foreign debt. The FSLN inherited a debt of $1.6 billion when it took power in 1979, and much of that money was misused by the Somoza regime. The inability of the FSLN to keep the balance of payments within reasonable bounds has led to a debt of roughly $3.5 billion, with a corresponding rise in the annual cost of servicing the debt. Nicaragua's annual projected debt payments are now equivalent to annual export earnings. The regime has begun to fall behind in its payments, including payments to the World Bank, but the FSLN maintains that it will honor its financial commitments.

Prospects for help from abroad do not appear bright. West Germany all but ended direct aid to Nicaragua in 1984, and the

Netherlands is reportedly in the process of doing so. The governments of both countries are increasingly critical of the FSLN. Sweden and Spain are the only West European countries with substantial aid programs in Nicaragua. An increasing number of aid projects are sponsored by Soviet-bloc countries, but they do not provide hard currency.

The country's deepening economic distress, which appears to be more acute than at any time since the 1979 revolution, is felt by all Nicaraguans. Consumers complain loudly about chronic shortages, especially of imported goods or products made from imported materials. Domestically produced goods that are available, including many fruits and vegetables, are often prohibitively expensive to lower class consumers. Spare parts of all sorts are difficult to find; thus buses, trucks, tractors and even factories are incapacitated. Roads are not well maintained, telephone service is deteriorating, and medicine is in short supply.

The government spends 10 percent of its budget subsidizing the shelf prices of 13 basic goods, including sugar, meat, milk and cooking oil. However, despite the subsidies and stiff price and wage controls, real per capita income for all classes has declined since the revolution. Estimates of inflation range from 25 to 35 percent. Unemployment is estimated at 20 percent. Economic problems have caused a great deal of cynicism about the FSLN, even with groups otherwise supportive of the revolution. Nicaraguan peasants, with characteristic wit, sometimes dismiss the revolution with such expressions as, "The same garbage, only the flies are different."

Still, the FSLN is confident that with increased experience and an ultimate end to United States aggression it can succeed in its bid to improve the welfare of Nicaraguans. Despite the need to direct resources to defense, the FSLN has continued many investments, ranging from hydrothermal energy projects to the construction of schools and hospitals to the building of what is planned as the largest sugar refinery in Central America. Most economic investments are in the agricultural sector. The government is anxious to increase the production of both agro-exports and of foodstuffs, especially maize. Concomitantly, the government has steadily moved to increase its role in the distribution of goods and services.

### The Private Sector

Still, between 60 and 70 percent of Nicaragua's economic production remains in private hands. The private sector is fearful of nationalization and resentful of the wide range of government policies that regulate private activities. Most of these policies entail intervention in the major markets for the products affecting producers—the markets for the products they consume and sell, and for land, labor and capital. To maintain production in the private sector, the FSLN has had to offer concessions to those with economic strength and not the reverse, despite the revolutionary rhetoric.

The state has made sufficient concessions to large producers of agro-exports like the Pellas family, which singlehandedly produces half of Nicaragua's sugar, and to the farmers who grow cotton, the linchpin of the economy. Generous credit has been made available; the state has held down wage increases for labor and has even used its organizations to help producers find labor during the harvest season; and, most important, the state has provided special price concessions. The rhetoric of the government suggests that despite these concessions large producers do not have a future in Nicaragua, but the concessions lead many producers to conclude that "there is money to be made in every tragedy," and for the most part they maintain existing production.

The state's need for revenue, especially foreign exchange, has prompted it to expropriate nearly all the wealth generated by private production when any specific sector or class does not have the bargaining chip of withdrawing from production. Nicaragua's small coffee producers demonstrate that this is true even if the class status of the sector in question suggests it should benefit from the revolution. There are an estimated 27,000 coffee producers, and 85 percent of them are small, marginal producers with yields only a fifth or sixth of those of most large producers. Unlike cotton, coffee is a fixed investment; once plants begin to bear they do so for years. Though one of the rationales for the establishment of state monopsonies was to aid small producers, small coffee producers report a marked deterioration in their real income. The value of the national currency has fallen precipitously, yet producers are paid for their crops on the basis of a highly overrated exchange rate minus taxes. Since small coffee producers have a fixed investment and lack the resources to withdraw from production, they can only hope for a better future.

The FSLN's agrarian reform program has continued to distribute land to peasants. Nearly 20 percent of Nicaragua's cultivated land has been redistributed. For many peasants, access to land is a long-coveted goal, especially in the northwestern departments where competition for land has always been intense. Unfortunately, for the most part the government has not been able to provide the technological assistance to small producers that would enable them to raise yields. Raising yields would not only contribute to national production, but would also help raise depressed incomes. There are many difficulties, including the sheer number of small peasant producers and their concentration in isolated regions, the emigration of many agricultural technicians and, perhaps most important, the competing need of state farms for agricultural technicians and resources.

Government policies directed at peasants have apparently facilitated access to land for peasants rather than improving the net income from agriculture. On the other hand, diverse changes have influenced the costs and returns for the principal crops of peasants—basic grains. The scarcity of foreign exchange, stemming in large measure from the decreased production of the "bourgeoisie," has driven up the prices of many goods, particularly imported goods. The government has sought to compensate by controlling the prices of many domestically produced commodities—especially food. Of course, since food is grown by peasants, low food prices mean low peasant income. Thus, the advantages to peasants of greater availability of land, made possible by the seizure of large estates, are offset by the low prices paid to peasants in order to protect consumers suffering from shortages because of reduced agricultural exports.

Ironically, the sector that has been asked to make perhaps the greatest sacrifices for the consolidation of the revolution has been the poorest, the landless and nearly landless agricultural workers. The FSLN labored for years to convince the peasants that they were being exploited and that a better future awaited them on the triumph of the revolution. Yet after it seized power, the FSLN switched its propaganda from stressing the unnecessary poverty of most Nicaraguans to emphasizing the politics of austerity and production.

This change in orientation involved a shift: from promoting labor militancy to stressing labor discipline. More important to laborers, the political line of the government has resulted in limitations on salaries. Only in the first year of the revolution were salaries for agricultural workers raised above inflation levels. Declining real incomes have led to tension, exemplified by the embarrassing strike in 1984 at the country's largest sugar refinery, San Antonio.

*The Counterrevolution*

Resolving Nicaragua's grave economic problems has been stymied by the counterrevolution. From the onset, the Sandinista regime has been confronted by armed resistance, at first isolated and poorly organized. United States assistance for the remnants of Somoza's National Guard, which fled to Honduras, and the concurrent cooperation of Honduras have resulted in a well-organized and financed counterrevolution. Serious fighting began in December, 1982, and has continued unabated.

The Sandinistas dubbed their foes *countrarevolucionarios* (counterrevolutionaries) and the term, shortened to "contras," has become the name for all the anti-Sandinista guerrillas. They include not only the 10,000 members of the Honduras-based Nicaraguan Democratic Force (FDN) initially organized and funded by the CIA, but a couple of thousand guerrillas in Costa Rica as well, most of whom have been fighting under the banner of the Democratic Revolutionary Alliance, known by the Spanish acronym ARDE, and led by the former Sandinista, Eden Pastora.

The Miskito Indians that inhabit the sparsely populated Atlantic coast are also fighting the FSLN. Almost from the start of Nicaragua's revolution, the Miskito Indians have resented the FSLN's efforts to change their traditional way of life. The FSLN has admitted it was initially heavy-handed with the Miskitos. The forced resettling of Miskito Indians in camps away from battle-torn areas has only aggravated the Miskitos' animosity toward the FSLN, despite the provision of building materials, social services, and food at the camps. The Miskito Indians started fighting with hunting rifles, but they are now heavily armed and pose a threat to government troops stationed on the Atlantic coast.

The counterrevolution suffered a number of setbacks in 1984, but has managed to continue its assault on the FSLN. First, the United States Congress refused to approve President Ronald Reagan's supplemental $21-million aid request for the rebels, effectively cutting them off from their most important source of funding—the CIA. (However, the rebels managed to raise between $15 million and $20 million in cash, military equipment, and medical supplies from individuals, groups and other governments, like Israel, Argentina, Taiwan and Honduras.) Second, Pastora was badly wounded by a bomb at a newspaper conference in May, 1984. Pastora has returned to the northern bank of the San Juan River, which forms a wide, muddy boundary between Costa Rica and Nicaragua. Third, the Miskito faction has been torn by rivalry between its two principal leaders, Steadman Fagoth and Brooklyn Rivera. Still, Miskito guerrilla columns continue to make the east coast the most inhospitable part of Nicaragua for the FSLN.

The contras have established solid footholds along the mountains of northern Nicaragua, mauled FSLN army patrols, and lured thousands of recruits to their cause. Many recent recruits are FSLN deserters or poor peasants. FDN guerrillas have operated as far south as Boaco, only 60 miles northeast of Managua, although their most permanent strongholds are in the northern provinces of Jinotega, Nueva Segovia Madriz and Chinandega, all along the Honduran border. Along the eastern end of the border with Honduras, guerrillas from the Misurasata alliance of Miskito, Sumo and Rama Indians control a barren and thinly populated strip of savannahs and swamps and strike at government forces along the Atlantic coast.

ARDE controls some territory along the San Juan River. However, the guerrillas have yet to carry their fight into the strategic lowlands or the cities. Now, the struggle is for the support of the rural poor on what is referred to in Nicaragua as the agricultural frontier.

The FSLN claims that fighting has taken the lives of over 8,000 Nicaraguans. There has likewise been considerable material damage. The areas of fighting are relatively marginal to the economy. The bulk of Nicaragua's gross national product (GNP) is generated in the Pacific region, which has been free from fighting. To date, the most consequential material cost to the new regime of the counterrevolution has been the cost of devoting attention and resources to defeating the counterrevolutionaries, and to preparing for a feared United States intervention. Many of Nicaragua's arms have been donated by Soviet-bloc countries; Nicaragua's regular army and mobilized reserves now total 62,000—in a country of 2.7 million. Defense officially absorbs 25 percent of the Nicaraguan government budget, but the figure is undoubtedly higher.

The Sandinista leadership has responded to counterrevolutionary efforts to recruit the rural poor with moral suasion, acceleration of the land reform in troubled regions and, when necessary, subtle coercion. Sandinista propaganda equates the counterrevolutionaries with Somoza's National Guard, using, in fact, the same nicknames. This is a persuasive tactic since nearly all poor Nicaraguans hated Somoza's National Guard. The government also appeals to nationalism by suggesting that counterrevolutionaries are United States puppets, and by evoking the memory of Sandino's armed resistance to the United States occupying force. One common slogan is, "After 50 years, the enemy is the same."

Some poor rural Nicaraguans have joined the counterrevolution. (All the country's Miskito Indians have joined, but for unique reasons.) More poor rural Nicaraguans have joined the government's bid to defeat the counterrevolution. Most poor rural Nicaraguans, however, appear to have adopted a calculated air of indifference. Peasants interviewed by the author outside Matagalpa said that they did not support the Sandinistas but that they did not support the counterrevolutionaries either. Certainly, Nicaragua's economic difficulties have led to cynicism about the FSLN. However, the political apathy in rural Nicaragua seems largely a matter of calculations about benefits and costs: the benefits are reckoned to be for "the government" and the costs are personal.

Peasants see their behavior as eminently reasonable. For the government, the apathy of many rural laborers and peasants must be seen as an annoying lack of political consciousness at best and threatening ingratitude at worst. The government must try to mobilize political support among the supposed beneficiaries and heirs of the revolution. Indeed, both the FSLN and the counterrevolutionaries seem to be using coercion not as a response to the perceived success of the opposition, but rather as an antidote to the peasants' indifference.

While United States support was decisive for the formation of the counterrevolution (total United States government support has been $63.5 million), the counterrevolution has become an independent force, complicating the chances for a negotiated settlement between Nicaragua and the United States. The war between the FSLN and the contras is a stalemate, with time perhaps on the side of the contras. The danger is that either side will attempt to end the war by seeking more sophisticated weapons or, less likely, foreign assistance. Either alternative could inflame great power rivalry and spark United States intervention. The Reagan administration's panic over the supposed arrival of Soviet MG-21 interceptors in November, 1984, showed Washington's anxiety.

Given the intractability of Nicaragua's economic problems, the strength of the counterrevolution, and the threat of United States intervention, it is not surprising that a recent slogan painted on a wall of the Central American University in Managua proclaimed: "Yesterday Somoza, Today Sandino, Tomorrow Who Knows."

---

## AN INTERVIEW WITH
## MIGUEL D'ESCOTO BROCKMAN,
## FOREIGN MINISTER OF NICARAGUA[2]

---

On Oct. 19, 1985, Miguel d'Escoto Brockman, a Maryknoll priest now serving as Foreign Minister of Nicaragua, spoke with me in his room at the United Nations Plaza Hotel in New York City. He had accompanied President Daniel Ortega Saavedra to the 40th anniversary session of the United Nations, where on Oct. 21 Mr. Ortega addressed the General Assembly.

The son of a Nicaraguan Ambassador to the United States, Father d'Escoto was born in Hollywood, Calif. He attended Maryknoll College in Glen Ellyn, Ill., spent a year in the novitiate and then studied theology at the Maryknoll Seminary in New York before being ordained in 1961. Immediately after ordination, he received an M.S. from the Columbia University School of Journalism.

[2]By Thomas H. Stahel, an associate editor of *America*. *America*. N. 16, '86. pp. 318–323. Copyright 1985 America, Inc. Reprinted with permission.

As is well known, Pope John Paul II has long desired that Father d'Escoto relinquish his Government post, in accord with the new code of canon law. Because Father d'Escoto did not meet the deadline indicated by the Vatican in this matter, he has been required to relinquish, instead, the exercise of his priesthood until such time as he complies with canon law.

He discusses that issue in this interview, as well as the state of the church in Nicaragua, the recent suspension of civil liberties there and other issues touching on relations between the United States and Nicaragua.

**You have lived for some years in the United States, I understand, and therefore you have the experience of living in the cultures of both North and Central America. Why is it that the statements of the Nicaraguan Government seem, from a North American point of view, to be so obsessed with the United States?**

Well, more than any other country in continental Latin America, we have suffered the consequences of U.S. official interventionism. We have been invaded, we have been occupied time and time again. We suffered the imposition of one of the most hideous regimes in the history of Latin America for close to half a century, and we are at this present time experiencing a war that is characterized, even by people in the U.S. Congress, as not only illegal, but also immoral, and that has resulted in the systematic murder, kidnapping and torture of thousands upon thousands of our fellow citizens. I think we have reason to be concerned about the United States.

As a matter of fact, I many times wonder what the reaction of the United States would be if it were to find itself in our situation. For that to be a possibility, there would have to be a country that is as least a thousand times more powerful than the United States. Of course, there is no such country. But I wonder what would happen if there were a country a hundred times larger in territorial size (which is the least important thing), and thousands of times more powerful economically and politically, and if that country were to be clearly committed to the overthrow and the destruction of American society! What would be the reaction?

**You spoke about immorality and illegality. That word "illegality" reminds me of the action in the World Court at the**

**moment. May I ask, how did you conceive that idea? Was it your idea, in fact, to sue the United States in the World Court?**

From the beginning of the application of Mr. Reagan's policy against the Nicaraguan revolution, it was quite clear to me that there was an illegality. But the United States has never been characterized by respect for law, in spite of the image that it likes to project internationally and within the United States. I think the fundamental principle is to do as much as you can possibly get away with. But you always try to keep a façade.

I had thought about going to the court, but never too seriously until the invasion of Grenada. But it was not the fact of the invasion that moved me to propose seriously to the President that we go to the court. It was that I decided to monitor American reaction to the invasion of Grenada, as presented mainly in editorials and op-ed pieces in the basic, leading newspapers across the country. I was concerned to see—there were a few notable and important exceptions—that the majority were willing to accept the fact of the invasion. They would formulate their argument in the following manner. They would say: "Surely, if one were to evaluate the decision to invade Grenada from the point of view of international law, this is an action outside the norms. But then again, international law has become obsolete"—I am summarizing. "Why? Because the interrelation between nations is increasing more and more, and as a result of this, one must redefine the principle of nonintervention."

This is really what they are saying, the vast majority. That's what I saw reflected in the United States. Well, where does that leave the small countries of the world?

Then, during an afternoon walk with the President, I said: "Daniel, you know I seldom lose sleep about anything. But I am thinking and thinking that this is *really* something. With international law, there can be war; but without it, for sure there will be nothing but war." We have to have more than only law. We have to have justice also, and a new international economic order, and other things besides. But there can be no greater damage to international peace and security than the destruction of the international legal order. So I said: "I think, Daniel, we have to go to the World Court. I am very concerned: I am very afraid. What I see happening cannot be taken just as a Reagan move, because look at what he has done and look at the reaction."

The other thing that concerned me was that international public opinion kept rather quiet. I mean, President Reagan comes out and says the most flagrant things. For example, he says publicly, for the world to hear, that he believes in the right of the United States to utilize covert action, which is the euphemism to signify activities to destabilize or overthrow another government. He says that he believes in the right of the United States to utilize covert actions against another nation whenever, in the mind of the President of the United States, that serves the interests of the United States. And everyone keeps quiet!

**About freedom of the church, another subject I wanted to raise with you: What is your view of the cause of the tension between the Nicaraguan hierarchy and the Government? Do you have better relations with some bishops than with others? It is well known that there is tension between Monseñor Obando y Bravo [Cardinal Miguel Obando y Bravo, Archbishop of Managua] and the Government.**

Well, it is a sad fact, but something that is a part of history, and undeniable: The church has never ever, as church, in our history in Latin America at least—and in the whole world, I think—supported *profound* changes in society that are being promoted precisely to benefit the majority of the people. On the contrary, the church historically—and this is sad—has defended the maintenance of the most un-Christian status quo by fomenting something that can only be characterized as sin, because the church has preached resignation in the face of exploitation and injustice. This is in total contradiction to Chirst's mandate that we should be a leavening agent in society, a transforming agent. To transform what into what? Selfishness into brotherly concern for one another.

The Lord's words, "The poor you shall have always with you," are manipulated to justify a political quietism, which again is sinful. No wonder the church was characterized until not too long ago—even in the Rockefeller Report when Mr. Nixon became President—as one of the fundamental pillars of the maintenance of the system, together with the military.

How has this happened in practice? Well, just look at the time when we were trying to become independent from Spain. The Holy Father was Pope Pius VII—at that time he was living not in Rome, but in France. He received the emissary from Spain, heard one side of the story and wrote in the name of Christ to his dear children in the Lord, and ordered us to submit to the Spanish Crown and desist from trying to become independent. In the name of God. What abuse!

And you know what happened? We were on the verge of the biggest schism in the history of Christianity. For years we did not have bishops in Latin America, until Muzi finally came on his mission to Chile, you remember. [The Muzi Mission, 1823–25, by Giovanni Muzi, Bishop of Città di Castello and first papal representative to the Americas. He came with faculties to name and consecrate bishops in the new Spanish American republics without further recourse to Rome.]

You know, Our Lord says He came to bring fire to the earth and that He wanted this fire to be enkindled—the fire of His transforming love, to push forward to new heights of brotherhood. But many of us church people have acted like frustrated firemen, putting out the fire. We question change, any change. Fffffttttt [sound and gesture of a fireman managing a firehose]. Dangerous, you know. So put it out with the hose.

It's not surprising that, in Nicaragua, where we are embarked at this time, also, on a profound change, you see a church whose leaders—like the rest of us priests—have been formed in a reactionary and anti-Communist tradition when it comes to social doctrine, and expecially those who make it to higher echelons of authority within the church. Not all, of course, but a great majority are of that bent. I always say to newspeople that it is not worth commenting on, because if you tell me that there is a revolution somewhere and the church is against it, I will say, "What else is new?" I mean, what *would* be newsworthy is to tell me that the church is for it. So in Nicaragua the new thing is, and the question is: How come so much of the church is in favor of it [the revolution]? How come so many of the priests, even of the bishops?

**Now, that was a question I wanted to ask: How many of the bishops?**
I do not like to speak for the bishops, but I can tell you that, in my very serious opinion, the fundamental problems are in Managua and a couple of other dioceses, and that the rest of the bishops understand the situation quite well. Now, we have a difficulty in Nicaragua. You see, some of our bishops are not Nicaraguans.

From our point of view as Christians, we should not even consider whether or not someone is Nicaraguan. But what is sad is that the local bishops really make the nonnationals feel that they are not Nicaraguans—although they have given their lives in our country because they came as missionaries and have been there a long time, 30 years or whatever. So they are intimidated, in the face of people like Monseñor Obando. I mention his name, because this is a fact.

**As far as I know, we get the impression in this country that the Nicaraguan bishops speak as a unified bloc, under the leadership of Monseñor Obando y Bravo.**
I have myself clearly established in many cases that at least some of the bishops knew nothing about these documents that have come out. They saw them only when they returned to the country, had never even read them, no draft being presented to them, or anything of that kind. Sometimes they are signed only by Monseñor Bosco Vivas, who is Auxiliary Bishop of Managua and acts as secretary to the bishops' conference. Oh, yes, that happens.

They have some kind of lamentable principle that any Christian should find hard to accept: They will not say something about a certain issue unless everyone says it. How can that be? That is, if *one* decides to keep quiet on something that another feels morally obliged to say something about, this other will not say it because there is an agreement not to say anything unless everyone agrees to it. We can't say that to our Lord on the day when we come to Him: "I kept quiet because the others didn't speak."

**You are saying that the bishops, or some of them, are not speaking up as they ought.**
They are not speaking up. They say it is very difficult; they are intimidated by Monseñor Obando. But of course in the final analysis the responsibility does not end with Monseñor Obando. There is an authority higher than his that has a very important responsibility in this whole issue.

**Let me ask you another question about the freedom of the church. That was how we started this part of the discussion, and then I asked you about the bishops. How do you think the**

church will be affected by President Ortega's recent announcement about the suspension of civil liberties in Nicaragua? Will
the Cardinal be prohibited from traveling around the country,
as is said in some newspapers here?
No one is prohibited from traveling anywhere. There is no restriction on the mobility of people from one place to another.

**What about a prohibition on his assemblies?**
There is a prohibition on assemblies, but it must be clearly understood what is meant by that. It does not mean, for example, that
if a political party wants to have an assembly tomorrow, it cannot
have it. What it means is that now, because of certain things that
are happening, they have to ask for permission, and they will get
it. Now, let us say there is going to be a procession. They ask for
it, and they will get it. But you can be sure that they will be told,
again, that it has to be a religious procession, and not an occasion
for political parties ( and all those with whom the Cardinal is especially identified) to use the church. An abusive utilization especially of the Cardinal, to project him as a symbol—this really has
been the role that the Central Intelligence Agency has assigned
to Cardinal Obando. I am sorry to say it, but I will say it here.
This is his role, and it is not surprising that he got a medal from
the C.I.A. Who is Constantine Menges?

**Excuse me?**
Who is Constantine Menges? The director of the C.I.A. in Latin
America, or he was. Along with Michael Novak and other people,
he created this Institute on Religion and Democracy. For what
purpose? It has been amply written up in the United States. It is
clearly a C.I.A.-front organization, and the first medal they gave
was to Cardinal Obando. For what? He is regarded as their most
valuable asset in Central America, and in Nicaragua in particular.
Has he knowingly accepted this role? Is he being used? Well, a
person does not make a long trip to get a medal without having
investigated previously why they are giving him such an honor,
and who it is that is giving him the honor.
   The thing is this. Nicaragua will always have freedom of conscience, freedom of religion. Nicaragua is truly committed, not
hypocritically committed, like Mr. Reagan, to democracy. We
fought to overthrow a regime that was sponsored by the United
States, because we could never have democracy under that re-

gime. We are building our democracy. But even the most important of all human rights, which is the right to life, can have
exceptions. Catholic morality accepts the principle that one can
kill in self-defense, and talks about "just war." The U.S. Government throws its arms up to the skies in horror because of the limi-
tation of rights in Nicaragua. But this is done precisely to defend
our most basic right, which is to sovereignty and the life of our
people. We will not allow the use of liberties that never existed
in Nicaragua before, but that now exist because of the revolution,
to reverse the revolutionary process—in the way, for example,
that freedom of the press in Chile was used in El Mercurio to do
in President Allende [Salvador Allende Gossens, the democratically elected Marxist President of Chile, overthrown in a bloody
coup of September 1973].

No one who is doing the proper type of activity has anything
to fear, and as a matter of fact there is no properly religious activity that is in any way, shape or form going to be limited. But, of
course, what we are talking about is not only not a religious activity, it is an activity that I myself—not the Government of Nicaragua, but I myself—call treasonous activity. And history will
condemn the church, and the Cardinal—and not only the Cardinal, but many of the bishops—for having kept what I call a silence
of complicity in the face of the aggression of the strongest and
richest nation in the world against our people. Even the American bishops have said a few things against it. But what have the
Nicaraguan bishops said? Nothing to condemn it, and a few
things—some of them—to support it. I have spoken to certain
bishops, and I have said: "Don't you see what you are doing to the
church? Don't you see how you are hurting the church?" And
they have acknowledged to me that that's right. They do not
know what to do because this other man won't move.

I am speaking more than I have ever spoken. But some bishops have acknowledged to me that they are very concerned about
the future of the church. They are guilty of high treason by becoming accomplices of a foreign power in its efforts to destabilize
and to overthrow our Government. And how are they manifesting this behavior now? At this point in time by going against the
draft. What would the United States do if it were being attacked
by another country and the church came out against the draft?

They say that the draft is to defend a party. Now they know
that in Nicaragua we had elections that were broad-based, and

with great participation, for the first time in history. Every political party that wanted to participate could participate, and in fact seven participated. Unlike elections in other parts of Latin America, there were no candidates in jail, and no one was prohibited from becoming a candidate. It was a direct vote, by the people. So we had elections, and we have a Government that is the result of those elections. President Reagan has acknowledged that he is trying to overthrow the Government, and then the bishops have the gall to say that the army, in defending our Government, a system that was voted in democratically by the people, is being used to defend a party. You know, this is extremely damaging to the church. Anyway, the church may have betrayed the people, but we must defend the wishes of the people, and we must defend them legally, through the established Government, and we must not allow the church to blemish further the name of Christianity and abuse the cross of Christ to spread imperialistic ideals, political ideas that would have Nicaragua become submitted again to United States dictates. This was the position of the bishops during the colonial days, and that is why for many, many years there were no bishops after independence. They were total lackeys.

**Let me put the question in another way. Some American bishops, as you say, have tried to speak out against U.S. interference in Nicaragua. But the deprivation of civil liberties—or whatever you want to call this statement by President Ortega on Tuesday, Oct. 15, 1985—makes it more difficult for U.S. bishops to defend Nicaragua's right to self-determination.**
We don't want the American bishops to defend Nicaragua. We don't need the American bishops or anyone to defend us. We are more than able to defend ourselves. I would ask the American bishops to defend themselves and their own souls. The hands of every American are bloodied with the blood of innocent Nicaraguan people. The American Catholic Church is very big. It is also American. It is an accomplice, unless it protests. These are crimes in which every American citizen is implicated because this is—or isn't it?—a democracy. Is not everyone co-responsible?

What would happen if a few American bishops really wanted to put an end to these crimes that their country is committing in their name? If they decided to take some dramatic sort of action until the policies ended, and appealed to the rest of the American Catholics and community of believers to protest? They can do it.

Especially since this President of the United States has the nerve to say that he does what he does to defend the most sacred values of our Judeo-Christian tradition. He is now the spokesperson, the defender of God. And he is allowed to play that role. He sprinkles all his speeches—I have heard him many times—with references to the Pope, and "God bless you" here and "God bless you" there, and he gets away with it. Let him take full responsibility for his actions but not implicate God, much less give an appearance that he is doing all this to defend persecuted Christians.

**Some of the U.S. bishops might say, "We are trying to protest, but we have to do it through means of political discourse, and the suppression of civil rights in Nicaragua makes it more difficult for us."**
Through means of political discourse? How did the prophets protest? No one is trying. Our Lord would say, "Close, but no cigar." They should protest. And one is better than none, and then maybe others will follow. But not only bishops.

**How do you feel, as Foreign Minister, about the fact that this pronouncement by President Ortega about the suppression of civil liberties was made just before you and he came up to the United Nations? Do you find that an embarrassment? It seems from a political point of view such an odd moment to have made that pronouncement.**
We are not in a propaganda campaign. Circumstances are there that oblige us to move. Others, more Madison Avenue–oriented, would have said: "Go to the United Nations, give a great exhibition, and then come back and do it." After all, this is the way some other Latin American countries have done things. No, we do things when we have to do them, and we have nothing to be embarrassed about.

**Let me shift over to the matter of your Christian ministry. Is that an acceptable topic?**
Any topic.

**Do you feel you are exercising your priesthood in your present work?**
I think so, in a unique, strange, unsought kind of way—a way that I never envisioned because it had never occurred to me. Basically, as a priest, I must try to excel always in those virtues that should

be the virtues of a *man,* and especially of a man who is a Christian, because I am first a man, and a Christian, and then by the grace of God also a priest. Now, the specifically priestly functions, the sacramental ones, have been deprived me by wishes of the Holy Father—not by my Society, and not by my bishop in Nicaragua, who would not do that.

**Who is your bishop in Nicaragua?**
Rubén López Ardón, who is the Bishop of Estelí. He is the bishop with whom I have been associated in Nicaragua, and with whom I have most cordial, fraternal relations.

**And the same with your Maryknoll superior?**
By the grace of God I have never had any but the best relations with all my superiors. Now we very much wanted to speak to Rome—because this thing [the order to leave the Government post] came from Rome—and Rome ended up saying there was nothing to speak about, that the law was the law, and it must be complied with.

Well, if it comes to that, and with all due respect to canon law—which I do in fact respect and mean never to disrespect—if it comes to the law being the law, I have to establish a priority. And the law of God has to come before canon law. I find that I would be in radical violation of the law of God, which is basically to love my neighbor, if, in the situation where my country finds itself, I were to comply with canon law and leave this post, which I never sought, never wanted . . . even now. They talk about the "honor." Where is the honor? It's work. To me there's no difference—and I say this before God, because it's true—between being a doorman or being a foreign minister. It's service.

I was asked at a certain point in time: "Would you help us do this? We need to establish decent and honorable and just relations with the international community. We need people to help us because of the conditions in Nicaragua, and the availability of human resources. We are among the privileged few who have had an opportunity for some degree of formal education, and everyone has to pitch in. And to be a bridge of understanding between your nation and others is a very noble and also, in a sense, priestly work."

I am not in a parish, but I never have been in a parish since I was ordained. I do not know why this post should be less priestly than my work in Orbis Books [a Catholic publishing house run by Maryknoll in New York].

**Is that what you did before?**
I founded Orbis Books. I began it, and I was director of communications at Maryknoll, and before that in Chile I was giving technical assistance.

So, it's very, very sad. But even my bishop was angry when I opened up the subject once (not that I was saying that I was going to leave my post). He told me how much it would hurt the church and the people. That is what matters, because we are transitory. The Lord may call us—we do not know when, today, in a minute. And so my idea is this: If I were to leave my post in order to have the satisfaction of saying Mass, I could not have that satisfaction as a matter of fact.

**Because you feel you could not celebrate the Mass?**
No, I would be in sin. I would be a traitor. And there has never been anything more important to me in my whole life, since I was a young man, than the Holy Sacrifice.

**Do you look forward to resuming your sacramental priesthood someday?**
Yes, but I am perhaps living that Mass now, with the pain, even more than if I did not have this difficulty. It is like the case of other priests who have been kept from saying Mass because they are in jail, for example. It is precisely in my fundamental commitment to living the Mass that I accept this prohibition from celebrating the Holy Sacrifice. Our Lord says, "Do this in commemoration of me." He did not mean that we repeat the words only, because we are not parrots, but that we repeat those words as human beings; that is to say, that we take on the inner dispositions that He had when He said, "This is my body and this is my blood." We make those inner dispositions our own, and *then* we say the words, because we speak as human beings, conveying what we feel. So, to live the Mass is to have that inner disposition of availability to God, including the giving of your life for the service of the people, and to ask to be strengthened in your love for the cross and the acceptance of the cross in whatever shape or form God decides you should carry it.

## THE WAY OF THE SANDINISTAS[3]

At the airport in San Jose, Costa Rica, a well-dressed man in his seventies begins a conversation with a young woman as they wait in line to board the Aeronica flight to Managua. She comes from Scotland, she says, and is eager to begin her volunteer work in Nicaragua.

The old man grows angry. "You're an intelligence agent for those communists," he shouts. "I'm a Nicaraguan, and I know that when you start giving out land the next thing you have is communism. I've been to Warsaw."

The woman ignores the mysterious Polish reference and declares that she is proud to be a Scottish Sandinista. "You're an old reactionary," she tells him.

The man mutters: "Look how well she speaks Spanish. Intelligence agents, that's all they are."

The Aeronica attendant interrupts the argument to announce the flight's boarding.

The trip lasts about forty-five minutes. The routine in the Managua airport begins with a required exchange of $60 for 4,200 cordobas, seventy to one, far less than the official exchange rate of 900 or the black-market rate of 1,800. The difference in currency rates troubles me. How can an economy function, I ask myself, with three different exchange rates?

This is my seventh trip to revolutionary Nicaragua. On each visit, I have noticed a gradual deterioration of the quality of everyday life. The erosion of comfort and convenience wears worst on people who were used to the material benefits of the middle class. In part, the shortages of consumer goods can be blamed on the United States—the U.S. trade embargo and blockade of badly needed loans from international lending agencies, the U.S.-sponsored low-intensity war, the U.S. propaganda bashing of the Sandinistas, and the U.S. diplomatic bullying.

In part, the shortages can also be attributed to the disruption of the old economic system. Nicaragua today is a Third World society in transition from the Somoza "kleptocracy"—as the Kiss-

[3]Reprint of an article by Saul Landau, a senior fellow at the Institute for Policy Studies in Washington, D.C. *The Progressive*. Ag. '86. pp. 21–25. Copyright © 1986, The Progressive, Inc. Reprinted by permission from The Progressive, Madison, WI 53703.

inger Commission described the dynasty that ruled from 1933 to
1979—to a more egalitarian model. If the United States will allow the transition to continue.

The war, the economic breakdowns, the inability of Managua's old pumps to keep pushing water through the taps seven
days a week, twenty-four hours a day, the corruption that seeps
from the old bureaucracy and parts of the new, the accelerated
pace of life without a corresponding catch-up in resources and
technology—all of this turns daily life into an endurance contest,
especially for those who have known better times.

But most Nicaraguans never had comforts or conveniences.
For them, life is ambiguously better. They now enjoy basic rights
in certain areas but have had to postpone their hopes for rapid
improvements in material well-being. The less tangible benefits
can be important.

About 8 P.M., at a bus stop in Managua, a woman is complaining to a Sandinista officer about mismanagement and corruption.
A man nearby sneers. "Have you no shame?" he asks. "Talking to
a *piricuaco* in public?" (*Piricuaco* is a pejorative Indian word meaning "dog from hell.")

The woman snaps back, "Perhaps you have forgotten that one
never talked to the *Guardia*, that one couldn't even be out at this
hour of the night, that we would be home worrying if our teen-
age daughter was not yet back that she would have been raped,
or that our teen-age son would have been murdered. I can talk
with tranquility to the *piricuaco* and so can you. You are not beat-
en, shot, or even arrested. This *piricuaco* has not said a word, or
unholstered the pistol," she says, ponting to the officer. The man
"hhrumphs" and strides away.

The Sandinista thanks the woman for her words. "I am not
with the FSLN," she replies. "I think you people are making very
bad mistakes. But I don't believe that you will ever carry out the
kind of brutality that we once had."

The bus arrives. It is filled to capacity, jammed so tightly that
the shapes of individual bodies melt together. The temperature
has dropped by this hour to the high eighties, but it is several degrees warmer inside the bus. The straining vehicle belches out a
cloud of acrid black smoke as it carries off its human cargo.

Only those with autos or motor bikes can avoid this kind of
daily exercise in crowding, and the woman who complained had

been unable to find a part for her car. Anti-Sandinista sentiment is strong and vocal among some sectors of the middle class.

But it does not make them pro-*contra*. Nicaraguans understand that the *contras*, should they win, will not form a benevolent democratic government. They know that Colonel Enrique Bermudez and most of those in the *contra* command structure used to be officers in Anastasio Somoza's National Guard. The *contra* military command was picked by the CIA. Adolfo Calero, former chief of Coca-Cola in Managua and also part of the *contra* political leadership, is also dismissed by top Sandinista officials as a CIA agent, an assertion they say was confirmed recently by a high U.S. national-security figure.

On the street in Managua, Masaya, Leon, and Chinandega, the names of Alfonso Robelo and Arturo Cruz—two of the *contras*' more liberal leaders—are virtually unknown. Members of the urban business class remember Robelo as one of the wealthiest entrepreneurs. Cruz has spent most of his adult life outside Nicaragua and has wider name recognition in Washington than in Managua. In any case, they are dismissed as cosmetics to hide the CIA's right-wing agenda.

The CIA had agents throughout the National Guard's high command when Somoza was in power. One CIA adventurer whisked away more than a hundred Guard officers in July 1979, under cover of the Red Cross, just as the revolutionaries marched victoriously into Managua to take power. A Sandinista official told me that the CIA began its war against the Nicaraguan people even before the triumph of the revolution. He reminded me that the National Guard and CIA worked together to launch the Bay of Pigs operation in April 1961, and he claimed that the Agency regularly provided information to the Guard's intelligence arm in exchange for a free hand in Nicaragua.

That was before the current undeclared war that has now dragged on for five years, before the mining of Nicaragua's harbors by the CIA's UCLAs (Unilaterally Controlled Latino Assets), before the CIA wrote and distributed assassination manuals, before the Reagan Administration imposed a trade embargo.

"If the *contras* would win by some miracle," confides an elegantly dressed lawyer in the bar of Managua's Intercontinental Hotel, "we would have to prove ourselves to them—here he runs his finger across his throat—"that we actively opposed the Sandinistas, that we belonged to the underground, wherever it is." He is drinking imported whisky at an outlandish price; rum drinks are cheaper. "Under Somoza, the Guard suspected every citizen of being a subversive. So if they come back how will it change? How can I prove to Colonel Bermudez that I am anti-Sandinista?"

"So," I ask, "what's your solution?"

He shrugs nonchalantly. "I can leave the country for Miami, where I have a sister," he says. "I can learn to live with the Sandinistas, or hope that your country will change its policy."

"In what way?"

"Send the Marines. That's the only way to defeat these people. The way you are doing it now, this slow war of attrition, is pure *mierda*, man."

The U.S. Government has waged low-intensity warfare for five years against the government of a destitute country, and the war has added immensely to the suffering of the poor. The most serious suffering is death—not only for the dead, the teen-agers who fall to *contra* fire at the front, but also for the mothers, wives, families. Then there are the one-legged, one-armed, wheelchair-bound young people, hundreds of them. The Sandinistas say the war thus far has taken 16,000 casualties, military and civilian, most of them under thirty years of age.

Ironically, the military front is the Sandinistas' one clear success story. In direct fighting between Sandinista forces and U.S.-paid *contras*, everyone agrees that the government troops are—to quote an American clergyman—"kicking *contra* ass." In the first five months of 1986, the Sandinistas claim to have inflicted more than a thousand casualties on the *contras* and to have inspired the desertion of more than a thousand others. Elite units acting in coordination with regular army and militia terms have routed the CIA forces from several provinces where they had been well-entrenched.

Unlike last year's, this year's coffee harvest—vital to Nicaragua's balance of trade—proceeded without serious *contra* destruction. Armed Sandinistas and volunteer pickers brought in a sizable crop—a feat they could not have accomplished two years ago in, say, Matagalpa. Coffee prices are high, thanks to frost in Brazil. A record coffee profit might have been made, had the government not already pledged part of this year's crop against prior loans and had the shortage of foreign exchange not curtailed outlays for imported pesticides and fertilizer. Still, the harvest boosted morale and showed that cooperative work and defense efforts can succeed.

Such encouragement is needed. Daily life is an ordeal for the typical resident of Managua; the shortages of basic goods, the transportation difficulties, and the frustration of dealing with bureaucracy and corruption all make survival for one more day a reason to celebrate. Stress and mental illness have become understandably more common. Nicaragua is not only engaged in a multi-front war against the United States; it is also in the midst of a profound social revolution. It is a society in transition from one way of organizing social and economic life to another, and what that other will be like is not year clear.

Nicaragua today is neither capitalist nor socialist. To use the word "mixed" confuses meaning, since it connotes a neutrality that is not present. Sandinista leaders are committed to independence and social justice as the primary goals of their revolution, an orientation that does not bode well for the future of capitalism in their country. The leaders of COSEP (Superior Board of Private Enterprise), a group representing the large-scale private owners, understand that a continuation of Sandinista government in Nicaragua is incompatible with their interests. This is not a matter of any one government policy, such as tax incentives, but rather a premise about who controls economic life, and for whose benefit.

The Sandinistas are clear on their economic priorities, and these are linked to substantive human rights. The poor, who constitute the vast majority of the population, have first place on the national agenda, and their needs are at odds with those of big business. The Sandinistas will invest to build a new social infrastructure of mass education, health care, and agrarian reform before spending to secure the fortunes of a handful of business people. The revolution is consciously class-oriented.

What the future holds for the people at the bottom—the unemployed, the landless—remains unclear, but there is no question for the country's big-business types. They will lose much of the power and privilege they enjoyed under the Somoza dynasty. That's why they favor the overthrow of the Sandinistas and the installation of a regime friendly to both traditional capitalism and the United States.

The Sandinistas don't want to eliminate the COSEP immediately, or the large growers of coffee or cotton or cattle. But they do want to control their operations, handle foreign-exchange transactions, regulate wages, and ensure the ecological health of their country—hardly the traditional formula for a long-term future for big business. In Managua, it is difficult to imagine the realization of the classic scene from the film *Red River*, in which enterprising cattle baron John Wayne puts his arm on the shoulder of young Montgomery Clift, motions to the vast expanse of land all around them, and says: "Son, one day all of this is gonna be yours."

The Sandinistas discourage the accumulation of large estates and have handed the titles for small parcels to some 100,000 landless people. Some of this acreage was confiscated by the government from the Somoza clan, and some was purchased from large ranchers who were underutilizing the land's productive potential. The big growers who cooperate with the government receive state credit, machinery, and other resources. These incentives, however, are temporary measures designed to maintain some stability in agricultural production during the transition to a different agrarian model.

To ensure that existing large growers keep producing, the Sandinistas pay them good prices in cordobas and bonuses in dollars. But the government, after negotiating with the growers, manages the labor force and controls some of the marketing and prices.

Agrarian reform has created a new peasant class rather than push people onto state or collective farms. Members of this new peasantry, whose holdings allow them to be self-sufficient and also produce for market, coexist with the shrinking rural proletariat, many of whom await the titles to their own small parcels of land. They do not see their interests as coinciding with the older, larger farmers, but they share a common concern for the prices paid for agricultural goods.

Nicaragua has plenty of food, but some days it's hard to find. The old market system—under Somoza a version of Adam Smith's invisible hand coupled with institutional theft by the National Guard—and the new Sandinista controls often conflict with each other, so a kind of distributional chaos reigns. In one of Managua's wholesale markets, farmers sell their produce to middlemen who then supply vendors at the retail markets, restaurateurs, and speculators. Cabbage, green peppers, carrots, onions, melons, citrus fruit, squash, tomatoes are plentiful—but the supply of staples like rice and beans, which are state-controlled, fluctuates. Some of the state-controlled markets do not have enough produce to meet demand at the low, controlled price. Speculators, hustlers, and hoarders abound; some become rich overnight. There is a tale, now legendary, of an airplane pilot who quit his high-status, high-salary job to sell cheese in one of the markets because he could make so much more money.

Neither efficient capitalism nor equitable socialism is at work. And, of course, the war dominates the economic equation. The military absorbs half the budget, and its needs continually disrupt productive life by removing people from civilian jobs and transferring other resources to the war.

Some of the foreigners who have worked for the revolution, even those who fought in the guerrilla war, now show signs of fatigue.

"I don't know sometimes if I will have enough energy to get myself to the office," a Mexican technician tells me. "I forget to store my water up the night before the pumps are to be worked on [two days each week] and then I go to the store and there is no bread, no eggs, no milk. My car won't start and I know that it will take months before I can find a spare part if that is the cause of it. The bus is so crowded that I think I have cracked a rib by the time I get off, and then my phone isn't working. Some of the people I work with are underqualified by ten times and screw up every operation and cover it up with militant slogan-shouting. But somehow I manage to get through the day and start again the next morning."

Revolution is the supreme test of will, and it rarely occurs without war—insurrectionary, counterrevolutionary, or both. In the wars, foreigners often play crucial roles. But then there comes a time when nationalism prevails and the foreigners become objects of resentment. They occupy positions that should be held by natives. They tend to behave with a certain arrogance, coming as most do with more education, from more developed societies. They are cosmopolitans; at least they appear to be.

And so, in Nicaragua, foreigners who have loyally braved the daily travails of revolutionary life find themselves shunted aside. The posts of secondary leadership that many of them once occupied now belong to Nicaraguans, some of them clearly less competent. Salaries are not changed, but perquisites and power relations are altered in favor of the natives.

Like most other nationalist revolutions in the Third World, the one in Nicaragua seeks to control and redistribute the nation's wealth. It is also anti-Yankee and anti-imperialist—one and the same in Latin America.

The real issue is what kind of culture will Nicaragua develop: elitist or egalitarian? A culture that preaches individualism and personal accumulation or one that finds the common good in collective cooperation to better the lot and establish the rights of the poor?

The battle rages in the censored press, in conversations and shouting matches on the streets, in slogans, on billboards, within the Catholic Church in Rome, Managua, and remote villages, and ultimately on the front, with bullets and artillery. The war is for the will of the people as much as it is for territory and wealth.

Common interests unite the White House in Washington with the businessmen and Cardinal Obando y Bravo in Managua. Such international class interests provide the thread that ties Nicaragua's internal opposition to the U.S. Government's war. Either property interests or human interests will define the social system, but few of the anti-Sandinistas state their cause this way. Instead, they argue the indivisibility of civil liberties and electoral democracy, free from the language of class conflict.

A Sandinista comandante in his early fifties recalls that the most ardent espousers of democracy and civil liberties for Nicaragua today had little interest in those subjects during the Somoza years. The op-ed pages and letters columns of major U.S. newspapers did not carry items from Cardinal Obando attacking repression or from leaders of the business sector and right wing complaining of the gross violations of civil liberties perpetrated by the Somozas for almost half a century. Except for the last year of Somoza rule, little attention was paid by the official church and business sectors in general to the Somoza abuses. The definition of substantive human rights, or of a democracy involving real participation in the allocation of national wealth, is still rejected by the people Ronald Reagan refers to as the democratic opposition, the "freedom fighters."

It should be clear to any observer that the Sandinistas stand for the rights of the poor. Their opposition, except for those on the extreme Left, stands for the rights of the wealthy.

The twelve parties of the political opposition in Nicaragua today, seven of which have representatives in the National Assembly, offer little in the way of program. The old Liberal and
Conservative parties want to abolish key parts of the agarian reform—their way of stabilizing agriculture and ending the economic crisis. The hundred of thousands of Nicaraguans who now
live on their own land as a result of the reform do not look favorably on this suggestion. The ultra-leftist parties, Trotskyist in orientation, demand immediate socialism, beginning with the
nationalization of all productive property, the formation of workers' soviets, and other remnants of 1917-style bolshevism.

As the *contra* war drags on, the National Assembly debates a
new Nicaraguan constitution. Discussion about the nature of the
future government takes place formally and informally. Lawyers
and barely literate workers and peasants are exposed for the first
time to dialogue about the ideal form of government for Nicaragua. Yet the implacable opposition ignores the constitution; little
has appeared in *La Prensa* and the bishops barely mention it in
their sermons.

The Cardinal poses a serious threat. The Pope chose Obando
y Bravo to be the Church's standard-bearer in Nicaragua, the
keeper of orthodoxy. He has prestige among all classes in this
most Catholic of nations, and he maintains a broad following
based on personal status and demands for loyalty to the Pope. He
has proposed no clear programmatic alternative to the Sandinistas, apart from advocating dialogue with the *contras* and the lifting of all restriction on the Church, press, and radio.

Cardinal Obando appeared at a May Day mass at Calvario
Church, opposite the old Thieves' Corner, near the Eastern Market, half a mile from the Plaza where President Daniel Ortega was
giving a speech. Ortega drew 75,000 people on a very hot day.
Provincial celebrations brought out another 200,000. About
1,000 squeezed into the church to hear the Cardinal, but the figures are deceptive: Obando has proved himself a tough and wily
enemy, the only man in Nicaragua with the name recognition and
stature to unify an opposition.

The Sandinistas understand that Obando's strength *is* his
ability to draw a crowd, to mobilize large numbers under religious banners and then turn them to politics with clever use of
Biblical texts. So the Sandinistas keep controls on him to prevent
the religious demonstrations from turning into militant political

rallies. The Sandinistas know that Obando and the publishers of *La Prensa* are committed to the overthrow of the government. They recall the scenario played out in Chile to destabilize Salvador Allende, involving both press and segments of the Church as key opposition elements.

People in the pro-Sandinista crowd passed Calvario Church on their way home from the May Day rally. Tension developed quickly when some of them exchanged words and slogans with placard-carrying members of Obando's congregation. Police defused the situation, blocking the passage of the most provocative groups, but the anger lingered. It is class-based and fueled by personal grudges and deep-seated feelings of righteousness on both sides.

The hostilities between some of the elite of the official Church on the one side, and the revolution and "popular" or "church of the poor" on the other, symbolize an international struggle within Catholicism. The church of the poor, with its liberation theology, views the world through the prism of class and casts its lot with the have-nots. Obando wants orthodoxy and, like the Pope, eschews class struggle. (There is an embarrassing photograph, taken in the mid-1970s, of Obando being embraced by Somoza.) The Cardinal has not been eloquent on the rights of the poor or on how he would protect them should the Sandinistas be overthrown.

And that is the most important political point in Nicaragua. There is no visible alternative to Sandinista rule. For all of their errors and misfortunes, the Sandinistas have a vision of a good society that remains unchallenged by any political imagination among their enemies.

On my last night there, at dinner with two Sandinista officials, we heard complaints from the next table, two other officials griping about corruption and bureaucracy. Everyone laughed. On television, a co-op leader from Minnesota sang the praises of the agrarian reform and pledged to buy Nicaraguan agricultural products to sell in the United States. A rock video followed, Madonna singing "Material World," then a film featuring Jack Nicholson and Bruce Dern.

In Nicaragua last March, President Reagan's speech against the Sandinistas was played in its entirety, but a reporter from a U.S. television network laughed when I suggested that Ortega's May Day speech be played in the U.S.—an absurd idea. The

United States is culturally important to Nicaragua and has been
for more than a century. Yet, after seven visits to the Central
American nation, I cannot understand why the U.S. Government
should be in such a sweat over a pauperized land of fewer than
three million people—save for the remote possibility that its experiment in social reform and independence might produce some
positive results if left alone.

## NICARAGUA'S SOVEREIGNTY AND INDEPENDENCE SHOULD NOT BE JEOPARDIZED BY MILITARY ACTIVITIES, INTERNATIONAL COURT OF JUSTICE DECLARES[4]

The International Court of Justice has ruled that Nicaragua's
right to sovereignty and political independence should not be
jeopardized by any military or paramilitary activities, and that the
United States should cease restricting access to and from Nicaragua's ports, particularly through the laying of mines.

The Court indicated these provisional measures in an Order
made on 10 May.

While the 15-judge Court was unanimous in calling for an end
to actions endangering access to ports, the vote was 14 to 1 on the
paragraph referring to military and paramilitary activities. Judge
Stephen M. Schwebel of the United States cast the dissenting
vote, arguing that the Court's emphasis on the rights of Nicaragua alone was unwarranted and incompatible with the principles
of equality of States and of collective security.

Nicaragua had requested the Court to indicate "provisional
measures of interim protection," pending the final decision of
proceedings initiated on 9 April. ("Provisional measures" may be
requested under article 41 of the Court Statute when a State considers that the rights which form the subject of its application are
in immediate danger.)

In its Application, Nicaragua charged the United States with
using military force against Nicaragua and intervening in its in-

[4]Reprinted from *UN Chronicle*, vol. xxi, Ap. '84, pp. 3–10.

ternal affairs, "in violation of Nicaragua's sovereignty, territorial integrity and political independence and of the most fundamental and universally accepted principles of international law." It asked the Court to call on the United States to immediately cease all use of force against Nicaragua and to pay reparations for damage to "person, property and the Nicaraguan economy."

In indicating the provisional measures sought by Nicaragua, the Court was unanimous in ordering both Parties to "ensure that no action is taken which might aggravate or extend the dispute submitted to the Court" or "prejudice the rights of the other Party in respect of the carrying out of whatever decision the Court may render."

Nicaragua appealed to the Court five days after the United States vetoed a Security Council draft resolution that would have called for an "immediate end to all threats, attacks and overt and covert hostile acts against the sovereignty, independence and territorial integrity of Nicaragua, in particular, the mining of its main ports."

A request by the United States that the case be dismissed on jurisdictional grounds was unanimously rejected by the Court. The United States had moved to block consideration of Nicaragua's Application and request for interim measures on the grounds that Nicaragua had never formally consented to the Court's jurisdiction and that the Court, therefore, lacked the authority to hear the case. After reviewing letters from the United States of 13 and 23 April and a letter from Nicaragua of 24 April, the Court concluded "that it had then no sufficient basis for acceding to the request of the United States."

The Judges decided that "the provisions invoked by the Applicant appear, prima facie, to afford a basis on which the jurisdiction of the Court might be founded." Nicaragua claimed to found the jurisdiction of the Court on the declarations of both Parties accepting compulsory jurisdiction under article 36 (2) of the Court's Statute—Nicaragua's declaration as deposited in 1929 with the Permanent Court of International Justice, the Court's predecessor under the League of Nations, and the United States' declaration deposited with the Court in 1946.

The Judges stated that their decision to indicate provisional measures "in no way prejudges the questions of the jurisdiction of the Court to deal with the merits of the case or any questions relating to the merits themselves." Further Court proceedings

will address those issues. Deadlines for written proceedings on
the jurisdictional question have been set at 30 June for
Nicaragua's "memorial" and 17 August for the United States'
"counter-memorial."

The provisional measures indicated by the Court will remain
in force until a final Judgment is delivered in the case.

### Nicaragua's Request

Nicaragua, in asking the Court to indicate provisional measures of interim protection, cited a series of events between
March 1981 and April 1984 from which it claimed to have suffered "grievous consequences."

According to Nicaragua, the activities of a mercenary army
of more than 10,000 men, "recruited, paid, equipped, supplied,
trained and directed by the United States," combined with the
"direct action" of United States Central Intelligence Agency personnel and United States armed forces, had resulted in the deaths
of more than 1,400 Nicaraguans, serious injury to more than
1,700 others and property damages in excess of $200 million.

The United States' activities were "mounting in intensity and
destructiveness," Nicaragua alleged. In March 1984, 6,000 United States–backed mercenaries had initiated the largest assault to
date on Nicaraguan territory. Simultaneously, the mercenary
forces announced they had mined the Nicaraguan ports of Corinto, Puerto Sandino and El Bluff. Five foreign commercial vessels
had been disabled by exploding mines, and many other scheduled
shipments to and from Nicaragua had been cancelled for fear of
the mines.

"Taken together with the previous bombings of international
airports, these new actions represent not only an effort to cut Nicaragua's vital trade and communications with the outside world,
but constitute a mortal hazard to third parties engaged in peaceful international commerce and travel," declared Nicaragua.

"The overriding objective" of Nicaragua's request for provisional measures, it alleged, was to prevent further loss of life. Ordering the United States to stop assistance of any kind to the
mercenary forces and to desist from any military or paramilitary
activity by its own officials and forces would be effective in preventing the anticipated harm, since, "as the United States administration has itself recently acknowledged, the mercenaries'

attacks would dry up without further infusion of U.S. aid," Nicaragua said.

"The lives and property of Nicaraguan citizens, the sovereignty of the state and the health and progress of the economy are all immediately at stake," claimed Nicaragua. "The situation has already resulted in a dangerous level of tension, not only between the United States and Nicaragua, but between Nicaragua and Honduras and other Central American neighbours."

Nicaragua said the United States' actions had persisted despite the repeated efforts of Nicaragua and "disinterested third parties." The United States continued to refuse to negotiate, contended Nicaragua, and there was "no reason to believe" it would voluntarily desist from that course of action while the case was pending before the Court.

*Jurisdiction Question*

In letters to the Court and in public hearings, the United States reiterated its position that, on jurisdictional grounds, the Court should not proceed on Nicaragua's Application—"and most certainly should not indicate provisional measures." Nicaragua's 1929 declaration purporting to accept the Court's jurisdiction had never entered into force, and no instrument of ratification had ever been deposited with the League of Nations, the United States argued, citing the *Yearbook* of the Court as evidence.

Nicaragua asserted that it had ratified "in due course" the Protocol of Signature of the Statute of the Permanent Court and said there were also "in force other treaties which provide this Court jurisdiction over the Application." It did not, however, specify which treaties. At the hearings on 25 April, Nicaragua pointed out that it had been a party to Court proceedings in the past—a fact of which the United States was "clearly aware," said Nicaragua, because it had participated in the mediation effort at the time to bring both Nicaragua and Honduras before this Court."

On 27 April, the United States called on the Court to ask Nicaragua "at this very moment to produce the evidence that [it] has accepted the compulsory jurisdiction of this Court," and, if it was unable to do so, to "preclude any further proceedings in this matter."

The Court said that while it could summarily dismiss a case in which the Applicant—while inviting the State named as Respondent to accept jurisdiction *ad hoc*—itself conceded it had no subsisting title of jurisdiction, that was not the situation in the present case. At issue in *Nicaragua v. United States* was whether or not Nicaragua could claim to be a "State accepting the same obligation" under Article 36 (2) of the Court Statute, so as to invoke the United States declaration notwithstanding the fact that it appeared that no instrument of ratification for Nicaragua had been received by the Permanent Court of International Justice.

The second jurisdictional argument advanced by the United States turned on the modification of its 1946 declaration. On 6 April, three days before Nicaragua instituted proceedings, the United States informed the Secretary-General it would not accept the Court's jurisdiction in any disputes related to events in Central America for the period of two years, "effective immediately." The reason proferred for what the United States called a "temporary and limited action" was to "place Nicaragua on notice that the United States would not permit the Contadora process to be subverted by further Nicaraguan efforts to take the issues of Central America out of the appropriate regional arrangements."

Nicaragua argued, however, that the United States' attempt to suspend its acceptance of the Court's jurisdiction was invalid, quoting the United States' 1946 instrument of ratification, which states that "this declaration shall remain in force for a period of five years and thereafter until the expiration of six months after notice may be given to terminate this declaration."

Nicaragua held that as the United States had not given the requisite six-months' notice for modification or termination of its declaration, its declaration regarding the Court's jurisdiction in cases concerning Central America did not apply. Nicaragua said the United States' advance knowledge of the impending suit was the real reason it had tried to withdraw its acceptance of the Court's jurisdiction.

The United States countered that the six-month notice proviso did not apply in the current case, as the 6 April 1984 declaration "did not terminate or purport to terminate" the 1946 declaration and was "narrowly limited in time and geography." Nicaragua's primary argument appeared to be that "because the United States did not reserve a right to modify or suspend operation of its 1946 Declaration, it could not do so." But that argument, said the United States, was "inconsistent with the practice of the Statute and this Court."

The Court said it would make no final determination at the current time on the jurisdiction questions raised by the Parties.

## Central American Issue

According to the United States, there were "compelling reasons" in addition to lack of jurisdiction why the Court should deny Nicaragua's request for provisional measures. Nicaragua's claims were "inextricably related" to the claims of other Central American States against Nicaragua, the United States contended, and those other States were "indispensable parties in whose absence this Court cannot properly proceed."

The Contadora effort was the "properly instituted regional process" to resolve the "current turmoil" in Central America, argued the United States. The Court could not "take cognizance of Nicaragua's Application or indicate the interim measures Nicaragua requests without detrimentally affecting that process in unpredictable and irremediable ways."

The United States said that Nicaragua's suit "improperly" called on the Court to "impose measures potentially impairing the inherent right of States to individual and collective self-defence under Article 51 of the United Nations Charter." Any determination that "unjustified use of force" was occurring, as Nicaragua claimed, fell more properly within the purview of "the political organs of the United Nations and the regional arrangements" than that of the Court.

Nicaragua's counter-argument was that its legal claim against the United States could not be resolved "or even addressed" through the Contadora process. "The United States has no standing or other basis to use Contadora as a pretext for avoiding legal scrutiny of its actions against Nicaragua," it told the Court on 25 April. "In fact," Nicaragua added, the Contadora Group had "sharply criticized" recent United States actions against Nicaragua as "disruptive of the peace process."

Regarding the United States' claim that interim measures could "irreparably prejudice the interests of a number of States," Nicaragua asked by what right the United States acted as "guardian" of those countries before the Court. The measures

Nicaragua sought—for the Court to ask the United States to stop violating international law—"cannot possibly cause prejudice to other countries," Nicaragua held.

Nicaragua said the Court should not decline an essentially judicial task merely because the question before it was intertwined with political questions.

## Opinions

*Separate Opinion:* Judges Hermann Mosler (Federal Republic of Germany) and Sir Robert Jennings (United Kingdom), in a separate opinion appended to the Order of the Court, emphasized that the obligation to refrain from illegal use of force or threat of force, and from intervention in the affairs of another State, applied to Nicaragua as well as to the United States. Both States, they said, were under an obligation to pursue negotiations in good faith in the context of regional arrangements approved by the Security Council and endorsed by the Organization of American States.

*Dissenting Opinion:* Judge Schwebel, in a dissenting opinion, observed that although he had supported the Court's indication of three of the four provisional measures, he had "emphatically" dissented from the provision holding that:

The right to sovereignty and to political independence possessed by Nicaragua, like any other State of the region or of the world, "should be fully respected and should not in any way be jeopardized by any military or paramilitary activities, which are prohibited by the principles of international law, in particular the principle that States should refrain in their international relations from the threat of use of force against the territorial integrity or the political independence of any State, and the principle concerning the duty not to intervene in matters within the domestic jurisdiction of a State, principles embodied in the charter of the United Nations and the Charter of the Organization of American States."

He characterized that paragraph's emphasis on the rights of Nicaragua—"in a case in which Nicaragua itself is charged with violating the territorial integrity and political independence of its neighbours"—as "unwarranted" and "incompatible with the principles of equality of States and of collective security."

Judge Schwebel said that the charges advanced by the United States against Nicaragua were "of a gravity no less profound" than Nicaragua's charges against the United States. Moreover, he observed, similar charges had been made against Nicaragua by El Salvador, Honduras and Costa Rica. Those three States were not parties to the case. Nonetheless, Judge Schwebel held that claims that Nicaragua was violating their rights might be made by the United States and acted on by the Court. The rights at issue did not depend, he said, on "narrow considerations of privity to a dispute before the Court" but on "the broad considerations of collective security."

Every State has "a legal interest in the observance of the principles of collective security," Judge Schwebel said. The United States accordingly was justified in invoking before the Court what it saw as wrongful acts by Nicaragua against other Central American States, "not because it can speak for Costa Rica, Honduras and El Salvador but because the alleged violation by Nicaragua of their security is a violation of the security of the United States."

Judge Schwebel explained that he had voted in favour of the provision concerning mine-laying, although it was directed only to the United States, because the United States had not submitted charges to the Court that Nicaragua was mining the ports and waters of foreign States.

Judge Schwebel said he had supported the Court's rejection of the United States' jurisdictional challenge, "despite the cogency of the United States argument," because the facts were sufficient at the current stage to provide a basis on which to indicate provisional measures.

"The nub of the matter appears to be that, while in deciding whether it has jurisdiction on the merits, the Court gives the defendant the benefit of the doubt, in deciding whether it has jurisdiction to indicate provisional measures the Court gives the applicant the benefit of the doubt. In the present case," said Judge Schwebel, "the Court, in my view, has given the Applicant the benefit of a great many doubts."

*International Court of Justice: How It Works*

The case concerning *Military and Paramilitary Activities in and against Nicaragua (Nicaragua v. United States)* is the fifty-second contentious case brought before the International Court of Justice since it was set up in 1945 as the principal judicial organ of the United Nations.

The first case dealt with by the Court—*Corfu Channel (United Kingdom v. Albania)* in 1947—also involved a mining incident, as the present case does in part. In that dispute, the main issue concerned Albania's responsibility for the explosion of mines in Corfu Channel that damaged British warships and killed crew members.

The 15-member Court, which sits at The Hague, Netherlands, settles international disputes on the basis of international law. Most of its work involves hearing "contentious cases" (disputes between States). Since 1946, the Court has delivered 43 Judgments and made 181 Orders in connection with contentious cases involving at least 44 States.

The Court is also empowered to give advisory opinions on legal questions as requested by the General Assembly, the Security Council, or other United Nations bodies so authorized. Between 1946 and 1984, the Court dealt with 17 requests for advisory opinions, delivering 18 opinions and making 24 Orders in the cases concerned.

*Access:* In contentious cases, only States—not individuals—may be parties in cases before the Court. The Court is automatically open to all States Members of the United Nations, who are *ipso facto* parties to its Statute. Other States may refer cases to the Court on conditions determined by the General Assembly at the Security Council's recommendation, or by filing declarations by which they agree to accept the Court's jurisdiction and comply in good faith with the Court's decisions.

*Jurisdiction:* The jurisdiction of the Court extends to all questions that States refer to it and to all matters provided for in the charter of the United Nations or treaties and conventions currently in force. The Security Council may also recommend that a legal dispute be referred to the Court.

A State cannot be made a party to proceedings without its consent in some form. Nor can States be forced to submit cases to the Court. Settlement of disputes at the international level, in contrast to national level, remains optional. The United Nations Charter requires Members to seek peaceful settlement of disputes first by "negotiation, enquiry, mediation, conciliation, arbitration, judicial settlement, resort to regional agencies or arrangements, or other peaceful means of their own choice."

States may bind themselves in advance, however, to accept the jurisdiction of the Court in disputes which have not yet arisen by signing various treaties or conventions, or by making a formal declaration to that effect. In their declarations accepting the Court's compulsory jurisdiction, States may exclude certain classes of cases or set other conditions.

Forty-seven States have accepted compulsory jurisdiction. They are: Australia, Austria, Barbados, Belgium, Botswana, Canada, Colombia, Costa Rica, Democratic Kampuchea, Denmark, Dominican Republic, Egypt, El Salvador, Finland, Gambia, Haiti, Honduras, India, Israel, Japan, Kenya, Liberia, Liechtenstein, Luxembourg, Malawi, Malta, Mauritius, Mexico, Netherlands, New Zealand, Nicaragua, Nigeria, Norway, Pakistan, Panama, Philippines, Portugal, Somalia, Sudan, Swaziland, Sweden, Switzerland, Togo, Uganda, United Kingdom, United States and Uruguay.

In adjudicating cases, the Court applies, in accordance with Article 38 of its Statute, international conventions, international custom, the general principles of law of nations, and judicial decisions and teachings of the world's most highly qualified jurists.

States are under no compulsion to recognize the jurisdiction of the Court, but once their consent to it has been established in a given case, it is incumbent upon them to comply with the Court's decisions. A Judgment of the Court is final and without appeal.

There is no formal means of enforcing Court decisions, but Article 94 (2) of the Charter provides that if a party to a case fails to perform its obligations under a Judgment, the other party may have recourse to the Security Council, which may decide on measures to be taken to give effect to the Judgment. To date, that provision has never been invoked.

*Procedure:* Contentious cases are brought to the Court either by special agreement—notification to the Registry that both of the parties agree to refer the dispute to the Court—or by an application by one of the parties founded on a clause in the Statute providing for compulsory jurisdiction (Article 36).

The parties are represented by agents, assisted by counsel and advocates. The proceedings consist of both written and oral parts. The written part usually involves the presentation by each of the parties of pleadings which are filed within certain time-limits. In principle, only two pleadings are filed—a "memorial" by the applicant and a "countermemorial" by the respondent. Sometimes, however, they are followed by a "reply" and a "rejoinder." The oral part consists of public hearings by the Court, at which witnesses and experts may appear, as well as the agents, counsel and advocates.

Following the written and oral proceedings, the Court deliberates in private to prepare its Judgment. All questions are decided by a majority of Judges present. In the event of a tie, the President of the Court or Presiding Judge casts the deciding vote.

As in cases before national courts, the question of the Court's jurisdiction is an important issue. In *Nicaragua v. United States,* for example, the United States asked the Court to dismiss Nicaragua's suit on jurisdictional grounds.

*Composition:* The Court is composed of 15 Judges elected to nine-year terms by majority votes of the General Assembly and Security Council, acting independently. They are chosen on the basis of their high moral character and their expert legal qualifications. No two Judges may be of the same nationality, and care is taken to ensure that all the world's principal judicial systems are represented on the bench.

Care is also taken to ensure impartiality. A Judge may not participate in the decision of a case in which he has previously taken part in any capacity, and Judges will sometimes decide to abstain from sitting on a case for special reasons. A country which does not have one of its nationals on the panel may appoint one to serve as a Judge *ad hoc* for a case to which it is a party.

The composition of the Court as of April 1984 was, in order of precedence: Taslim Olawale Elias (Nigeria), *President*; José Sette-Câmara (Brazil), *Vice-President*; Manfred Lachs (Poland), Platon Dmitrievich Morozov (USSR), Nagendra Singh (India), José-María Ruda (Argentina), Hermann Mosler (Federal Republic of Germany), Shigeru Oda (Japan), Roberto Ago (Italy), Abdallah Fikri El-Khani (Syrian Arab Republic), Stephen M. Schwebel (United States), Sir Robert Jennings (United Kingdom), Guy Ladreit de Lacharrière (France), Kéba Mbaye (Senegal) and Mohammed Bedjaoui (Algeria). The Registrar of the Court is Santiago Torres Bernárdez.

[For more information on the Court, see "Perspective," *UN Chronicle*, 1983, No. 11.]

The International Court of Justice stated in its Order of 10 May that although it could not make "definitive findings of fact" in the proceedings on Nicaragua's request for provisional measures, the respondent State—the United States—had the right to dispute the facts alleged by Nicaragua in its request and to submit arguments to the Court in respect of the merits of the case.

The United States raised several objections to the granting of interim measures of protection as requested by Nicaragua, apart from its jurisdictional objections to the Court's consideration of the case. It argued that:

• The subject of Nicaragua's Application and its claims therein were "committed to a regional arrangement"—the Contadora process—approved by the Security Council and endorsed by the Organization of American States, and that Nicaragua was obliged therefore to pursue negotiations in the context of that process. "It would be singularly inappropriate for this Court to substitute itself in the circumstances of this case for the mechanism provided for in the Charter for resolving disputes involving armed conflict," said the United States.

• Nicaragua's Application and request for provisional measures "inevitably implicate the rights and interests of other Central American States," the United States contended. Those other States were indispensable parties, and the case could not proceed in their absence.

• Nicaragua had "improperly" called on the Court "to make judgements and to impose measures potentially impairing the inherent right of States to individual and collective self-defence under Article 51 of the United Nations Charter," according to the United States. Nicaragua seemed to be asking for a determination that an unjustified use of force was occurring. However, questions regarding use of force during hostilities were more properly within the purview of the political organs of the United Nations and the Organization of American States.

The United States told the Court that Nicaragua's Application tried to convey the impression that the problems facing Central America today were "essentially a bilateral dispute between the Government of the United States and the Government of Nicaragua." But the problems were not those of isolated violence affecting Nicaragua's security alone; the question was how best to bring peace to the region as a whole. The United States did not feel that the judicial forum was the appropriate place to address that issue.

The Contadora process, which had been accepted by all parties concerned, including Nicaragua, had made substantial progress towards the achievement of a comprehensive and enforceable resolution to the multifaceted problems of Central America. The nature and status of those regional negotiations were directly relevant to the issues confronting the Court in the present proceedings, the United States contended.

The 1980s had brought "profound change" in the societies of the Central American countries—Costa Rica, El Salvador, Honduras, Guatemala and Nicaragua—and a transformation in the character of the problems of the area from largely internal difficulties to region-wide strife. Nicaragua's "Junta of Government of National Reconstruction" had come to power in 1979 committed to pluralism, electoral democracy and respect for human rights, but had turned instead to an increasingly authoritarian internal policy. It had initiated a massive build-up of military forces "unprecedented in the region," numbering 75,000 persons by 1983, plus some 3,000 Cuban military personnel.

Nicaragua had not only become deeply involved in insurgencies in neighbouring countries but had experienced violence in its own territory as well. Many leaders of the 1979 revolution and former high-ranking members of the Sandinista Government itself had gone into armed opposition to achieve the original goals of the revolution.

Nicaragua had accused other nations of instigating and supporting the opposition movements within its own territory. "But just as it cannot be argued that violence in El Salvador or other neighbouring countries is exclusively the result of Nicaraguan and Cuban aggression, Nicaragua's Government cannot pretend that its armed opposition is solely a creature of outside forces."

The problems of Central America were "too complex and interrelated to be dealt with on a piecemeal basis," according to the United States. The Cancun Declaration issued by the Contadora Group (Colombia, Mexico, Panama and Venezuela) in July 1983 had proposed a comprehensive agenda to address the security, economic, social, political and compliance issues facing the region. Nicaragua had countered with proposals of its own which, while "unbalanced and focused almost entirely on security issues, did recognize the need to address these problems on a regional basis."

In September 1983, the Contadora Group and the five Central American States had prepared a 21-point document of objectives listing the issues and principles on which regional peace must be based and establishing the framework for negotiations. Since then, however, Nicaragua had repeatedly tried to separate from the regional negotiating process issues of special concern to Nicaragua and divert them to other forums, and to portray the problems of the region as a product of United States antagonism towards Nicaragua, while excluding the concerns of its neighbours.

In April 1984, Nicaragua had again sought to raise complaints in the Security Council and on 9 April had filed its Application with the Court.

The other States of the region had expressed the view that Nicaragua's request for indication of provisional measures directly implicated their rights and interests, and that indication of such measures would intefere with the Contadora negotiations. Costa Rica, El Salvador and Honduras had communicated their concern directly to the Court, and Guatemala had issued a public statement to that effect. Those communications made it clear that Nicaragua's claims were linked inextricably to the rights and interests of the neighbouring States.

The United States had from the outset shared concern that attempts to separate individual aspects from that comprehensive regional process for address in other fora would impede the prospects of a negotiated solution. There had been "no choice but to place Nicaragua on notice that the United States would not join in such a diversionary exercise and would continue to do all it could to give the regional negotiating process the time it needs to accomplish its work successfully."

For the Court "to grant Nicaragua in these proceedings the relief it seeks in the Contadora process, in whole or in part, can only prejudice the ability of the other Central American States to have their grievances, too, satisfied," said the United States. "Any decision to indicate the interim measures requested, or a decision on the merits, would . . . cut those States off from their right to seek and receive support from the United States in meeting the armed attacks against them."

There was a final reason, argued the United States, why the Court should not recognize Nicaragua's Application in general or indicate the interim measures in particular: Nicaragua sought to enjoin the United States from a "wide range of actions, the legitimacy of which might not be adjudicated for an indefinite period. A request of this nature, raising very fundamental questions, is absolutely unprecedented in the history of this Court and its predecessor. It strains incidental proceedings beyond any reasonable bounds," the United States contended.

---

## THE UNITED STATES AND THE WORLD COURT[5]

---

I welcome this opportunity to discuss the background to the President's decision of October 7 terminating our acceptance of the compulsory jurisdiction of the International Court of Justice (ICJ). This decision will take effect 6 months from that date. I will discuss what the President's decision means in practical terms before turning to some of the reasons for it.

### Jurisdiction of the Court

The ICJ has limited jurisdiction, based on its Statute and on the consent of states. Under Article 36(1) of the Court's Statute, the ICJ has jurisdiction when states sign a special agreement referring a dispute to it or are parties to a treaty providing for ICJ dispute resolution. The President's action does not affect this basis for jurisdiction. Indeed, we have just agreed with Italy to submit an important dispute, involving millions of dollars, to the Court for adjudication. We also are party to some 60 treaties providing for adjudication of disputes by the ICJ.

The second basis for ICJ jurisdiction exists when a state accepts the Court's compulsory jurisdiction under Article 36(2) of the Statute—the so-called optional clause. Historically, acceptance of compulsory jurisdiction has been less important as a basis for the Court's work than specific agreement between the parties to a dispute.

[5]Reprint of a statement by Abraham D. Sofaer, legal adviser to the United States Department of State, before the Senate Foreign Relations Committee, Washington, D.C., on December 4, 1985. *Department of State Bulletin.* D. '85. pp. 1–4.

A state accepts compulsory jurisdiction by depositing with the Secretary General of the United Nations a declaration to the effect that it agrees to be sued by any state depositing a similar declaration. In return, the filing state may bring suit under compulsory jurisdiction against any other state filing such a declaration. Generally, a state has no way of knowing in advance by whom or on what issue a suit may be filed. A declaration covers any issue of international law, except to the extent that the state excludes specific disputes or categories of disputes. A state faced with a suit under compulsory jurisdiction may invoke any exclusion in its declaration and, on the basis of reciprocity, any exclusion in its opponent's declaration to seek defeat jurisdiction. It also may raise nonjurisdictional objections to the Court's taking the case. If the parties disagree over the scope of a declaration or its exclusions, the Court itself decides the issue.

Under the Court's Statute, a state is free to accept or to decline the Court's compulsory jurisdiction. A state accepting the Court's compulsory jurisdiction likewise is free to terminate or modify its acceptance whenever the state concerned believes that doing so would serve its interests. The President's action terminating our 1946 declaration, thus, is entirely consistent with our international legal obligations.

The President's action also is consistent with his domestic legal authority. Declarations under Article 36(2) of the Statute are not treaties under either international law or the Constitution. Nevertheless, in 1946 the executive branch considered that congressional approval of the declaration was necessary for several reasons. Any such a declaration necessarily entails an open-ended exposure to suit, including potential financial liability. In addition, Congress traditionally had been reluctant to allow the President to enter into compulsory third-party dispute settlement arrangements, as the fate of repeated executive efforts to have the United States accept the jurisdiction of the predecessor Court, the Permanent Court of International Justice, showed.

The terminating of the 1946 declaration, on the other hand, does not expose the United States to new commitments or obligations. On the contrary, it reduces or eliminates that exposure. Furthermore, by its terms, the declaration authorizes termination on 6 months' notice, and our October 7 note is consistent with that condition. Finally, the Constitution allows the President unilaterally to terminate treaties consistent with their terms; and his authority is even clearer with respect to lesser instruments such as the 1946 declaration.

## Reasons for U.S. Review

Our experience in the case instituted against the United States by Nicaragua in April 1984 provided the chief motivation for the Administration's review of our acceptance of the Court's compulsory jurisdiction. The principal basis of jurisdiction cited by Nicaragua in bringing that case was the 1946 U.S. declaration accepting compulsory jurisdiction. We believed at the time, and still believe, that Nicaragua itself never had validly accepted the Court's compulsory jurisdiction. More important, Nicaragua sought to bring before the Court political and security disputes that were never previously considered part of the Court's mandate to resolve. In our view, the Court's decision last November that Nicaragua had, indeed, accepted compulsory jurisdiction and that Nicaragua's claims were justiciable could not be supported as a matter of law. These considerations led the President to decide last January that we would no longer participate in the case.

The Court's decision also caused us to undertake a thorough evaluation of our 1946 declaration and its place in the system of compulsory jurisdiction extablished by Article 36(2) of the Court's Statute. That we were evaluating these questions was well known. The issues at stake were considered and debated in government and private groups interested in this question. All the relevant points were carefully considered.

We recognized, first of all, that the hopes originally placed in compulsory jurisdiction by the architects of the Court's Statute have never been realized and will not be realized in the foreseeable future. We had hoped that widespread acceptance of compulsory jurisdiction and its successful employment in actual cases would increase confidence in judicial settlement of international disputes and, thus, eventually lead to its universal acceptance.

Experience has dashed these hopes. Only 47 of the 162 states entitled to accept the Court's compulsory jurisdiction now do so. This number represents a proportion of states that is substantially lower than in the late 1940s. The United Kingdom is the only other Permanent Member of the UN Security Council that accepts compulsory jurisdiction in any form. Neither the Soviet

Union nor any other Soviet-bloc state has ever accepted compulsory jurisdiction. Many of our closest friends and allies—such as France, Italy, and the Federal Republic of Germany—do not accept compulsory jurisdiction. Moreover, a substantial number of the states accepting compulsory jurisdiction have attached reservations to their acceptances that deprive them of much of their meaning. The United Kingdom, for example, retains the power to decline to accept the Court's jurisdiction in any dispute at any time before a case is actually filed.

Compulsory jurisdiction cases have not been the principal part of the Court's overall jurisprudence. Of some 50 contentious cases between 1946 and the end of 1983, 22 were based on the Court's compulsory jurisdiction, of which only five resulted in final judgment on the merits. The last case decided under the Court's compulsory jurisdiction, the *Temple of Preah Vihear,* was completed in 1962. In the remaining 17 cases, objections to the Court's jurisdiction were sustained in 13; four were dismissed on other grounds.

Another consideration we weighed is the fact that, although we have tried seven times, we have never been able successfully to bring a state before the Court. We have been barred from achieving this result not only by the fact that few other states accept compulsory jurisdiction but also by the principle of reciprocity as applied to our 1946 declaration. That principle allows a respondent state to invoke any reservation in the applicant state's declaration to seek to defeat the Court's jurisdiction. Thus, respondent states may invoke reservations in our 1946 declaration against us. The so-called Connally reservation in our 1946 declaration provides that the United States does not accept compulsory jurisdiction over any dispute involving matters essentially within the domestic jurisdiction of the United States, as determined by the United States. In other words, we reserve to ourselves the power to determine whether the Court has jurisdiction over us in a particular case. Any state we sue may avail itself of that power on a reciprocal basis to defeat jurisdiction.

This is, in fact, precisely what happened when we tried to sue Bulgaria in 1957 on claims arising out of the loss of American lives and property when Bulgaria shot down an unarmed civilian airliner that had strayed into its airspace. Bulgaria claimed that the Court had no jurisdiction because the matter in dispute was within Bulgarian domestic jurisdiction as determined by Bulgaria. Even though we had pledged never to invoke our Connally reservation in bad faith to cover a manifestly international dispute, we were compelled to acknowledge that its invocation in any case would be binding as a matter of law. Hence, Bulgaria's reciprocal invocation of the Connally reservation forced us to discontinue the case.

On a more general level, other countries, the international legal community, and, indeed, the executive branch have severely criticized the "self-judging" nature of the Connally reservation. Some commentators even argue that the Connally reservation made the 1946 declaration a legal nullity because of its wholly unilateral and potentially limitless character. Certainly, that reservation has undercut the example the United States tried to set for other countries by its acceptance of compulsory jurisdiction.

For these reasons we have never been able successfully to bring another state before the Court on the basis of our acceptance of compulsory jurisdiction. On the other hand, we have been sued under it three times: by France in the *Rights of Nationals of the United States in Morocco* case in 1950–1952; by Switzerland in the *Interhandel* case in 1957–1959; and, finally, by Nicaragua last year.

The terms of our acceptance of compulsory jurisdiction contain an additional weakness. Nothing in it prevents another state from depositing an acceptance of compulsory jurisdiction solely for the purpose of bringing suit against the United States and, thereafter withdrawing its acceptance to avoid being sued by anyone in any other matter. Students of the Court long have recognized that this "sitting duck" or "hit-and-run" problem is one of the principal disadvantages to the system of compulsory jurisdiction under article 36(2). It places the minority of states that have accepted compulsory jurisdiction at the mercy of the majority that have not.

The Court's composition also is a source of institutional weakness. At present, 9 of 15 judges come from states that do not accept compulsory jurisdiction; most of these states have never used the Court at all. Judges are elected by the General Assembly and Security Council, frequently after intense electioneering. One reasonably may expect at least some judges to be sensitive to the impact of their decisions on their standing with the UN majority. Whereas in 1945 the United Nations had some 50 members, most of which were aligned with the United States and shared its views regarding world order, there are now 160 members. A great many of these cannot be counted on to share our view of the original constitutional conception of the UN Charter, particularly with regard to the special position of the Permanent Members of the Security Council in the maintenance of international peace and security. This same majority often opposes the United States on important international questions.

### The Nicaragua Case

None of the weaknesses deriving from the Court's composition and our 1946 declaration is new. We have hitherto endured them on the assumption that the respect states owed to the Court and the Court's own scrupulous adherence to its judicial role would insulate us from abuses of the Court's process for political or propaganda ends. The Nicaragua case showed that it would be unrealistic to continue to rely on that assumption.

Several aspects of the Court's decisions in the Nicaragua case were disturbing. First, the Court departed from its traditionally cautious approach to finding jurisdiction. It disregarded fundamental defects in Nicaragua's claim to have accepted compulsory jurisdiction. This question involves more than a legal technicality. It goes to the heart of the Court's jurisdiction, which is the consent of states. International law—in particular, the Court's own Statute—establishes precise rules that states must follow in order to manifest that consent. The purpose of such technical rules is to ensure that a state's consent is genuine and that all other states are given objective notice of it. Nicaragua never complied with those rules, and the historical evidence makes clear that its failure to do so was deliberate and designed to ensure that Nicaragua could never be sued successfully under article 36(2). A majority of the Court, on the other hand, was prepared to discover an exception to those rules that allowed Nicaragua to bring suit, an exception that is inconsistent with the Court's prior jurisprudence on the subject. The result-oriented illogic of the majority's position was vigorously exposed in the opinions of the dissenting judges.

Furthermore, the Court engaged in unprecedented procedural actions—such as rejecting without even a hearing El Salvador's application to intervene as of right—that betrayed a predisposition to find that it had jurisdiction and that Nicaragua's claims were justiciable, regardless of the overwhelming legal case to the contrary. In the particular case of the Salvadoran intervention, the Court ignored Article 63 of the Statute, which deprives the Court of discretion to reject such interventions. The Court sought to cover itself by holding out the possibility of accepting the Salvadoran intervention at the merits stage—at which point Salvadoran objections to the Court's jurisdiction and the justiciability of Nicaragua's claims would have been too late.

Even more disturbing, for the first time in its history, the Court has sought to assert jurisdiction over a controversy concerning claims related to an ongoing use of armed force. This action concerns every state. It is inconsistent with the structure of the UN system. The only prior case involving use-of-force issues—the *Corfu Channel* case—went to the Court after the disputed actions had ceased and the Security Council had determined that the matter was suitable for judicial consideration. In the Nicaragua case, the Court rejected without a soundly reasoned explanation our arguments that claims of the sort made by Nicaragua were intended by the UN Charter exclusively for resolution by political mechanisms—in particular, the Security Council and the Contadora process—and that claims to the exercise of the inherent right of individual and collective self-defense were excluded by Article 51 of the Charter from review by the Court.

I cannot predict whether the Court's approach to these fundamental Charter issues in the jurisdictional phase of the Nicaragua case will be followed in the Court's judgment on the merits. Nevertheless, the record gives us little reason for confidence. It shows a Court majority apparently prepared to act in ways profoundly inconsistent with the structure of the Charter and the Court's place in that structure. The Charter gives to the Security Council—not the Court—the responsibility for evaluating and resolving claims concerning the use of armed force and claims of self-defense under article 51. With regard to the situation in Central America, the Security Council exercised its responsibility by endorsing the Contadora process as the appropriate mechanism for resolving the interlocking political, security, economic, and other concerns of the region.

*Implications for U.S. National Security*

The fact that the ICJ indicated it would hear and decide claims about the ongoing use of force made acceptance of the Court's compulsory jurisdiction an issue of strategic significance. Despite our deep reluctance to do so and the many domestic constraints that apply, we must be able to use force in our self-defense and in the defense of our friends and allies. We are a law-abiding nation, and when we submit ourselves to adjudication of a subject, we regard ourselves as obliged to abide by the result. For the United States to recognize that the ICJ has authority to define and adjudicate with respect to our right of self-defense, therefore, is effectively to surrender to that body the power to pass on our efforts to guarantee the safety and security of this nation and of its allies.

This development particularly concerned us as a matter of principle and for reasons bearing directly on the capacity of the ICJ to reach sound, correct decisions on use-of-force issues and to enforce principles it eventually may articulate on our communist adversaries. The Court has no expertise in finding facts about ongoing hostilities or any other activities occurring in areas such as Central America. Based on my years as a trial judge and considerable experience with complicated cases, I doubt that the 16 judges sitting on the Nicaragua case may reliably resolve the evidentiary problems presented. The ICJ is similar to an appellate Court, more at home with abstract legal questions than with competing factual claims. Moreover, the Court's rejection of El Salvador's application to intervene deprived it of that nation's indispensable contribution to a true picture of the situation in Central America, a contribution that goes to the heart of our legal position.

Even if the Court were inclined to allow participation by all necessary parties, it has no power to compel that participation. We have, for example, no doubt that Cuba, and quite probably the Soviet Union, help Nicaragua's efforts to subvert the democratic regime in El Salvador as well as to undertake unlawful acts against Costa Rica and Honduras. But, in view of their consistent refusal to submit to the Court's jurisdiction in any other matter, neither Cuba nor the Soviet Union can be expected to join in the proceedings, and the Court cannot force them to do so. These facts render even more questionable the capacity of the Court to determine the facts concerning Nicaragua's aggressive acts.

The Court's lack of jurisdiction over Soviet-bloc nations, especially the Soviet Union, also has long-term significance for the strategic acceptability of ICJ review of self-defense issues. The Soviets have long advanced the view—by the Brezhnev doctrine and otherwise, and by their actions in places like Czechoslovakia and Afghanistan—that force is acceptable in order to keep a nation in the socialist orbit or to promote a socialist revolution but have not hesitated to condemn responsive uses of force as violating the UN Charter.

We reject this view. We believe that, when a nation asserts a right to use force illegally and acts on that assertion, other affected nations have the right to counter such illegal activities. The United States cannot rely on the ICJ properly and fairly to decide such questions. Indeed, no state can do so. If we acquiesce in this claimed authority, we would be bound by the Court's decisions that limited our ability to confront Soviet expansionism, even though the Soviets could and would do as they pleased. That most of the Court's judges come from nations that do not submit to its jurisdiction, including Soviet-bloc nations and other states that routinely support that bloc, is of special concern on these fundamental issues.

Mr. Chairman [Sen. Richard Lugar], in considering this complex and important subject, I hope that you and the other members of this distinguished committee weigh carefully the national security implications of accepting the Court as a forum for resolving use-of-force questions. For example, would the Court be the proper forum for resolving the disputes that gave rise to such actions as the Berlin airlift, the Cuban missile crisis, and, most recently, our diversion of the *Achille Lauro* terrorists? Each event involved questions of international law.

At the same time, however, at stake on each occasion were interests of a fundamentally political nature, going to our nation's security. Such matters cannot be left for resolution by judicial means, let alone by a court such as the ICJ; rather, they are the ultimate responsibilities assigned by our Constitution to the President and Congress. We did not consider such issues to be subject to review by the ICJ at the time we accepted the Court's compulsory jurisdiction, and we do not consider them to be encompassed by that acceptance now. The Court's apparent willingness to construe our declaration otherwise left us with no prudent alternative but no terminate that aspect of our use of its facilities.

We carefully considered modifying our 1946 declaration as an alternative to its termination, but we concluded that modification would not meet our concerns. No limiting language that we could draft would prevent the Court from asserting jurisdiction if it wanted to take a particular case, as the Court's treatment of our multilateral treaty reservation in the Nicaragua case demonstrates. That reservation excludes disputes arising under a multilateral treaty unless all treaty partners affected by the Court's decision are before the Court. Despite Nicaragua's own written and oral pleadings before the Court—which expressly implicated El Salvador, Honduras, and Costa Rica in the alleged violations of the UN and OAS [Organization of American States] Charters and prayed for a termination of U.S. assistance to them—and statements received directly from those countries, a majority of the Court refused to recognize that those countries would be affected by its decision and refused to give effect to the reservation. Furthermore, merely having filed a declaration is enough for the court to indicate provisional measures against the filing party, whether or not the Court later found it had jurisdiction under the declaration. Finally, the 1946 declaration expressly provides only for its termination, and we would not wish to have the legality or effectiveness of any lesser step open to question.

*Conclusion*

Looked at from the standpoint of the reality of compulsory jurisdiction today, the decision to terminate our 1946 acceptance was a regrettable but necessary measure taken in order to safeguard U.S. interests. It does not signify a lessening of our traditionally strong support for the Court in the exercise of its proper functions, much less a diminution of our commitment to international law. We remain prepared to use the Court for the resolution of international disputes whenever possible and appropriate.

We recognize that this nation has a special obligation to support the ICJ and all other institutions that advance the rule of law in a world full of terror and disorder. Our belief in this obligation is what led us to set an example by accepting the Court's compulsory jurisdiction in 1946 and by continuing that acceptance long after it became clear that the world would not follow suit and that our acceptance failed to advance our interests in any tangible manner.

Yet, the President also is responsible to the American people and to Congress to avoid potential threats to our national security. The ICJ's decisions in the Nicaragua case created real and important additional considerations that made the continued acceptance of compulsory jurisdiction unacceptable, despite its symbolic significance. We hope that, in the long run, this action, coupled with our submission of disputes under article 36(1), will strengthen the Court in the performance of its proper role in the international system established by the UN Charter and the Court's own Statute.

## ICY DAY AT THE ICJ[6]

"The Court's decision of November 26, 1984, finding that it has jurisdiction [in the case brought by Nicaragua against the United States], is contrary to law and fact. With great reluctance, the United States has decided to participate in further proceedings in this case." With that, the U.S. Government turned its back not only on the International Court of Justice but on 40 years of leadership in the cause of world peace through law.

It cannot have been an easy decision. Those in Washington who took it must have known that it would be costly to the national interest, in both the long run and the short term. In the long run, it deprives the United States of whatever moral superiority accrues from a continued commitment to restraint based on neutral reciprocal principles in a world of rampant opportunistic self-aggrandizement. In the short term, the decision not to participate in the "merits" phase of the case will also be seen by many as confirmation that the United States is guilty as charged by Nicaragua.

In announcing its decision, the State Department argued that "much of the evidence that would establish Nicaragua's aggression against its neighbors is of a highly sensitive intelligence character. We will not risk U.S. national security by presenting such

[6]Reprint of an editorial comment by Thomas M. Franck, Professor of International Law, New York University School of Law, and editor in chief, *American Journal of International Law. American Journal of International Law.* Ap. '85. pp. 379–84. Copyright 1985 The American Society of International Law, publisher of the *American Journal of International Law.* Reprinted with permission.

sensitive material in public or before a Court that includes two judges from Warsaw Pact nations." Yet those who drafted his statement undoubtedly realized that it would be greeted by nearly universal skepticism. The State Department itself has engaged in detailed public recitations of unclassified evidence to support its contention that its covert retaliation against Nicaragua is an exercise, with Honduras and El Salvador, of the right of collective self-defense. It is not really credible that a 4-year-long effort at large-scale training, supply and direction of Salvadoran insurgents by Nicaragua and Cuba would have remained entirely invisible except to highly classified sensors. Most observers, even those of pro-American leanings, will reluctantly group this explanation with the too familiar use by national governments of the "national security" rationale to withhold evidence of their own wrongdoing. In this they may be wrong, but their response will be both human and predictable.

Given these almost inescapable long- and short-run costs, why was withdrawal considered the only acceptable option open to the U.S. Government? Careful reading of the U.S. statement suggests that Washington's decision was based on two conclusions. The first is that the Court's decisions in the proceedings to date are so blatantly biased as to foreclose the possibility of a fair hearing on the merits. The Government's statement asserts unequivocally that the decision of November 26 "is erroneous as a matter of law and is based on a misreading and distortion of the evidence and precedent." Ambassador Jeane Kirkpatrick earlier hinted at this conclusion when, at the 1984 Annual Meeting of the American Society of International Law, she noted that the judges of the ICJ are elected by the very same political process that generates the resolutions of the United Nations.

The second conclusion follows from the first: that the time has come to undertake a basic rethinking of U.S. relations with the Court and, indeed, all multilateral institutions of world order. "We have seen in the United Nations, in the last decade or more," the U.S. statement on withdrawal continues, "how international organizations have become more and more politicized against the interests of the Western democracies." Those developments "compel us to clarify our 1946 acceptance of the Court's jurisdiction." And, for that matter, our membership in most multilateral institutions. The United States travels more surely and swiftly, the Reagan administration now appears to believe, when it travels alone.

In a recent statement, Allan Gerson, the acting counselor for legal affairs to the U.S. Mission to the United Nations, noted that the Nicaraguan suit really did not turn on a question of law—the right of collective self-defense is well established by Article 51 of the UN Charter and in customary international law—but on complex facts: is there a Nicaraguan "attack" to which U.S. actions are part of a collective response? "Do we," he asked, "really want the World Court to be in a position to second guess the House Committee on Intelligence, the Senate Committee on Intelligence, the Bipartisan Commissions established for that purpose?" To his own question, the counselor gave an emphatic no, because, by submitting to the Court, we would risk a negative decision, in which case "U.S. freedom of action in the region will be impaired." Moreover, even if we were to win, he argued, the United States would gain nothing except to serve as a "good example" to other states. "But does it make sense," he continued,

for the United States to agree to a fact-finding reviewing role by the Court, in matters of U.S. national security, at a time when we have no reasonable assurances that our posture will contribute to inducing other states to take similar risks, and indeed when all available evidence points in the other direction? That the process of setting a good example does not yield results—not, at least, in terms of getting others to follow our example in accepting the compulsory jurisdiction of the Court—is empirically verifiable.

In walking away from the Court, the United States thus expresses despair with its politicized, anti-Western bias, as revealed by its preliminary decisions in the Nicaraguan case, and with multilateral institutions and the neutral reciprocal principles by which they were intended to operate. Why should we be the last ones to play by the rules, the Reagan administration seems to be asking, long after they have been abandoned by everyone else? Moreover, why should a superpower, in matters of essential national interest, ever subordinate its power of initiation to a system that it does not control and that may even be controlled by our enemies?

These are fundamental questions. They are not new, of course. Senator Borah, in joining to frustrate U.S. adherence to the PCIJ in 1935 said, "I am not in favor of an international judicial tribunal, so called, which is political and advisory in character." That the questions are now asked again creates a fundamental challenge to the basic assumptions held for 40 years by American international lawyers, in particular, and shared by most of the nation's foreign policy establishment. It's a dog-eat-dog world out there, we are being told, so let's stop acting as if it were otherwise.

Whatever, the merits of this reality-testing challenge, when directed towards UNESCO or the UN General Assembly, it seems exaggeratedly alarmist, to the point of paranoia, when addressed to the ICJ. This is, after all, the same Court that, despite its socialist and Third World membership, overwhelmingly endorsed the U.S. complaint against Iran during the hostage crisis in 1980. Does the Court's conduct to date in respect of the Nicaraguan complaint provide clear-cut evidence that it has now been politicized by America's enemies?

In its Order of the Court of May 10, 1984, the ICJ directed certain provisional measures to the parties and to other states in the region and the world. However, by specifically naming the United States while referring to Nicaragua only anonymously, the Court left itself open to the suspicion that its unexceptionable injunction against the illegal use of force by any party incidentally demonstrated a bias against one of the parties. It was an unfortunate beginning to a case in which the Court should have gone out of its way to demonstrate its unimpeachable impartiality. Equally unfortunate was the Court's Order of October 4, 1984, which decided not even to hear El Salvador's oral argument on behalf of its Declaration asking to be allowed to intervene in the proceedings on the question of jurisdiction and admissibility under Article 63 of the Statute.* While the Court, both at the time and in its opinion of November 26, 1984, reiterated the possibility of El Salvador's intervening at the merits stage of the proceedings, this curt treatment further reinforced the suspicion in Washington that the majority of judges had already made up their minds and would brook no delay in reaching their preconceived decision. Once again, by refusing to bend over backwards to give the utmost consideration to the respondent's side, the Court seemed to bow in the direction of the plaintiff.

Nevertheless, the United States continued to participate in the Court's proceedings. This took considerable courage on the part of the State Department's Legal Adviser, since there were already voices within the administration arguing for abandonment of the Court. No doubt that courage was reenforced by a

*The author participated in the preparation of El Salvador's Declaration seeking to intervene as of right on the questions of jurisdiction and admissibility.

certainty that the United States had the law entirely on its side in the matter of jurisdiction and admissibility. When a sizable majority of the Court voted otherwise, Washington's suspicion of judicial bias became a vested conviction.

Is the conviction justified? The issues before the Court, at this stage, were numerous and complex. Nevertheless, the four most important findings of the Court should now be examined by every American international lawyer as if he or she were engaging in a form of judicial review, for it is now the Court itself that has been placed on trial by the U.S. Government. The appropriate standard for such review is the same as might be fashioned by any appellate tribunal: Are the findings of the ICJ so patently unreasonable—in another section of this issue, Monroe Leigh calls one "preposterous"—as to permit no other conclusion than that they reflect the willfull anti-American bias of the judges?

The Court's first finding is that Nicaragua has accepted the ICJ's compulsory jurisdiction. The United States had demonstrated that Nicaragua, while having formally declared its intent to accept the optional compulsory jurisdiction of the predecessor Permanent Court of International Justice, had nevertheless failed—deliberately or not—to ratify that Court's Protocol. The United States had argued that this technical noncompliance entitled it, reciprocally, to refuse to be sued by Nicaragua despite Washington's conditional acceptance of the Court's optional clause (Article 36 of the ICJ Statute). To reach its conclusion, the majority of judges (by 11 to 5) held that the defect in the Nicaraguan acceptance of the PCIJ's compulsory jurisdiction had been cured, in part by the wording of the provision in Article 36(5) of the ICJ's Statute by which the new Court inherited the jurisdiction of the old. It further held that the conduct of the ICJ Registry, the UN Secretary-General and Nicaragua itself evinced an intent that Nicaragua be seen to be bound by operation of Article 36(5) of the Statute. These deductions are certainly arguable and a reader may well conclude that the dissents of Judges Oda and Schwebel on these points make more convincing deductions from the ambiguous historical evidence. The Court's treatment of the estoppel argument is particularly thin. Still, it would be hard for a fair-minded reader of the majority's reasoned opinion to conclude that this result could not be reached by a dedicated and impartial judge. Indeed, it would have been more surprising if the Court had refused to take jurisdiction on the basis of Nicaragua's technical failure, in 1939, to follow up its telegraphed notice of ratification with an actual delivery of the instrument, particularly since, after 1945, separate ratification of the new Court's constitutive instrument became unnecessary, it being subsumed in ratification of the UN Charter by operation of Article 93.

The Court's second major finding is that the United States is also bound by its 1946 acceptance, with reservations, of the compulsory jurisdiction of the ICJ under Article 36(2). In reaching this conclusion, the Court held that the United States was obliged to act in accordance with its self-imposed requirement of 6-months' notice for termination set forth in the U.S. acceptance of the Court's compulsory jurisdiction. It rejected the notion that the "1984 notification" merely suspended, rather than selectively terminated, U.S. adherence under Article 36(2) of the Statute. It also rejected the U.S. contention that, since Nicaragua had imposed no such 6-month notice period on itself, the principle of reciprocity should release the U.S. from that obligation. Instead, the majority thought that Nicaragua's acceptance was subject to an implicit requirement of "reasonable" notice, but that, in any event, such self-imposed procedural requirements are not subject to the reciprocity concept. Even if they were, a reciprocal "reasonable notice" test would not have been satisfied by U.S. conduct. Once again, the Court's conclusions, whether one agrees with them or not, cannot be dismissed as mere window dressing for a hanging party. The last-minute effort by Washington to escape from the Court's jurisdiction, once it learned that Nicaragua was about to start a lawsuit, may be explicable in terms of leaving no legal stone unturned, but it was a dodge that could not reasonably have been expected to appeal to a majority of the judges, particularly in view of the rather ostentatiously self-imposed 6-month notice requirement which sought to demonstrate U.S. resolve never to employ so unworthy an evasion.

A third major holding of the Court, and one that is backed by all but two judges, is that the Court has mandatory jurisdiction under the terms of Article 24(2) of the U.S.-Nicaraguan Treaty of Friendship, Commerce and Navigation of 1956. This provides: "Any dispute between the Parties as to the interpretation or application of the present Treaty, not satisfactorily adjusted by diplomacy, shall be submitted to the International Court of Justice, unless the Parties agree to settlement by some other pacific means." Article 19 provides for "freedom of commerce and navigation" and other articles (1, 14, 17, and 20) mandate friendly and equitable relations. The history of this and comparable treaties can be, and was, used to argue convincingly that these provisions were intended to deal with commercial relations and not with armed hostilities. It cannot, however, be maintained that a reasonable judge—Sir Robert Jennings, for example—could not have decided that the language of the Treaty patently applied, regardless of what the parties may have contemplated at the time it was concluded, and that the actual meaning of the Treaty in this dispute could only be determined at the merits stage of the proceedings.

Finally, the Court rejected the notion that this is the sort of dispute which, because it involves ongoing hostilities and complex facts, is beyond its competence. What else could 16 jurists at the ostensible pinnacle of the international legal system have been expected to say? Previously, it was the Soviet judge who could be counted upon to urge that, faced with a hot political issue such as the appropriate *Conditions for Admission to Membership in the United Nations* or the mandatory allocation of *Certain Expenses of the United Nations,* the Court could do the parties no good and itself much harm if it did not stay out of it. Soviet Judges Krylov and Koretsky may have been more sensible than we then recognized, but neither then nor now is it to be expected that a majority of judges would agree to circumscribe their powers so radically.

These four issues do not exhaust the matters considered in the November 26 decision. No part of that decision, however, appears to this American international lawyer to be insupportable in law and thus, evidently, a manifestation of "politicization." It is a decision as to which reasonable men and women versed in the law can and will differ.

That brings us to the second conclusion that appears to underlie the administration's decision to walk away from the Court: that the U.S. interest is better protected when the nation relies on its own power than when it is submerged in a multilateral system which it cannot control, and to which we adhere solely in the quixotic hope, Mr. Gerson says, of setting a good example.

That, of course, was not the view in Washington when a virtually unanimous ICJ backed us against Iran. The Court deserves some credit for helping to generate the diplomatic climate in which Iran felt impelled to release the hostages and, incidentally, to submit the rival monetary claims of the United States and Iran to another system of international adjudication. The unilateral use of U.S. power had failed utterly to achieve that desired result.

Surely, the point is that self-reliance and submission to law are not alternatives, but eminently compatible components of a superpower's strategy, at least for as long as it proposes to be law-abiding. The United States does not adhere to the Court primarily to "set a good example," but, rather, because, as a richly endowed but not omnipotent member of the international community, it tends—as a matter both of principle and of self-interest—to conduct itself in accordance with those neutral reciprocal principles to which it has voluntarily committed itself. When others fail to live up to those commitments, it is useful to be able to demonstrate this, credibly, in open court. *That* is why we joined, and that is why we should not have walked away.

---

## THE UNFINISHED AMERICAN REVOLUTION AND NICARAGUA TODAY[7]

Like the rest of Central America, Nicaragua has had an unfavorable relationship with the United States, starting practically from when the United States became a nation and replaced its original project of liberty and democracy with Manifest Destiny.

Due to our unfortunate geographical proximity to the United States and Nicaragua's geographic possibilities for an inter-oceanic canal route, we have been in the geopolitical sights of one North American administration after another. This proximity and the insatiable thirst for domination fired by the idea of empire which some in the United States used to encourage the perpetual expansion of its borders—and they still want to continue expanding them—created a fundamental historical contradiction. For centuries, Nicaragua has struggled to survive as a nation in the face of the United States' imperial ambitions. From 1855 when we were invaded by the first filibusters until 1979 when the

[7]Reprint of a speech given by Sergio Ramírez Mercado, a member of the Government Junta of National Reconstruction, on July 14, 1983, to the "Conference on Central America" sponsored by the Sandinista Association of Cultural Workers. In Marlene Dixon and Susanne Jonas, *Nicaragua under Siege*, Synthesis Publications, '84, pp. 208-15. Copyright 1984 Synthesis Publications. Reprinted with permission.

revolution definitively proclaimed national independence—a period which included General Sandino's heroic fight against the 1927 intervention when he laid the ideological foundation for this age-old struggle—now we are again fighting the struggle of all Latin America in these small but solid trenches.

*Since this is also a political and ideological struggle, and the arguments of imperialist propaganda only try to mask and justify the military aggression armed, organized, directed, and financed by the Reagan administration, it is useful to look at some of the more blatant falsehoods entoned, like songs of death and perfidy, against our right to independence and to look at them under the light of reason, which is the right of a poor people to struggle for their national identity against the growing attacks of Manifest Destiny, in order to see this web of lies and deceptions so often repeated:*

### "The Serious Error of the Sandinistas Is That They Try to Export Their Revolution."

Throughout history, revolutions have been exportable, if we care to use that rather commercial term when talking about the dynamic by which ideas circulate across borders. Without the revolution of the 13 North American colonies, there would never have been a French Revolution, nor would Jefferson's ideas have existed without the inspiration of the French Encyclopedists, nor would General Lafayette have left France to fight in the fields of Virginia had he not believed that revolutions have no borders, nor would Benjamin Franklin have spent so many years plotting in European courts had he not thought that his American revolution was exportable.

So the revolution which gave rise to the United States' nationhood has been the most exported revolution in modern history, and the one which employed the greatest number of imported ideological elements as the basis for its thinking, its liberation war, and its innovative laws.

Confronting the despotism of the Spanish monarchs in Hispanic America, a colonial absolutism just like that practiced by England over the then future United States, our creole liberators found that the most brilliant and convincing formulas for ending the colonial yoke came from the north (just like later all our calamities would come from the same place): the example of an implacable and bloody war fought by men intent on substituting the

colonial regime with a new political and social order; the crystalli-
zation of European Enlightenment's utopian ideas about democracy first put into practice in the New World, a promised land for
those philosophical dreams which until then were considered ex-
travagant—a constitutional government and the balance of powers. All these concepts were considered extremist and subversive
by the monarchical order, and when they clandestinely spread
through Hispanic America they met with persecution, jail, and
exile. Reading James Madison then was a *les majesté* crime, just as
reading Marx can cost you your life in Guatemala or El Salvador
now.

The new United States Constitution and the explosive ideas
which inspired it traveled by muleback through Central America
as clandestine literature. That nascent republic, governed by radical madmen, extremists, and exporters of revolution, believing
only in their own model and rejecting any other, represented a
threat to Spain's internal security and strategic interests in the
New World when her great colonial empire was ready to crack
open. In 1823, when independence had been won in Central
America, the first federal constitution was adopted as an attempt
to concretize the ephemeral dream of a united Morazán-like Central America, beginning with the same introduction, copied word
for word, as the Constitution written by Madison in 1787. Thus
the United States was exporting a model and exporting the
bloody lesson that such a profound change—the defeat of the
British Empire in America—could not be moved forward without rifles, without militarily crushing the enemy, and without em-
ulating the Minutemen, guerrilla combatants as brave as those of
El Salvador's FMLN. Facing the emergence of a new order based
on new, necessarily subversive ideas, the old order was destroyed
in the war, and the old ideas and hundreds of thousands of counterrevolutionary theories underwent a mass exodus to Canada,
because revolutions always produce an exodus.

The continent's first armed revolution occurred in the United States. The United States exported its revolution to Spanish
America, and in spite of everything that the crown did to repress
these clandestine ideas quickly and secretly circulating throughout the Viceroyship of Guatemala and through New Granada, it
was impossible to prevent them from taking hold in the minds of
thousands of other bearded, barefoot, hungry, and ragged extremists who trafficked in books and pamphlets containing those

incendiary speeches and subversive laws. They also trafficked in rifles and ammunition, since those ideas, which already had the power of truth, had to be imposed by force. And they did not hesitate to seek and accept the weapons they needed to assure their liberation army's victories. As Bolívar admitted in his Angostura Speech: "Our army lacked military elements, it had always been unarmed with justice but also with force . . . such great advantages are due to the unlimited generosity of some foreigners who have seen humanity groan and have seen the cause of reason perish, and they have not observed this calmly but rather have rushed to extend their protectful aid . . . these friends of humanity are the genuine custodians of the Americas. . . . "

It would not have been possible for Jefferson, Washington, Bolívar, or Morazán during those days of forging a new world on a continent in revolution to prevent their revolutions from being exported, because it was not a matter of ruses to impose models by force, but rather of leading a historical crusade for radical changes which buried the old colonial world.

Morazán, as the ideologue of the great dreams of the Central American federal republic, never thought in provincial terms; nor did he believe that his liberalism would stop at Honduras's borders. On the contrary, his political and military movement, the largest in the 19th century in Central America, led to the emergence of a large revolutionary party throughout the region, which opposed ideas against ideas and advanced its ideas of change by the force of the federalist weapons. Then the struggle was not between Hondurans and Salvadorans nor between Guatemalans and Nicaraguans, but between liberals and reactionaries, between the armed revolutionaries of that period and obscurantist clerics and feudal landlords and a gloomy Central America of the friars of the Inquisition and the lords of the gallows and knives. And Morazán, like Washington and Bolívar, was a great exporter of revolution, of subversion, and of extremism because he wanted to change reality.

So for the Sandinistas, who are repeating the revolutionary feats of Morazán in the 20th century, it is impossible to prevent their idea of revolution from being exported. We export ideas, ideas of change and renovation, ideas that provide a foundation for a new world being born, we export the proven possibility that an armed people, when they set about to do so, can overthrow tyranny and establish a nascent and innovative world on the wastes of that tyranny; we export the news that in Nicaragua the revolution has brought with it literacy, agrarian reform, an end to poliomyelitis, the right to life and hope. How can one prevent a peasant from another Central American country from hearing, from finding out, from realizing that in Nicaragua land is given to other poor and barefoot peasants like him? How can you avoid his realizing that here children—not his children—are being vaccinated while his children still die of gastroenteritis and polio?

Now, like then, the struggle is not between Nicaraguans and Hondurans, but between peons and bosses, between the New Man and the specters of the past, between those who struggle for a better order and those who try to maintain for all eternity the worst of orders.

In that sense, we export our revolution.

### "The Sandinistas Have Betrayed Their Original Revolutionary Project."

The original revolutionary project of the United States began to be betrayed very early, such that James Madison himself, father of the American Constitution, already feared by 1829 that the perpetual expansion of the new nation, controlled by manufacturers and businessmen, would end the experiment of a republican government.

Soon after, Madison's fears were changed into Manifest Destiny and the Americas in revolution, a continent lit by the bonfires of change, were soon turned into the America on top and the America on bottom, the oppressors and the oppressed, the plunderers and the plundered, the expansionists and the occupied. And the sons of Washington and Jefferson not only took the huge territories of Mexico in that first great push to dominate but also took the name of America, and since then the dream of liberty and justice has been turned into a nightmare of hegemony. The United States of 1898 were no longer the same United States of 1776; the original revolutionary project had been left behind and in its place was started the expansionist counterrevolution that swallowed up Cuba and Puerto Rico and prepared to assault the entire Caribbean, including Nicaragua and Panama. This was carried out, not in the name of that old republican ideal for which so many soldiers during the struggle for independence spilled their blood on the snow covering the battlefields, but instead in the name of that imperial ideological aberration of Manifest Destiny, an aberration which would later be veiled by Pan-Americanism—the United States allied with the rest of the continent in a crafty and opportunist way, only to destroy the possibilities for identity and identification of nations that now appear conquered or conquerable. All the scaffolding of constitutional law, division of power, and courts of justice began to succumb under the worst elements that those weak and poor countries could offer, the political dealers and dark exploiters who divided up presidential gangs, who negotiated with the grandchildren of the founders of that first liberatory republic, already hidden among the shadows of history.

We know what the original revolutionary project of the United States was. But when they talk about the Sandinistas' betrayal of our original revolutionary project, what project are they talking about?

During Reagan's 1980 Presidential campaign, the New Right's spokesmen—who had already conquered the positions of ideological leadership within the Republican Party—declared that the United States would never again commit the mistake of not fighting to the end for an ally like Somoza; they felt guilty and ashamed for having abandoned him. Later they confirmed preferring Somoza a thousand times over the Sandinistas. And even later they armed the old supporters of the Somoza regime—the Guard no less—to destroy the Sandinista revolutionary project and to retake power through the counterrevolution's arms.

The original project that the United States government refers to is not ours. Their project is the same one as always—not changed or even retouched—it is that of the National Guard created in 1927 by the United States itself to replace the Yankee occupation army in 1933, which sustained the Somoza dictatorship for almost half a century.

The United States' project intends to reinstall the National Guard as the decisive force within the country, to be faithful to North American interests in the region, like the army of General Alvarez in Honduras is faithful to those interests.

Why do they want the National Guard to occupy Nicaraguan territory again like they did for almost 50 years? To give us Jefferson's Constitution and George Washington's political model? To fulfill the American Dream of 1776 in Nicaragua? That dream doesn't exist but the National Guard does, thanks to the Reagan administration.

The Reagan administration's miracle workers cannot really think that we have betrayed our original revolutionary project because they radically and viscerally reject all revolutionary ideas. The word revolution is incompatible with their views and conception of the world. Of course, the revolution that we have been unable to make and from which we have separated ourselves they will entrust to the Somocista Guard's colonels and paid assassins, who murdered thousands of young people and peasants, who bombed neighborhoods and villages, who raped women and filled the jails.

But it's not only the Reaganite ideologues who declare that we have betrayed the original revolutionary project. The people who feel materially and ideologically affected by the revolution also say that they don't see, in its path or its actions, what they thought was the original ideological project; that is to say, their original project which would impetuously ignore the privileges that they had for so many decades, their excessive riches, their feudal plantations, their businesses, and corporations with the dictatorship. It would have been impossible to make a revolution with so much sacrifice and blood that could fit that model, a selfish, not very Christian, and not at all altruistic model. We have truly betrayed this meaningless idea of revolution.

However, one must not forget that we Sandinistas did not make fundamental promises to the United States—to whom we never made any type of promises—nor to Nicaragua's privileged groups. The basic promises were made to the country's poorest people, the promises that they have defended with weapons and their herosim. The original project is still there, growing and being multiplied for those people, in the cooperatives, schools, health centers: land, dignity, and sovereignty. There was never any other revolutionary project besides this one; this was the original project.

We believe that the United States is the one which should return to its original project of liberty and democracy, the project of Washington, Madison, and Jefferson, that beautiful revolutionary project that was betrayed by capitalist greed, by the wanton accumulation of riches and by this perverse expansionist will that has forced the United States' borders so many times to our border, as they are once again doing by pushing it to the Honduran border.

## "The Sandinistas Have Copied a Model
## Of Revolution That Is a Totalitarian Model."

The same ideological device that justified the invasion of these lands of the Americas and the confiscation of our free destiny also created the pretext of the invader's racial superiority and that of the invaded people's inferiority: if we as marginalized people were perpetually condemned to live off the rich's crumbs, it was because of our own historical inabilities. The adventure of the Yankee conquest thus became an adventure for the white race, master of initiative and spirit of conquest, capable of dominating nature and of creating all science and technique, machinery and unceasing progress; we not only became the conquered but also the slow and lazy mestizos and were illiterate because of desire and inertia, poor due to our hopeless destiny, violent and anarchical, quarrelsome and vengeful.

God was associated with the United States and with its prophetic mission to conquer the world; the people of the Second Coming found their promised land wherever they could lay down their claim to conquer frontiers and tame the tumultuous savages, who according to William Walker's beliefs, only deserved slavery because they were racially inferior.

Since then, our country has been subject not only to divinely dictated submission, but also to a model of political conduct which meant accepting foreign domination along with all that conquering race's superiority and their advantages which were never trusted: civilizations and progress were gifts offered to us, but under that ideological condemnation to which we were subjected, they were impossible to obtain.

Therefore, the dogma of a political and cultural domination could not inspire hope to aspire toward any independence or individual thought; the North American political system which our forefathers coveted and fought for turned into the permanent expansion of the armed Puritans to conquer, and this was a destiny that had to be accepted, no matter how bitter it was. The triumph of the business of domination presupposed the draining of all our national identity and ideas, of any hopes of creating a political model or developing our own creative capacity. The almighty, strong, and wise Yankees owned all initiative and the future; we, the cause and product of underdevelopment, could only own our misery, our poverty which created more poverty, condemned to live off the ideological leftovers of the perfect model of Yankee democracy that elects a President every four years among colored balloons, willing nonetheless to tighten the screws of domination in our countries in the name of the bankers and financiers whose claws neither Jefferson nor Madison envisioned.

That is why when the New Right, which now governs the United States, hears us talk about our own model in Nicaragua, they raise their eyebrows disdainfully and unhappily, and their first reaction changes from surprise to fury. "Their own model, they do not have the historical capability to generate models, they can only aspire to have an immutable role in the ideological and political division of labor!" For such a mentality, the initiatives, whatever they may be, and historical projects can only be generated in the metropolitan centers and never in the periphery, as if the United States itself had not originally been on the periphery, where the new model of bloody revolution emerged.

But as Madison bitterly lamented, political models also waste away when they begin to serve interests they were not intended for. For us, the efficacy of a political model depends on its capacity to resolve the problems of democracy and justice. Effective democracy, like we intend to practice in Nicaragua, consists of ample popular participation; a permanent dynamic of the people's participation in a variety of political and social tasks; the people who give their opinions and are listened to; the people who suggest, construct, and direct, organize themselves, who attend to community, neighborhood, and national problems; the people who are active in the sovereignty and the defense of that sovereignty and also teach and give vaccinations; a daily democracy and not one that takes place every four years, when at that, or every four, five, or six years when formal elections take place. The people don't go as a minority but in their totality, and they consciously elect the best candidate and not one chosen like a soap or deodorant, a vote freely made and not manipulated by an advertising agency, a vote for change to improve the nation and not in favor of a transnational finance company or an industrial military trust.

Maybe when Madison wrote his Constitution, he was thinking about this type of democracy, which no longer exists in the United States.

On the other hand, for us democracy is not merely a formal model, but a continual process capable of solving the basic problems of development and capable of giving the people that elect and participate in it the real possibility of transforming their living conditions, a democracy which establishes justice and ends exploitation.

Because a political model emerges from concrete reality and from the needs that that reality imposes in order to change it, the Sandinista model—our own model—emerges from the long period of U.S. domination in Nicaragua, a domination that was political, economic, and even military as well as social, ideological, and even cultural. It is in the face of this domination that our model responds and establishes a vital necessity that independence be our own model, and together with this national independence, the recovery of our natural resources and of the will to develop an economic project that while transforming the nation, will give us the possibility not only to generate riches but also to distribute them fairly.

When they speak about copying models, we must remember that during half a century Somocismo slavishly copied the model imposed by the United States. Nicaragua was branded with the most radical capitalist model, a market economy which impoverished the country and ravished the possibilities for its true development. With this destructive capitalist model came the destructive dependency on markets, raw materials, and financial resources; Nicaragua became a satellite of the United States; Nicaragua was behind a true iron curtain with a solid, triple-locked bar. Of course, the Somoza family also imported the political model of elections every four years, and elections existed here, a bi-partisan system existed here, and there was a two-chamber legislative system, a supreme court, and a constitution with laws. And it was all a bloody hoax.

And this imported, copied, and imposed model historically failed, and we are now seeking our own model. We are no longer a satellite of the United States, we are no longer behind the United States' iron curtain. We are free, sovereign, and independent, something that was always deceptively written into all the Somoza constitutions and only now is true, even though we still have not written our constitution.

To consolidate this national project, this genuine project of a sovereign revolution, we are willing to meet any challenge and make any sacrifice. To make this idea possible and to nurture it, the people of Nicaragua are ready to defend their project and their model of revolution with arms. They are ready to achieve a definitive peace so that this model may flourish, a model which we do not want to impose on anyone. Because it has real political borders, Nicaragua's borders. We are not a people chosen by God to fulfill any manifest destiny, we don't have capital to export or transnational corporations to defend beyond our borders. Our dreams are not to dominate, expand, or conquer but rather our dreams are the humble dreams of a humble people who aspire to true justice and independence.

That is why we want to live in peace and grow in peace, that is why we want to spread the news of our sovereign people's example in peace, a people who never thought to ask anybody for permission to make its revolution and will not ask anyone for permission to defend it.

Free Homeland or Death!

---

## STATEMENTS BY ROLLIN B. TOBIE, ANA MARIA LOPEZ, AND MODESTA MARTINEZ[8]

**Rollin B. Tobie:** Do I believe that I have a future in Nicaragua? Look, a myth has been spread that we Coast people are lazy, without ambition, don't care to work, and so on. So, to prove a point and, incidentally, because it's a good investment, I decided to go into the cattle business. I established a ranch, a big place near Bluefields. It was virgin land, and I started from the very beginning. In 1981 I bought the land, I had it cleared, and so on. I bought some stock. Now it is starting to produce. Someday it will be very successful. It was a sizeable investment, but it will pay off. Do I have confidence in my future in Nicaragua? What do you think?

This government has made tremendous efforts, particularly in the areas of health and education. But in matters of the cultural needs of the people of the Atlantic coast, of the traditions and history of our people, it has failed. I know. I speak as a Black man.

---

[8]From Alvin Levie, *Nicaragua: The People Speak*, Bergin & Garvey, '85, pp. 23–26, 78–81, 110–113. Copyright 1985 Alvin Levie. Reprinted with permission of Bergin & Garvey Publishers.

I was born in Zelaya, in the town of Bonanza, in 1938. My father was a miner.

From the beginning the Sandinistas have mistrusted us. We are Black and Indian. We have a different history, culture, religion. We even speak English, a language foreign to the people of the Pacific coast.

And the interesting thing is that we are all victims and inheritors of imperialist traditions. Here on the Pacific coast they have an inheritance of Spanish imperialism. We on the Atlantic side had British imperialism. Yet we are all Nicaraguans.

Perhaps if we had shared the revolutionary experience, things would be different. Perhaps if we had lived under the same oppression of the *Spanish* . . . But you see, under Somoza there was a laissez-faire attitude in the Atlantic zone. Certainly we were exploited—our gold, our timber stolen from us. But politically, culturally, Somoza ignored us.

There was a major war here on the Pacific side. Tens of thousands gave their lives in the struggle against Somoza. On the Atlantic coast, very little.

Then came the Triumph—and the Sandinistas. They didn't know us. They didn't understand us. They didn't want to know us. To them we were foreign—Indians, Creoles, Blacks. We were, in their eyes, enemies or potential enemies. They feared us as potential counterrevolutionaries. It wasn't so much a matter of racism. Racism as it exists in the United States has never been a problem in Nicaragua. Certainly, there have always been differences based upon class and wealth. But otherwise, we Nicaraguans tend to live and let live.

The attacks from Honduras certainly made the problem worse. But the Sandinistas made no secret of their contempt for us. They bullied us, they jailed us. Specific cases? Here's one, not earth-shaking, but typical: Some Miskito mothers visited their sons who had been imprisoned on various charges. The Sandinista guards insisted that Spanish be spoken. The poor women couldn't speak Spanish, only Miskito. So they had to return, many miles and days of travel along the river and through the bush without having talked to their sons. Another case: Many Spanish-speaking people in the Bluefields area are now wearing T-shirts embossed with the slogan "Atlantic Coast Culture is Imperialist Culture"—in English! What an insult!

I've heard of other, far worse, examples. But these simple practices demonstrate their insensitivity to us—their contempt.

So now we Nicaraguans, all of us, are paying for this. There is considerable counterrevolutionary activity on the Coast, particularly among the Miskitos. Before the Triumph we had few doctors, engineers, teachers, or other professionals. Now we have less. Most of them are in exile—in Miami, New York, Costa Rica. It's not that they are counterrevolutionary. It's simply that they've suffered ill will and chose to leave Nicaragua.

The rest of the Coast people, most of them, don't participate in anything. They have an "I don't care" attitude. They simply sit and watch events. Certainly they make no contribution to the defense or growth of Nicaragua.

I personally have always believed in investing, and I've never been able to simply sit and watch events. I told you of my ranch in Bluefields. Well, I also have a farm here near Managua. We grow corn, pepper, fruit. And I have a stable, too. I bought some Peruvian horses. Beautiful animals. I'm going to breed them.

I don't believe in simply accumulating money. It should be invested. It should be made to work. I believe that when I make these investments, I show confidence in the future of my country.

It has been proven that bureaucrats make bad administrators. They tend to look at politics rather than at profit and loss. The social aspects of the process are fine, but at the same time you cannot be losing money forever. These people aren't fools. They know this. They want Nicaragua to prosper, and to do so, those who wish to work must be allowed to do so. Those who wish to invest in our nation must be permitted to do so, and to profit by it.

As a businessman, I think that I've been investing both for myself and my country. Look, during the war and immediately after the Triumph, many people in my business, the hardware business, got frightened. They got nervous. They didn't know how the future would treat them. So they decided to dispose of their businesses and leave Nicaragua. All right. I decided to remain. So I bought a lot of merchandise at very good prices. As a result, I have a very large stock. Who benefited? I benefited. Nicaragua benefited.

Everything that happens in Nicaragua today is colored by the war. Everything must be viewed within that context. Look, our problems here, especially on the Coast, are intensified by the war, by fear. Other, *new*, problems are coming into being because of the war. With the war's end, things will settle down. We'll have a chance to breathe.

The United States must leave us alone. I don't think that the United States' talk of "democracy" and "liberty" has much credence in Nicaragua. Traditionally, the United States has supported regimes in Latin America that snuff out democracy and liberty. They don't have good credentials.

Negotiations with the counterrevolutionaries? Perhaps that would be possible if the counterrevolutionaries weren't led by Somocistas. But, negotiations with the Somocistas? Never.

I was here during the war. I saw the boys and girls running up and down the streets with guns. I saw what the Somoza people did to innocent people—the torture, the murder. I don't think it is realistic to expect Nicaraguans to sit down and negotiate with these people. The people won't have anything to do with Somoza's henchmen.

I'm optimistic, though. I believe that in the end justice will triumph. We will have peace and freedom in Nicaragua—far better than before. But first, I'm afraid, there will be much more suffering.

**Ana Maria Lopez:** I come from Jinotega city. My father was a campesino. My five brothers and sisters also worked on the land.

We were poor people, but no more so than many others I knew. For instance, we children had milk occasionally. Once or twice every week we had meat with our rice and beans.

When I was eleven years old I was finished with my schooling. Then I went to work as a maid in the houses of different people in Jinotega. Mostly I washed and ironed clothes, cleaned the houses, looked after the children. I did this kind of work for three years.

In those days I had some friends, maids like myself. We often talked about our lives, our work. We were children. We had nothing and we knew nothing. All we knew was work, work from morning till evening, every day of the week. We were all dissatisfied, and we talked about our unhappiness all the time.

Two of these girls, my friends, had become prostitutes. They worked in a house in Jinotega. They came to see us often, and they told us about this good life that they had. It was easy work, it was fun. They had pretty clothes, a lot of free time, things like that. They made it seem very attractive.

One day I went with them to that house. I became a prostitute. I was then fourteen years old. Now I know that those girls didn't think it was so good. The man they worked for made them go out and get girls like us. He paid them for that service.

At first I didn't mind it too much. I was fourteen. What did I know? Some of the men, the customers, were not so nice. But mostly they were pleasant enough. They were simple working men, campesinos. It was easy, it was quick.

We lived in that house—six, sometimes eight girls like me. We took our meals outside. The boss paid us half of all that we earned, and the rest he charged us for his commission and for rent. After paying for my food, clothing, rent, and everything else, I never had any money left over. But I didn't worry. I lived for the day. I was indifferent to the future.

Then later I began to think, what kind of life is this? Degenerate. Worse than an animal. But what could I do? Where could I go? My family? I couldn't face them. I was ashamed.

One time a man, a customer, came to me. He was a nice man. His name was Luis. He came back again and again, and he always asked for me. One day he said to me, "This is no life for a girl like you. Leave this house. Come with me. We'll get married."

I didn't have to think about it too much. He was a nice fellow. I liked him. So I left. One day I walked out of that house and I didn't return. I was then sixteen years old.

Luis was true to his word, and we got married. He was a truck driver and was good to me. But that was only in the beginning. Maybe, too, I wasn't such a good wife. I didn't know anything about keeping a house. Remember, I was still very young, and I had no mother, no sisters or friends to advise me.

The problem with Luis was that he drank too much. It became worse and worse. He never beat me or anything like that. But he began to abuse me, call me foul names. He would tell me how he had found me, how he had taken me out of that house, things like that. Then he did it more often, sometimes every day. I started to argue back, to fight with him.

It continued this way for a long time. Eventually, after we were together for three years, Luis started to see other women. Then he abandoned us. By then I had two children.

I had to feed my children. I had to support them. What could I do? Where could I go? I went back to that life. I became a prostitute again.

This new house where I went to work was owned by a Guardia officer. He was very strict. He insisted that the girls dress well.

He bought our clothes for us and charged us double for them. Now I needed money to pay someone to look after my children. I was often short, and he insisted that I borrow from him. He charged us rates that you couldn't believe. We all owed him a great deal of money.

This Guardia officer used to point his gun at us. He said that any girl who owes him money and leaves the house will be a corpse. We were terrified. But now there was no way out.

It went on like this for four years, until the Triumph of the Revolution. My Guardia boss disappeared. They say he went to Honduras. Prostitution was outlawed and the house was shut down.

I was liberated—but for what? I had lived this life for many years, and I knew nothing else. Still, I started to do different things. I cleaned people's houses. I washed clothes. I worked in the fields. I did everything, anything, to earn cordobas for my little family.

One thing was very bad. People knew me. The women in Jinotega wouldn't talk to me. The men, many of them, wouldn't leave me alone. To them I was only a whore. On several occasions I was forced to have sex with men who kept after me. These were hard times for me.

Finally, I took my two children and I left Jinotega. We came to Matagalpa city. Here it was a little better. People didn't know me, didn't know what I had been. Once again I started to do any kind of work to feed my children and myself. Mostly I cleaned houses and worked in the fields.

I began to attend my barrio CDS meetings and I helped in AMNLAE. You see, I was very lonely. I didn't know anyone in Matagalpa, and in this way I made friends. Now I made no secret of my past. But people here didn't seem to mind so much.

One time I worked on tomatoes in the Leonel Valdivia Cooperative. They had a big harvest, and they hired people to help bring it in. I worked hard, but it was enjoyable. The people were good to me. They were friendly. They were fair.

After the harvest a boy came to my home. He told me that the cooperative executive committee wanted to talk to me. I had no idea what they would want to talk to me about, so I went with the boy.

The committee invited to me join the cooperative. Just like that. They told me that I had worked very well in the harvest and, as they had recently opened their membership to women, they were looking for some "high class" people. Imagine that! High class. Me! I accepted on the spot.

Later I learned that the AMNLAE people had spoken to the cooperative executive committee and had asked them to consider me for membership.

These people here are more than only my fellow workers. They are my *compañeros*. They are my brothers, my sisters, my family. I belong here now as much as anyone else.

My children and I moved to the cooperative. We live in a room in the house of one of my *compañeras*. Soon, after the next harvest, when I have some money, I'm going to start to build a house, here, a home for my children and me.

**Modesta Martinez:** I was born in Ocotal, in the very same house I live in now. The house belongs to my mother. She lives with me. My son, Noel, lives with me. He's eleven years old. Also my sister and her two children. Another boy, Martino, lives in our house. He's thirteen, and he has no family, no place else to live. We're accustomed to tight living, but there's always room for a cot for one more, right?

My father, he was no good. He had many women and he wasn't home very much. He was a big drinker, too. He didn't work very much, but when he did work, it was in the woods, in the sawmills. My father died sixteen years ago.

We had two girls and five boys in my family, and we all lived together in our little *ranchito*. So you see, we're accustomed to being crowded. Most people in our barrio live tight like we do.

When I was growing up we had no electricity, no water—we still don't. We draw our water from the river at the bottom of the hill. For light we have a kerosene lantern. For cooking we use wood. Sometimes, when we can get it, we burn charcoal. That makes a good, hot fire. But charcoal is scarce, and it's expensive. So most of the time we use wood.

I had one year of school, and then my mother took me out because she needed me at home. I worked in the house with my mother. Then I began to clean other people's houses. In that way I made a few cordobas to bring home to my family.

I've been cleaning other people's houses all of my life. I don't mind the work. Someone has to do it. I never earned much money, but the little bit I earned has always helped.

Now I do the cleaning at the *Centro Desarrollo Infantil*. I like it here very much. I've been at the CDI for six months, and I think it's the best job I ever had.

Isn't this a beautiful place? The gardens—oh! This used to be a private home—for one family. It belonged to rich people. At the time of the Triumph they left Ocotal. Maybe they left Nicaragua. I think they thought that we were going to kill them [she laughs].

So now we have this house for the children. I love working here. Aren't the children beautiful? For me it's a pleasure to be here—to listen to them singing, laughing.

Since the Triumph of the Revolution life has changed for me. It's still hard, but at least we no longer know hunger.

Last year I was the CDS leader in my barrio, San Jose Rodriguez. That's 3,000 people in my barrio. Can you imagine me, with only one year of school, with such a responsibility?

In our barrio we have a health brigade. We learn first aid, we clean up places that breed sickness, we learn about the proper things to eat. The aim, you see, is to prevent sickness, so that we don't get sick, don't have to see the doctor.

As the leader of our CDS I helped to organize a volunteer brigade to pick coffee on the border. Honduras is right over the mountains, you know, and it's dangerous for us there. But the coffee, the coffee crop, is very important to our economy, and so we volunteer to pick it.

Our CDS, it organizes men and women to keep the streets fixed. We do many things like that. Everything we do is important because we don't have any money, and the people must do these things themselves. In this way we work for ourselves and for the barrio. That's why our CDS is so important.

Our CDS also organized our health care program. Very important. I myself took a course in preventative medicine.

Now when we get sick we go to the new health center. It only costs us 10 cordobas. That's nothing, just a fee. The medicine is free, but sometimes there isn't any medicine. Before the Triumph these was plenty of medicine, but no one, no poor people, could afford it. Now, medicine is free for us, but it's scarce. That's because of the war. All of our money goes into the defense against aggression, so there is nothing left for medicine. Most of the medicine that we get now is given to us by friendly countries.

But even so, it's better now. Before, when we were sick we had to pay a lot of money to see a doctor. Before, if you had no money, you could die for all anyone cared.

Our health care center is a long way from Barrio Jose Santos Rodriguez. We need a new one right in our own barrio. But I don't know. It doesn't look too likely as long as the war continues. But we keep agitating anyway. You have to agitate. You have to fight for what you need, or else you never get anything, right?

I'm active in my church, Iglesia San Jose. I'm on the parish council. The nuns there are North Americans. They've been very good to us, especially Sister Maria. She's a trained nurse, you know.

Life is better for us now. But it's still difficult. Every day the counterrevolutionaries are murdering our people. They are trying to destroy our economy. These people are beasts. They have no respect—not for old people, not for women, not for babies. All that those people know is killing, destroying.

Those counterrevolutionaries are Nicaraguans. But they don't look upon us as brothers and sisters. They receive pay from Reagan. That's why they want to destroy our country. That's why they kill us. Does your President Reagan have no heart? Doesn't he know that he's giving weapons to animals who have no feelings?

They say that we're Communists. Reagan says that. The rich people here in Nicaragua also say that we're Communists. Are we Communists? I don't know. We're Catholics. I know that. Can Catholics be Communists, too? I don't know. I have to think about that.

Look, I don't think that Communists are bad people. The Communists help Nicaragua. Fidel Castro, he's a Communist, and he is a friend to us. I really don't think that Communists are bad people. Meanwhile, I'm very busy. I do *vigilancia*. At night I patrol. I carry a gun. I'm trained to use it and I'm a pretty good shot.

Would I use my gun? Look, I never thought that I could kill another human being. But I'm ready. If the Contras come here, if anyone comes here, I'll kill. I'm ready to kill to defend my country.

# IV. SOLUTIONS: INCREASED HOSTILITIES OR A MODUS VIVENDI

## EDITOR'S INTRODUCTION

Solutions to the growing and costly U.S.-Nicaraguan antagonism are elusive. Many observers see the confrontation in global terms, and some perceive the specter of a long and bloody Vietnam-type conflict at the end of the road the United States is following. Those who hope for a change of heart from the Sandinistas or a change of policy under a new U.S. administration do not count on the inertial power of entrenched military-bureaucratic positions.

Shirley Christian, in the first article of this final section, taken from her book *Nicaragua: Revolution in the Family*, briefly examines the entire conflict, concluding that there is little hope for a "satisfactory exit" from the standoff.

The general features of the Contadora peace process are examined by the staff of the *UN Chronicle* in the second article. Then Susan Kaufman Purcell, an experienced observer of Latin America writing in *Foreign Affairs*, presents in the third article a detailed view of the complex history of Contadora and the reasons that the process has seemed constantly to be stalemated.

The fourth article, reprinted from *Commentary*, is by Max Singer, a Washington consultant on Latin America, and constitutes perhaps the gloomiest view of all: that Nicaragua will not be stopped from exporting its revolution throughout Central America and that within a decade the region could "be as Communist as Eastern Europe." The final article, by Maria Elena Hurtado, from South, a London-based Third World media service, briefly advances the position that any search for a regional peace is an ultimately futile exercise.

# EPILOGUE[1]

There seemed, in the first months of 1985, to be no satisfactory exit from this situation. On the one hand, there was a well-armed Marxist regime unacceptable to the United States and many other countries of the region for its external policies and unacceptable for its internal policies to those Nicaraguans seeking political pluralism. On the other hand, the large anti-Sandinista armed force raised moral and ethical questions for the United States, and its actions lacked the international emotional support that had helped justify the armed opposition to Somoza in 1978-1979.

The Sandinista Front probably would have become a footnote to history had a moderate regime been able to assume power in Nicaragua before the end of 1978. But the Carter administration could not make the decision to do what was necessary to bring this about, nor could it make the decision to resume military and political backing of Somoza, which would likewise have prevented the rise of the Sandinistas, though probably with other undesirable consequences. The United States ignored its own significance in Nicaraguan history in refusing to use its power to help Nicaragua evolve into a politically open society. The Carter administration would neither back Somoza nor tell him to go. Somoza himself was determined to stay, and faced with the indecisiveness in the White House, he thought he could win the United States back to his side in time to defeat the guerrillas militarily.

The rise of the Somozas and their permanence in power for nearly half a century is a shared burden of U.S. and Nicaraguan history, and the Sandinista quest for power was, in turn, aided by the refusal of the Somozas to open the political system to all who wanted to participate. But the thesis that dictatorship of the right begets dictatorship of the left is not fully applicable here. The Somoza dynasty, in fact, permitted a greater degree of political, social, and economic liberty than most such regimes, and in that ambience, moderate political alternatives to Somoza developed. Part of this came out of Nicaragua's own political history. In addi-

[1]Excerpt from *Nicaragua: Revolution in the Family* by Shirley Christian, winner of a Pulitzer Prize for international reporting in 1981 for coverage of Central America for the *Herald* and now a bureau chief for the New York *Times* in Buenos Aires. Random House, '85. pp. 305-311. Copyright 1985 Shirley Christian. Reprinted with permission.

tion, the United States contributed to the development of those
alternatives over two decades by directing its aid programs to
nongovernmental institutions as well as the government, by its
support of the Central American Common Market and independent labor groups, and by maintaining contact with opposition
politicians. What was missing when the whole thing came to a
head was the determination of Somoza or the Carter administration that a peaceful transition should occur. Because of its desire
to adhere to the nonintervention principle, the Carter administration could not make Somoza go at a time when a moderate succession could have occurred.

The leaders of the Sandinista Front intended to establish a
Leninist system from the day they marched into Managua, whether they called it that or not. Their goal was to assure themselves
the means to control nearly every aspect of Nicaraguan life, from
beans and rice to religion. This was demonstrated by such things
as creation of the block committees and other organizations under the FSLN banner, the pressure for the media to support the
FSLN program, the importance attached to making the Church
sympathetic to the FSLN, the political use of the army, the rapid
development and expansion of the state security apparatus, and
various statements and documents about future FSLN plans. All
of this was under way before the end of 1979, at a time when the
Carter administration's main operating premise toward the
Sandinistas was to do nothing that would make the United States
appear to have been responsible if Nicaragua took the path of
Cuba. Also, it was before the Republicans had nominated Ronald
Reagan the first time. This tends to negate the arguments that
antagonism from the United States nudged Nicaragua along a totalitarian path. Any indication the Sandinista leaders gave of
wanting something other than a Leninist system in Nicaragua
was, as they admitted several times, for tactical or strategic purposes, not for reasons of substance.

It cannot be argued that the Sandinista Front was created by
Moscow or Havana, but it is certain that the Sandinistas, from the
day in 1961 when they created the FSLN, anticipated close ties
to those countries. The Cuban connection was established
through military training, advice, and supplies that the Cubans
provided to the Sandinistas during and before the insurrection.
That support carried with it the obligation to assist other guerril-

la organizations. Once in power the Sandinistas turned quickly and willingly to Moscow, first accepting Bulgarian economic advisers, then seeking arms ties with the Soviets, and eventually offering themselves meekly to the Soviets in exchange for more and more weaponry. In a sense, they sold themselves for the means to stay in power in the face of failed policies and widespread unhappiness. But these ties were also the result of the Sandinistas' belief in their own principles, the ideological convictions that they themselves held, and for which they were willing to risk the wrath of the United States.

While a valid point may be raised about whether this military dependency on the Soviet bloc might have been avoided if the United States, in the first months of the new regime, had been willing to provide military equipment to the Sandinista Army, it is very likely that any such arrangement would have been hampered by the Sandinista leadership's ideological loyalty to Marxism-Leninism and by the fact that the United States would never have been willing to provide arms at the levels the Sandinistas thought necessary to consolidate their power internally.

Sandinista internal policies planted the seeds for the rise of the *Contra*. It was the broken commitments and the exercise of total power on the part of the FSLN that sent many of those who had earlier led the opposition to Somoza into subsequent armed opposition to the Sandinistas, finding common cause with the National Guardsmen of the old regime. It is also true that the Reagan administration, particularly by making CIA money available, encouraged some of those people to give up peaceful internal opposition and go into exile. Given all that happened inside Nicaragua in the first year or so after the fall of Somoza, armed opposition to the FSLN was inevitable, though the dimensions it reached were the result of U.S. support.

Two basic objections were raised to the *Contra*, even by many U.S. and foreign critics of the Sandinistas. One questioned the morality of the decision by the United States to fund and advise a paramilitary force, mine harbors and sanction—in a *Contra* training manual—the assassination of rural Sandinista officials. There was good reason for these objections, at least to some of the specific actions, but it was not as easy to argue against the general principle of backing the *Contra*. This had to be viewed in the light of the validity of the cause and the size of the military force the anti-Sandinista forces faced, and whether there were other means available.

The second objection held that the *contras* accomplished nothing except to contribute to death and destruction, including the killing of noncombatants, and that they gave the Sandinistas reason to institute repressive policies. This presumed they would not have adopted the policies they did if there had been no *contras* and ignored the sequence of events in 1979 and 1980. Had there been no *contras*, the Sandinistas might have had no justification to stockpile food, to institute the military draft, and to pressure people to join the militia. But the absence of the *contras* and other external pressures would also have made it easier for the Sandinista Front to crack down on the press, the church, and opposition groups without attracting international criticism. It is true, for example, that the state of emergency was instituted in March 1982 in reaction to the first significant *Contra* attack, but it is also true that the state of emergency decree basically formalized the restrictions already being applied on a de facto basis. It may be true that the *Contra* operations reduced the size of the coffee harvests in 1983 and 1984, but the *contras* also forced the FSLN to orient its agrarian policies away from state farms and toward individual ownership.

In essence, while it is true that, without the *Contra*, circumstances in Nicaragua may have been marginally better in economic terms, its existence—along with all of the other external and internal pressures—represented what little hope there was to force the Sandinista Front into accepting major structural changes toward an open political system.

The possibility always existed for a negotiated settlement of sorts between the United States and the FSLN, which had put enough pieces on the board that it could afford to remove a few without having to give up the one thing that really mattered: its own permanence in power. The Sandinistas appeared willing to satisfy U.S. national security concerns, including some kind of agreement terminating Sandinista support for the Salvadoran guerrillas. The Salvadoran army had become strong enough to convince the Sandinistas of the futility of this support anyway. In the FSLN's view, if it had to retreat from its "revolutionary internationalism" for the time being, then so be it. As long as the FSLN remained in power it could expect another opportunity to arise in the future to further the cause outside its borders, perhaps under a different U.S. administration.

However, the likely price to the United States for such an agreement was the end of the *Contra*. That, in turn, would amount to consolidation of the Sandinista regime internally, and tacit U.S. approval for policies that would never lead to the kind of political pluralism that was the goal of so many Nicaraguans, first when they opposed Somoza and later when they turned against the Sandinista Front.

This matter of internal political pluralism (and whether the United States has the right or obligation to intervene) is the real dilemma for the United States in much of its foreign relations and particularly in the Central American and Caribbean area—not only direct military intervention but also broader attempts to influence the internal politics of a country through all the methods at the command of the United States. Should we threaten to invade Nicaragua only if it introduces MiGs, or could we justify intervention or other forms of pressure in the interests of internal changes? Even if the tactics in question did not include invasion, could they be justified?

Just as the intervention issue had dogged the Carter administration, it also dogged the Reagan administration, which, while using different language, came no closer to resolving it. Much of the confusion about the goals and function of the *Contra* was linked to this debate.

Reluctant to pursue an overtly interventionist policy, the Reagan administration refused to address directly what was perhaps the most significant aspect of the Nicaragua problem—the internal policies of the FSLN. Thus the White House invented other reasons for training and financing the *Contra*. At first, it publicly claimed the *Contra* forces existed to interrupt arms supplies from Nicaragua to guerrillas of the Farabundo Martí National Liberation Front in El Salvador, though CIA officials were allowing *Contra* militants to think they were fighting to rescue their own country.

It was never fully clear whether the real purpose of the *Contra* in the mind of the Reagan administration was to bring down the Sandinistas or simply to put a piece on the game board that could be taken off in exchange for something else—such as concessions on the Salvadoran guerrilla question or the halting of Nicaragua's military buildup. If the Reagan administration, for example, had been serious about trying to bring down the FSLN, it would have supported *Contra* efforts to set off insurrection activities in urban areas—as the FSLN itself did in 1978–1979. Instead, this proposal was dropped in early 1983 because, according to the CIA, of media suggestions that the *contras* were trying to do something other than stop the Salvadoran arms supply.

While the evidence of logistical and advisory connections between the Sandinistas and the Salvadorans was strong—including the presence in Managua of the Salvadoran guerrilla high command—the hard evidence on arms shipments has always been sparse. At the same time, there was no proof that the arms from Nicaragua were the determining factor in the Salvadoran insurgency. As a result, critics of Reagan policies attacked the support for the *Contra* on these grounds, which tended to invalidate the *contras'* own cause, and that of the entire Nicaraguan opposition, in the eyes of the outside world.

Not the least of the ethical questions about the U.S. role in creating the *Contra* was whether the United States should have manipulated people who only sought for their country the things the United States had long encouraged them to seek in opposing Somoza—a chance to test political pluralism as the means of addressing its problems. The Reagan administration played on the legitimate desire of large numbers of Nicaraguans to change their government. No matter how often the U.S. government might say the *Contra* existed for another reason, the Nicaraguan opponents of the Sandinistas—whatever their own differences and personality clashes—always had internal change in Nicaragua as their goal. Yet, they came to be seen as mercenaries because of the way they were used by the United States.

Those in the United States and in other Western developed countries concerned with policy toward Central America have tended to view the area's crises as either the result of Soviet support for insurgencies or of economic and social woes. But the dispute in Nicaragua has been about how and by whom public policy is to be shaped, about the philosophical bases for decision-making, which the Nicaraguans, after a century and a half of independence, are still trying to determine. That issue set off the insurrection, though economic and social issues eventually contributed to it. Had the United States dealt with the political question, it would have been able to address its other concerns—

national security as well as human and civil rights. A political democracy on U.S. or European lines is not likely to forge military alliances and stockpile weapons contrary to U.S. interests. At the same time, it offers the possibility of ending political repression, dealing with social and economic injustice, and establishing a rule of law in which courts function as a check on the excesses of the military and the executive power.

But bringing about changes in the political system implies a more interventionist policy than the United States has been willing to commit itself to in recent history, except when events compelled outright military operations. Even when President Hoover withdrew the marines from Nicaragua at the beginning of 1933 he did it largely in reaction to the public outcry against intervention.

Part of the problem is the pejorative connotation to the word intervention. The basic tenets of international relations since World War II have been nonintervention and self-determination, though most Third World governments have been more concerned with demanding nonintervention in international forums than with practicing self-determination at home. Cuba and the Soviet Union get around the problem of the connotation of intervention by using another term—internationalism—to describe their attempts to assist the development of other countries along statist, totalitarian lines. Internationalism has a more positive ring to it than intervention.

It is valid to argue that the United States cannot intervene everywhere in the world where there are governments it does not like, that the United States cannot be a global policeman. But foreign policy must be formulated in response to the dynamics of specific situations, taking into account a country's internal situation, its location, and the history of its relationship with the United States. Only by promoting democratic political development on a long-term basis can the United States hope to avoid the hard choices between sending troops and accepting a regime that overtly opposes its interests.

A proposed Central American peace treaty drawn up in 1983 and 1984 by the governments of Panama, Venezuela, Colombia, and Mexico—and known as the Contadora Process, for the Panamanian island where writing of the treaty began—attempted to deal with all of the issues by committing the signatory nations to internal democratization as well as reductions in armaments and foreign military advisers. The FSLN said that it would sign the proposed treaty, but nothing known about the Sandinistas so far suggests that they would substantially alter their policies except in the face of real or implied military force or other insurmountable pressure.

The bitter lesson for the United States is that a democracy—especially one that allows broad participation in the formulation and conduct of foreign policy—cannot let a situation reach a point that demands black and white choices between national security and national conscience. The United States should not allow itself to fall into the trap of having to accept, in an area as closely tied to it as Central America, either a repressive right-wing dictatorship because it is not threatening to U.S. national security or a repressive left-wing dictatorship in exchange for commitments not to overthrow a neighboring government or acquire MiGs.

The hour was late for this lesson to be applied in Nicaragua. Those who wanted democracy there were left in a vise, forced to accept that their goals were hostage to other people's priorities—the level of weaponry acquired or the degree of Sandinista support for guerrillas elsewhere. The establishment of a totalitarian regime, tragically, was seen as secondary. As so often in the past, Nicaraguans faced the bitter realization that their own needs—and dreams—were subjugated to matters beyond their borders.

## CONTADORA: PEACE PROCESS IN CENTRAL AMERICA[2]

*On a tiny island off the Pacific coast of Panama in January 1983, the Foreign Ministers of Colombia, Mexico, Panama and Venezuela launched a process aimed at peacemaking in Central America. That initiative begun on the Isla de Contadora has resulted in continuing efforts among the countries of the region to achieve a political solution to the area's conflicts.*

[2]Reprinted from *UN Chronicle*, vol. 21, no. 3, Mr. '84, pp. 9–12.

On its first anniversary in January 1984, the peace effort gained new momentum. Meeting in Panama City, the Contadora Group and the Foreign Ministers of Costa Rica, El Salvador, Guatemala, Honduras and Nicaragua adopted specific measures designed to fulfil commitments made earlier in the year in an effort to restore harmony and stability in Central America. It was the twelfth meeting of the Contadora Group and the fifth held jointly with the Central American Foreign Ministers.

The measures called for include reduction of military forces in the region, withdrawal of foreign advisers, ending of foreign military interference and establishment of machinery to facilitate dialogue between countries of the region and to ensure fair and free elections.

Over the past year, the efforts of the Contadora Group have received widespread endorsement. The Security Council, the General Assembly, the President of the General Assembly and the Secretary-General have expressed their support, as have the countries of the Non-Aligned Movement and the Organization of American States (OAS). Leaders including Cuban Premier Fidel Castro and United States President Ronald Reagan have spoken in favour of the Contadora process.

"The question of Central America should be resolved within the context of the region and by peaceful means through negotiations," Secretary-General Javier Pérez de Cuéllar affirmed at his year-end press conference on 21 December 1983. "And I think we should give the most honest—I repeat, the most honest—support to the Contadora effort."

The General Assembly, in resolution 38/10 adopted on 11 November without a vote, expressed its "firmest support for the efforts of the Contadora Group" and urged States of the region and outside to refrain from military operations which might hamper the negotiations the Group was undertaking with the agreement of the Governments of Central America. The Assembly welcomed the Cancún Declaration signed by the Contadora Presidents in July 1983 and the "Document of Objectives" endorsed by the Governments of Costa Rica, El Salvador, Guatemala, Honduras and Nicaragua in October as the basis for the start of negotiations to ensure harmonious co-existence in Central America.

Last May, the Security Council, in resolution 530 (1983), which reaffirmed the right of Nicaragua and all other countries of Central America to live in peace and security, free from outside interference, urged the Contadora Group to "spare no effort to find solutions to the problem of the region."

(The resolution was adopted following the Council's debate on a Nicaraguan complaint of invasion by "Somozist forces operating out of Honduras and financed, trained and supported by the present United States Administration.")

Following is a brief history of the Contadora initiative.

### Contadora Declaration

"At our first meeting," the four Foreign Ministers of the Contadora Group later reported to the OAS (*document A/38/599*), "we emphasized the need to strengthen the Latin American dialogue as an effective way of dealing with the political, economic and social problems that are jeopardizing peace, democracy, stability and development of the peoples of the hemisphere."

In the Contadora Declaration (*document A/38/68*) issued by the Group after that first meeting (8–9 January 1983), they made an "urgent appeal" to the countries of Central America to "engage in dialogue and negotiation so as to reduce tension and lay the foundations for a permanent atmosphere of peaceful coexistence and mutual respect among States." Expressing their "deep concern about direct or indirect foreign interference in the conflicts of Central America," the Ministers agreed on the need to eliminate "the external factors intensifying those conflicts" and called on all States to refrain from actions which might aggravate the situation.

After reviewing "the various peace initiatives and their effects," the Group said, they analyzed possible new actions to bring peace to the region. In that regard, they emphasized the importance of having other countries from the Latin American community join in those efforts.

Their appeal was welcomed by the Co-ordinating Bureau of the Non-Aligned Countries at its 1983 extraordinary Ministerial session held in Managua, Nicaragua (10–14 January) to evaluate the situation in Latin America and the Caribbean (*document A/38/106*) and later by the Seventh Conference of Heads of State or Government of Non-Aligned Countries at New Delhi (7–12 March) (*document A/38/132*).

A visit by the Contadora Group to the capitals of Costa Rica, Nicaragua, El Salvador, Honduras and Guatemala from 12 to 13

April 1983 set the stage for the first joint meeting with the Foreign Ministers of those countries, held in Panama City (20–21 April). In an information bulletin following that meeting (*document A/38/164-S/15727*), the Contadora countries reported that "for the first time in the course of the present crisis, the Central American Ministers for Foreign Affairs had joined in a common effort to establish a dialogue."

Joint meetings in May and July 1983, along with the April meeting, "enabled us to make some progress," the Contadora Group reported (*document A/38/599*) "in defining an agenda covering matters of concern to each Central American country" and to consider procedures, approaches and possible ways of solving specific issues. "At all of them," said the Group, "the central objective was to create a climate of confidence for initiating substantive negotiations on each of the issues in dispute."

During that period, the four Contadora countries, meeting on their own in Panama City (11–12 May), discussed a request made of the OAS by Costa Rica, which has no army, to establish what Costa Rica called a "peace force, capable of effectively monitoring the area of Costa Rica bordering on Nicaragua."

The Contadora Foreign Ministers, recalling that the Group's "original and essential purpose" was to "fulfil a diplomatic role designed to seek the settlement of conflicts through political means" (*document A/38/234*), decided to send an observer commission to study the situation and submit recommendations. The commission's mandate was confirmed at the second joint meeting of the Central American Foreign Ministers and Contadora Group (28–30 May). It was decided then that the commission would continue to act as an advisory group on all matters relating to solution of border problems.

## Cancún Declaration

The Contadora initiative received new impetus—and concrete proposals for peace in Central America—from a meeting of the Presidents of Colombia, Mexico, Panama and Venezuela at Cancún, Mexico on 17 July 1983.

The Heads of State had decided to meet, they said, "in view of the worsening of the conflicts in Central America, the rapid deterioration of the regional situation, the escalation of violence, the progressive increase in tensions, border incidents and the threat of an outbreak of hostilities that could become widespread" (*document A/38/599*).

The Cancún declaration (*document A/38/303-S/15877*) drawn up by the Presidents outlined a general programme to be proposed to the countries of Central America that would lead, region-wide, to:

- effective control of the arms race;
- an end to arms traffic;
- the elimination of foreign advisers;
- the creation of demilitarized zones;
- the prohibition of the use of the territory of some States to destabilize others;
- prohibition of other forms of interference in the internal affairs of countries of the region.

Implementation of the programme, as envisaged in the Declaration, would require a series of political commitments. Among them would be commitments to end "all prevailing situations of belligerency" and "to promote a climate of détente and confidence in the area by avoiding statements and other actions that jeopardize the essential climate of political confidence required."

The Contadora Presidents also appealed to the chief executives of the Central American countries, Cuba and the United States, and the Secretaries-General of the United Nations and the OAS for support for their peace-making efforts.

## Document of Objectives

The impetus of the Cancún Declaration carried the peace process forward to the fourth joint meeting of the Central American Foreign Ministers and the Contadora Group, also in Panama (7–9 September). From that meeting emerged the Document of Objectives, containing 21 basic points for peace in Central America (*document S/16041*). It defined the specific areas of negotiation and the terms of reference for formulating the legal instruments and machinery essential to ensure harmonious coexistence in the region.

Among the objectives set out in the Document are those in which the countries of Central America declare their intention to:

- promote détente and end conflict in the region;
- ensure respect for human rights;

• adopt measures conducive to the establishment of democratic, representative and pluralistic systems;

• promote national reconciliation;

• create political conditions to ensure the international security, integrity and sovereignty of the States of the region;

• stop the arms race in the area and begin negotiations for reductions of weapon stocks and troops;

• prevent the installation of foreign military bases or any other type of foreign military interference;

• reduce the presence of military advisers and other foreign
elements involved in military and security activities, with a view
to their elimination;

• prevent arms traffic;

• prevent use of their territories for destabilizing other Central American Governments;

• undertake economic and social development programmes.

REPORTS OF SECRETARY-GENERAL

The Secretary-General, in transmitting the Document of Objectives to the Security Council, noted that the Minister for Foreign Affairs of Mexico had pointed out that it was a "single
consensus text . . . which contains the principles on which eventual solution of the Central American problems will have to be
based." The Secretary-General said that in his conversation with
the Mexican Foreign Minister, he had emphasized that "any attempt at a solution should take into account the profound economic and social imbalances with which the Central American
people have always struggled."

The Secretary-General said there had been frequent accusa-
tions and counter-accusations of foreign interference in the region and complaints of numerous border incidents as well as
incursions by sea and by air, causing deplorable loss of life and
material damage. In the view of some Governments, military and
naval manoeuvres in progress added to tensions in the region. "It
has also been pointed out that the presence of military advisers
and training centres, the traffic in arms and the activities of
armed groups, and the unprecedented build-up of arms and of
military and paramilitary forces constitute further factors of
tensions."

"The Governments of Colombia, Mexico Panama and Venezuela are motivated by an earnest desire to find solutions adapted to the realities of the region, without any intrusion derived from the East-West conflict," Mr. Pérez de Cuéllar said. "That is why they have the manifest support of the international community as a whole."

The Security Council, in resolution 530 (1983), asked the Secretary-General to report periodically on the Contadora effort. In a report issued on 9 December, he noted that the "pace of the efforts of the Contadora Group is accelerating" (*document S/16208*). He also reported "perceptible movement in the position of the Government of Nicaragua," consisting mainly of proposals submitted within the framework of the Contadora effort and measures which, "notwithstanding their domestic nature, take cognizance of certain requirements of the other countries of the area."

Nonetheless, the Secretary-General warned, the situation in Central America continued to be "exceedingly complex and unstable," and "any one of the multiple factors which account for its dangerous character" could aggravate it again from one moment to the next.

### HUMAN RIGHTS COMMISSION SUPPORTS CONTADORA EFFORTS

The Commission on Human Rights has expressed its "firmest support" for the efforts of the Contadora Group in providing its good offices to the Central American countries aimed at agreements for peace in the area.

In a resolution adopted without a vote on 12 March, the Commission said it "repudiates the acts of aggression against the sovereignty, independence and territorial integrity of the States of the region which are causing loss of human life and irreparable damage to their economies."

### SPECIFIC MEASURES

The "Measures to be taken to fulfil the commitments entered into in the Document of Objectives" (*document A/39/71-S/16262*), adopted at the fifth joint meeting of the Central American Foreign Ministers and the Contadora Group (Panama 7–8 January), are the most concrete step to date in the Contadora process. Those measures relate to questions of regional security, political matters and co-operation in the economic and social spheres.

**Security questions:** Steps to be taken by the Central American States regarding security include an inventory by each country of its military installations, weapons and troops, with a view to developing guidelines for reductions and ceilings to achieve a "reasonable balance of forces in the region." Other measures concern establishing a timetable for withdrawal of foreign advisers and other outside elements, elimination of support or toleration of "irregular groups or forces engaged in destabilizing Central American Governments"; stopping illegal arms traffic; and establishing "mechanisms of direct communication" to avert incidents between States.

**Political matters:** "The promotion of national reconciliation" and "establishment of machinery to facilitate dialogue between the countries of the region" are key measures set out in the political area. Others concern machinery to ensure free and fair elections, including guarantees for participation of political parties which represent the different currents of opinion.

**Economic and social questions:** Agreed measures include encouragement of intraregional trade and joint investment projects, strengthening of programmes of assistance to Central American refugees and the extension of full co-operation to the Central American Integration Bank, the Economic Commission for Latin America (ECLA), the Committee for Action in Support of the Economic and Social Development of Central America (CADESCA) and the General Treaty of Central American Integration (SIECA).

The Foreign Ministers also decided to establish three working commissions to prepare studies, legal drafts and recommendations on those questions and make proposals for verifying and supervising implementation of the measures agreed on. Representatives of the Governments of Central America will comprise the commissions, which will be convened by the Contadora Group and will carry out their tasks within the framework of the "Document of Objectives."

The working commissions were officially inaugurated on 31 January. Their recommendations are to be submitted to a Joint Meeting of the Foreign Ministers "not later than 30 April" (*document A/39/95-S/16304*).

At its most recent meeting (27–28 February), the Contadora Group reiterated its resolve to search for a stable and lasting peace in Central America. But it acknowledged that if that objective was to be obtained, the measures agreed on at the joint meeting in January had to be "scrupulously carried out" (*document A/39/126-S/16394*).

The Ministers noted with interest advances made with respect to elections in various countries of the area and highlighted the importance of making use of democratic processes as a means of bringing about domestic reconciliation in the various countries and détente in the region.

They also emphasized the growing international co-operation in tackling the serious social and economic problems "at the root of the crisis in Central America." The Group considered proposals made towards that end by the International Labour Organisation, the Pan American Health Organization and CADESCA. The Foreign Ministers expressed satisfaction at the convening of the CADESCA's first meeting, scheduled for 1–6 March 1984 in Mexico City, calling that body "a necessary instrument for the co-ordination of economic and social cooperation in the Central American area."

## DEMYSTIFYING CONTADORA[3]

Contadora is the code word used to mean the pursuit of peace in Central America through negotiations. Its main alternatives are widely believed to be a U.S. invasion, a regional war or both. Like motherhood and apple pie, Contadora is liked and supported by everyone.

Why, then, has a negotiated settlement within the Contadora framework proved so elusive? Critics of U.S. Central American policy argue that a diplomatic solution requires support from Washington and that, despite rhetoric to the contrary, Washington opposes Contadora because a Contadora treaty would prohibit unilateral action by the United States in protection of its interests. The facts are more complex than this reasoning conveys. The U.S. government remains divided, with some saying

[3]Reprint of an article by Susan Kaufman Purcell, director of the Latin American Program at the Council on Foreign Relations. *Foreign Affairs.* Fall '85. pp. 74–95. Copyright, 1985, by the Council on Foreign Relations, Inc. Reprinted by permission of FOREIGN AFFAIRS, Fall 1985.

that an imperfect treaty is better than no treaty and others arguing that no treaty is better. For their part, the countries of the
Contadora group—Mexico, Venezuela, Colombia and Panama—are divided in their interests and strategies. Some of them
share the fears and ambivalence of the United States, though
they have taken great pains to conceal this fact; the domestic political costs of agreeing with the United States in Central American matters are not negligible.

The impression that the United States and the Contadora
Four have few shared interests leads to two opposite conclusions;
either the Contadora process is a waste of time, since the United
States will ultimately impose its own solution on Central America,
or Contadora still offers a good solution, if only the United States
would support it. The reality is somewhere in between. Over the
past two and half years, the Contadora Four have been obliged
to move beyond empty rhetoric to deal with the complexities of
designing a treaty that takes account of the interests of the Central American countries and the United States. In the process, despite all the significant obstacles that remain, they have increased
the possibility of a negotiated settlement in Central America.

*II*

Contadora refers to both a regional grouping and the negotiating process in which it is engaged. The Contadora group was
originally created in January 1983, at the initiative of Colombian
President Belisario Betancur, as a diplomatic alternative to the
conflict escalating in the region. Nicaragua was aiding the Salvadoran guerrillas. In response, the United States organized the
"contras," who were increasing their forays into Nicaragua from
Honduras. The U.S. military presence and activities in the region
were beginning to expand. The Contadora countries feared that
the Sandinistas would retaliate against the contras and draw Honduras, and then the United States, into open armed conflict that
might eventually spill over into the rest of Central America.

Contadora aimed to fill a diplomatic vacuum. The Sandinistas
have preferred not to work with the Organization of American
States (OAS) since they believe the United States still controls its
members, despite considerable evidence to the contrary. They favor the United Nations, where the dominant Third World coalition is sure to favor Nicaragua over the United States. For this

reason, the United Nations has been an unacceptable mediator for the United States, which strongly advocates hemispheric solutions to hemispheric problems.

By joining forces under the Contadora umbrella, the regional powers believed that they might be able to constrain the United States from its habitual unilateral actions and thereby enhance their own role. They also hoped to offer a different interpretation of events in Central America. They believed that the United States, as a global and non-Latin power, tended to impose an East-West perspective on conflicts that essentially involved such North-South issues as poverty, inequality and exploitation. Their de-emphasis of the Soviet threat was understandable, since the United States, not the Soviet Union, had traditionally been seen as the danger to the countries of the region.

Finally, the contadora countries had a record of successful joint efforts. In 1976, Omar Torrijos of Panama had enlisted the support of Mexico, Venezuela, Colombia, as well as Costa Rica, to generate Latin American support for the Panama Canal treaties. Three years later, these same countries persuaded the not-yet-victorious Sandinistas to commit themselves to political pluralism, a mixed economy and international nonalignment in return for their support. In 1981, Torrijos again brought the group together, shortly before his death, to pressure the Sandinistas to abide by their commitment.

In January 1983, the presidents of Mexico, Venezuela, Colombia and Panama met on the Panamanian island of Contadora to discuss the deteriorating situation in Central America. Their meeting marked the formal beginning of the Contadora group.

The Contadora Four were not interested in protecting U.S. security interests in Central America. On the contrary, they were reluctant to acknowledge publicly that the United States even had legitimate security interests in the region. They had no such qualms about speaking publicly of the legitimate security interests of Nicaragua. In fact, the regional powers had joined forces precisely to counter a real or imaginary U.S. military threat against Nicaragua.

Since then, observers have repeatedly pronounced the Contadora process dead or dying. They take at face value the frustration of the participants who keep encountering new, seemingly intractable problems each time they solve old ones. They fail to understand that Contadora's mere existence is useful. It allows the four participating governments to affirm that they have kept the United States at bay and have avoided a regional war. This makes it difficult for any of them to desert the negotiating process. At the same time, the costs of failure are relatively low. If diplomacy leads nowhere, the Contadora countries can say that they did their best, but the hegemonic pretensions of the United States made their best not good enough.

*III*

The Contadora Four had first become active in Central America in the late 1970s. Venezuela, Colombia and Panama had helped arm Nicaraguan President Anastasio Somoza's opponents and all four had worked hard to isolate Somoza internationally. Yet the Four's familiarity with Central America remained limited. Contadora has helped teach them about Central America and about each other. It has also shown them that it is far easier to call for a diplomatic solution than to create one.

Contadora has forged a consensus around a number of objectives that could constitute the basis for a negotiated settlement. These are embodied in the 21 points of the Document of Objectives of September 1983, calling for democracy and national reconciliation, an end to support for paramilitary forces across borders, control of the regional arms race, reduction of foreign military advisers and troops, and prohibition of foreign military bases. These goals were incorporated into the draft treaty or "Acta" of September 7, 1984, which Nicaragua quickly accepted and the United States just as quickly rejected. These starkly different reactions created the impression that Nicaragua favored a negotiated settlement and the United States did not.

In fact, the United States rejected the Acta because it was a vague statement of goals without concrete limits on Nicaraguan action. Its provisions for verification and enforcement were totally inadequate, and it deferred negotiations on foreign military and security advisers and arms and troop reductions until after signature of the treaty. On the other hand, it required the United States upon signature to cease military exercises and support for the contras. Further military aid to El Salvador and Honduras was frozen, while Nicaragua was allowed to maintain its military advantage over these two countries. The provisions for democratization and internal reconciliation were hortatory and unenforceable as drafted. They would have allowed the Sandinistas to claim that the Nicaraguan elections scheduled for November 1984 were in compliance with the Acta despite charges by the democratic opposition, led by Arturo Cruz, that the electoral process was rigged.

Nicaragua accepted the Acta as a final document, not a draft for discussion, because it asked little of Nicaragua immediately and left no possibility for Nicaragua to be pressured in post-signature negotiations. Accepting the Acta also improved Nicaragua's image internationally, just as the U.S. Congress was to vote on aid for the contras and Nicaraguan President Daniel Ortega was to address the U.N. General Assembly.

When Nicaragua surprised U.S. friends in Central America by accepting the Acta, Honduras, El Salvador and Costa Rica began drafting what became the Act of Tegucigalpa of October 1984—a substitute draft that sought to correct what they and the United States had seen as the main problems of the September 1984 Acta. The timetable for disarmament and demilitarization procedures was changed to produce more simultaneous action on these issues, and the role of the Central American governments in the verification and enforcement processes was enhanced. The Nicaraguans immediately rejected the October draft and repeated that they would not accept any substantive changes in the September Acta. That is still their position at this writing.

With the process at an impasse, the Contadora countries looked to the bilateral talks in Manzanillo, Mexico, between the United States and Nicaragua to achieve a breakthrough. In the penultimate round in late 1984, Nicaragua hinted that it was willing to be flexible on key security issues in a strictly bilateral agreement. The United States pointed out that Nicaragua logically could not enter into two contradictory agreements, and eventually concluded that Nicaragua was proposing at Manzanillo the substitution of a limited bilateral agreement on security issues for a comprehensive Contadora agreement. It therefore suspended the bilateral talks in January 1985 to emphasize multilateral discussions within Contadora.

This worked for a time. In April 1985 an agreement in principle was reached on revised verification procedures involving concessions by both Nicaragua and the Central American drafters of the Tegucigalpa Act. But the negotiations bogged down again in the summer of 1985, when Nicaragua once more tried to substitute a series of bilateral security agreements for Contadora's comprehensive agenda. Nicaragua favors such an approach to avoid the issue of democratization and internal reconciliation, a shorthand term for talks between the Sandinistas and the armed and unarmed opponents (including the contras) leading to their eventual incorporation into a democratized political process.

Democratization and internal reconciliation may well be the most difficult issue of all, because it would, in the words of President Reagan, "overthrow the Nicaraguan government, in the sense of changing its structure." The Sandinistas, however, say it is a non-issue; they will not deal with the contras and Nicaragua is already democratic.

The democratization/internal reconciliation issue is also at the heart of the division within the U.S. government. While there is consensus that a more democratic Nicaragua would be more likely to abide by a negotiated settlement, the debate is over the more fundamental question of whether it is possible to democratize Nicaragua at all. Some argue that Nicaragua can be made to accept democratization and internal reconciliation under pressure and want the United States to hold firm for such an outcome. Others doubt that the Sandinistas will ever incorporate the rebels and democratize. They believe that the United States should therefore accept a treaty that deals with the conventional security issues but not with democratization and internal reconciliation.

The so-called Reagan Peace Plan on April 4, 1985, came out squarely in favor of continuing to press for democratization and internal reconciliation. President Reagan was not about to abandon the Nicaraguan "freedom fighters"; he called for a cease-fire and talks between the Nicaraguan government and the rebels. At the same time, he asked Congress to release an appropriation of $14 million in humanitarian aid for the rebels, which the United States would not make available if the talks did not succeed by June 1, 1985. The plan failed to obtain sufficient backing from Congress, which denied aid at that time, and from the Contadora Four, who wanted nothing to do with a plan that included aid for the contras. The Reagan Administration continues to emphasize the need to include democratization and internal reconciliation in any treaty. Progress thus depends on whether the Contadora process can devise such a treaty.

*IV*

The Contadora Four enjoy an image of unity. They oppose a military solution and unilateral action by the United States. They seek a negotiated settlement to end the fighting. They also believe that the Sandinista government of Nicaragua is here to stay and that its future, particularly its international alignment, can be influenced by outside actors. Beyond this consensus, however, there are important differences among the Four, which reflect their particular historical experiences as well as the political constraints they face domestically.

*Mexico.* Mexico's position has been most at odds with that of the United States. Although critical of Washington for supporting right-wing dictators in Central America and for failing to help eradicate poverty and injustice, in policy terms Mexico has not behaved very differently from the United States. Mexico has not actively supported right-wing dictators, but it did nothing to undermine their rule until the late 1970s, when it withdrew recognition from the disintegrating Somoza regime. Nor did Mexico pursue an active or generous aid program toward the area. In fact, Mexico "discovered" Central America at about the same time the United States did, belying the myth that Mexico knows and understands Central America better than the United States does.

Mexico's policy toward the Sandinistas has been protective and empathetic. As a country that had experienced its own modern revolution, Mexico could not condemn other revolutions. Mexico had also suffered multiple U.S. interventions and lost half its territory to its northern neighbor. It therefore sympathized with the Sandinistas' fear of a U.S. invasion or intervention in their affairs. Precisely because of its historical relationship with the United States, Mexico had earlier adopted a foreign policy based on the principles of nonintervention and self-determination. It applied them to the Nicaraguan revolution when it occurred in July 1979.

Mexico's definition of nonintervention, however, was tailored to its policy preferences. Mexico did not consider itself to be intervening in Central American affairs when it withdrew recognition from Somoza or joined in the Franco-Mexican declaration of August 1981 that recognized the Salvadoran rebels as a "representative political force."

Mexico's support of the Sandinistas and the Salvadoran rebels reflected its belief that revolutionary governments in Central America, including communist ones, would not threaten Mexico's interests. It felt confident that it could establish friendly relations with such goverments, as it had done earlier with Cuba. Mexico might even gain influence if left-wing governments triumphed in Central America. The United States would have little, if any, influence over such governments; Mexico, in contrast, could work with them and possibly replace the United States as the most important power in the region.

Finally, Mexico rejected the theory that it was the "last domino" that would fall if Marxist revolutionaries were successful in Central America. Mexico correctly viewed itself as different from its southern neighbors, considerably larger and more developed, with a more differentiated social structure. And, with the exception of Costa Rica, its political system was more effective and responsive than those in Central America.

Mexico's actions were, nevertheless, marked by a gap between rhetoric and reality. The Mexicans pursued a very different policy toward the right-wing military regime of Guatemala than toward other right-wing governments in the region. Mexico has neither broken with nor publicly criticized the government in Guatemala City; nor has it called Guatemala's Marxist guerrillas "a representative political force." Also, despite Mexico's rejection of the domino theory, it has reinforced its military presence along its southern border and implemented the so-called Plan Chiapas to help improve the standard of living of Mexican peasants in the lands bordering on Guatemala.

Over the past year, the perception has grown that Mexico's policy toward both the Sandinistas and Central America in general has changed. The presence of Mexico's foreign minister at the inauguration of President José Napoleón Duarte in El Salvador is often cited. The fact that Mexico no longer supplies petroleum to the Sandinistas on terms more favorable to Nicaragua than to other clients is another example. Mexico also has become less tolerant of the political representatives of the Salvadoran guerrillas operating in Mexico. President Miguel de la Madrid has also begun to balance references to U.S. intervention in Central America with references to Cuban intervention. And he seems less eager then his predecessor, José López Portillo, to engage in high-level meetings with Fidel Castro.

Mexico claims that its policy has not changed, but that circumstances in Central America and Mexico have changed. Yet the policy has also evolved. Under López Portillo, Mexico's initial unquestioning support for the Sandinistas, as well as its de-emphasis of the need for political pluralism in Nicaragua, had made Mexico ever more isolated within the Contadora group. Also, as growing numbers of refugees crossed the border into Mexico, Central America increasingly became transformed from a foreign policy issue to a domestic one. Ministries other than the Foreign Ministry became involved, weakening the previous consensus behind the government's approach and pushing it to adopt a more balanced policy toward Central America.

This shift does not mean that Mexico has abandoned the Sandinistas. Mexico does not want to drive the Sandinistas out of the negotiating process and into total isolation. Mexico was therefore critical of the October 1984 treaty drafted by the Central American allies of the United States because it feared that Nicaragua would abandon the Contadora process if it did not get favorable treatment. Mexico also supported the Sandinistas' stress on the importance of having bilateral talks with the United States. The Manzanillo talks were in part the result of a personal initiative by President de la Madrid during his visit to Washington in May 1984. Mexico therefore continues to work for a balanced settlement in Central America.

*Venezuela.* The Contadora country whose position has been most at odds with that of Mexico, and closest to the United States, is Venezuela. Unlike Mexico, Venezuela does not consider itself a revolutionary country; instead, its sense of identity is strongly based on its evolution into one of the most important democracies of the hemisphere. Support for the principle of democratization has been considerably more important in Venezuela, therefore, than it has been in Mexico. Venezuela has also been much more distrustful of Marxist revolutionaries than Mexico, since for years Marxist guerrillas had threatened the survival of Venezuela's democracy. Venezuela believed that democratic government could not develop in El Salvador if the guerrillas remained unchecked. Venezuela also has been wary of Cuba because of Havana's earlier support of Venezuelan guerrillas.

Unlike Mexico, Venezuela admitted from the beginning that the Central American conflict had implications for Venezuelan security and required a strategic, as well as an economic, political and social, response. For this reason, Venezuela sent military advisers to El Salvador. (The decision was facilitated because Christian Democratic presidents were in power in both Venezuela and El Salvador.) This policy became politically unsustainable after the United States sided with Britain during the 1982 Falklands War. Nevertheless, even after the transfer of the presidency to a Social Democrat, Venezuela's policy toward Central America did not change dramatically. Venezuela distanced itself initially from the interim government of Alvaro Magaña in El Salvador, when right-wing elements seemed ascendant. But once Christian Democrat Duarte was elected president, even Venezuela's Social Democratic regime supported him.

Venezuela also favored the incorporation of the Salvadoran guerrillas into the electoral process and, like the United States, opposed negotiated power-sharing. Venezuela had, after all, successfully incorporated its own guerrillas into its electoral process, and some had even been elected to important public offices.

As the Sandinistas became more authoritarian and closely tied to Cuba and the Soviet Union, Venezuela became more openly critical of them. More recently, it has terminated shipments of subsidized petroleum to Nicaragua and has increased its assistance to democratic elements in the labor movement, the church, universities and the private sector in Nicaragua. Former President Carlos Andrés Pérez, a prominent leader of the Latin American Social Democratic movement who has been highly critical of U.S. policy in the region, refused to attend Ortega's inauguration as president of Nicaragua to express his displeasure with the path that the Sandinistas were taking. Still, Venezuela has not yet given up on the possibility of some degree of political pluralism in Nicaragua.

The dramatic differences between Venezuela and Mexico demonstrate the fallacy in the judgment that the Contadora Four are united in opposition to the U.S. approach to Central America. Venezuela, in fact, shares some of the basic premises that underlie U.S. policy toward Central America.

Yet neither Venezuela nor Mexico wishes to see the United States return to the highly interventionist role it played in Latin America in the past. Both would like a solution that would avoid U.S. military intervention or other forms of unilateral U.S. action. The main differences between the Venezuelan and Mexican positions is that Venezuela seems more willing and able to cooperate on military-security dimensions with the United States than is Mexico, and Caracas places more importance than does Mexico City on the need to democratize the Nicaraguan government. At the very least, Venezuelans are divided over whether a Marxist regime poses a security threat and if so, whether Venezuela should play a military role in chainging or containing it.

*Colombia.* The Country whose attitudes and behavior changed most substantially with a change of governments is Colombia. Under former Liberal Party President Julio César Turbay, Colombia was supportive of U.S. policy toward Central America. In part, this reflected a traditional tendency on the part of his party to work closely with the United States. Turbay himself distrusted the Sandinistas' expansionist inclinations, particularly toward a number of Colombian islands claimed by Nicaragua. President Reagan backed Colombia in its conflict with Nicaragua, which reinforced cooperation between the two governments.

Colombia is the only Contadora country with an immediate guerrilla problem. Turbay had promulgated a National Security Statute less than one month after his inauguration in 1978. The attempted military solution to Colombia's guerrilla problem failed and so Turbay's successor, Belisario Betancur, tried a completely new tack when he took office in 1982.

Betancur's goal was to negotiate amnesty for the guerrillas in return for their peaceful incorporation into the political system. The new president believed that such a deal would not be possible while Colombia continued to align itself with the United States, whose Central American policy seemed to emphasize defeat of guerrillas by military means. On his inauguration day, he distanced himself from the United States by announcing that Colombia would apply for admission to the Non-Aligned Movement, chaired at that time by Fidel Castro. He also called for the restructuring of the OAS so as to exclude the United States and include Cuba. These steps paved the way for a new strategy for dealing with the guerrillas at home.

In pursuit of his new domestic policy, Bentancur successfully engaged the services of Nobel Prize laureate Gabriel García Márquez, who was close to Castro as well as to the Sandinistas. The idea was to get Castro and the Sandinistas to encourage Colombia's guerrillas to negotiate the terms of an amnesty with the Colombian government. If successful, the strategy would end Colombia's guerrilla problem and neutralize Cuba and Nicaragua, in the sense of ensuring their noncooperation with guerrilla groups in Colombia.

Betancur was trying to "Mexicanize" Colombia's foreign policy. By pursuing a "progressive" foreign policy that included friendly relations with Cuba and Nicaragua, Betancur hoped to discourage their support for the Colombian guerrillas and encourage them to cooperate with his government.

Batancur paralleled his domestic strategy toward the guerrillas with a more active role for Colombia within the Contadora group. Attracted to the role of international peacemaker, Betancur traveled incessantly throughout the region, engaging in marathon talks with governments and rebels, as well as with the other three Contadora countries and the United States. The last such effort ended in Washington, D.C., in April 1985, the same day President Reagan announced his peace plan. President Betancur endorsed the plan, but qualified (or some would say retracted) his endorsement several days later by stating that he could not side with the United States in supporting the contras. Since the plan clearly included a role for the contras from the beginning, Betancur had either endorsed it before reading it carefully or was persuaded to distance himself from the United States once the other Contadora countries objected to it.

Betancur's domestic policies continue to be debated within Colombia. Critics contend that they are failing. Although Betancur succeeded in signing truces with Colombia's two main guerrilla groups, one of them subsequently changed its mind. There is also evidence that some of the guerrilla groups used the amnesty to regroup and rearm. Betancur has so far rejected the use of force or pressure to achieve his objectives at home and abroad. The guerrillas, however, have not. Their use of force and negotiations has therefore put the Colombian government at a disadvantage.

Presidential elections are scheduled in Colombia for 1986. If guerrilla violence continues to increase, Colombia will probably return to a more hard-line policy toward the guerrillas after the election, whoever is elected. Colombia's role and posture within Contadora would also probably change, toward a lower profile and a more centrist approach.

*Panama.* The fourth Contadora country, Panama, resembles the Central American countries themselves; it is small, poor and weak. Yet Panama has never regarded itself as part of Central

America, and neither can it be considered a regional power like
Mexico, Venezuela and Colombia. Its membership in the Contadora group is mainly a reflection of the leadership qualities of
Omar Torrijos, who regarded Panama as too small a stage for his
ambitions and talents, and so played an active role in regional politics. Since his death, Panama has been governed by four different presidents, a symptom of the domestic political instability that
has focused Panama's attention inward.

Panama's diminished role in Contadora also reflects ambivalence regarding developments in Central America and in its relationship with the United States. On the one hand, Panama does
not wish to see the Sandinistas extend their influence in the region. The traits that Panama shares with its Central American
neighbors, in addition to its geographical proximity, make it
more immediately vulnerable than are its Contadora partners to
the destabilizing impact of regional conflict. Furthermore, the
Panamanian National Guard shares many of the anti-communist
sentiments that underlie U.S. policy toward Central America.

On the other hand, Panama does not want to appear too
closely aligned with the United States for fear of fanning domestic anti-U.S. sentiments. The United States has been a kind of colonial power in Panama, where its ownership of the canal gave it
extraordinary influence, if not control, over the course of events.
Despite a reduction in the U.S. role in Panama since the signing
of the canal treaties, the United States remains very involved.
The U.S. Southern Command is headquartered in Panama and
has grown considerably during the course of the Central American conflict.

Panama has resolved these tensions by focusing within Contadora on getting an agreement that would increase Panama's international prestige. Consistent with this goal, its position on
specific issues has been flexible and pragmatic.

In view of these differences among the four Contadora countries, how could they claim to be united in support of the September 1984 Acta that the United States and the Central American
countries found unacceptable? Mexico took the lead in pressing
for a draft treaty prior to the U.S. presidential election. It hoped
that if a draft treaty were in place prior to Ronald Reagan's expected reelection, the chances for unilateral action by the United
States would be diminished. Colombia agreed. Venezuela believed it important to have a treaty prior to the Nicaraguan elec-

tions, which were also scheduled for November 1984; after the elections it would be difficult to press Nicaragua to democratize. Nicaragua also wanted to move before its elections so the result would seem to be blessed by Contadora. There was no time to work out a perfect treaty before November. The decision was made, therefore, to leave the most difficult problems, such as arms negotiations, a timetable of withdrawal for security advisers, verification and processes for implementation, for later negotiations. Meanwhile, a treaty ending U.S. military exercises and support for the contras would protect Nicaragua and reduce the chances of direct intervention.

This strategy involved a decision to win Nicaragua's support at the expense of that of the United States, a reasonable decision in view of the fact that there was considerable doubt among the Contadora Four that the United States would ever find any draft treaty acceptable. Obtaining Nicaragua's acceptance of the draft, however, could probably be counted on to increase international pressure on the United States to go along as well. This is exactly what happened.

The Contadora Four did not accept the idea that un unenforceable treaty would threaten their security. This highlights a major problem that confronts the United States in the search for a negotiated settlement in Central America. Underlying any negotiations is the assumption on the part of the Contadora Four that if their security is *really* threatened, the United States will do something about it. Thus, they can take risks in the negotiating process that the United States is unwilling to take.

*V*

But there are, of course, players beyond the Contadora Four. Any negotiated settlement in Central America would have to win the approval of the Central American countries. Yet these countries do not see eye to eye with the Contadora countries, and the latter, especially Mexico, virtually ignore them in the mediating process. Costa Rica, Honduras and El Salvador are pitted against Nicaragua; Guatemala is also, but it seeks to project itself as more neutral than the other three.

Because the positions of Costa Rica, Honduras, and El Salvador are congruent to the United States' position, the conventional wisdom is that the United States has pressured these small, weak countries to do its bidding. This is, at the least, an oversimplification.

The views of the governments of Costa Rica, Honduras and El Salvador reflect the common reality they face. They all feel vulnerable to the activities of Marxist guerrillas operating in Central America and accept the much-maligned "domino theory." They do not trust the Sandinistas and, together with the United States, fear that Nicaragua will continue to support radical insurgents throughout the region. Their support of the contras is due to their belief that the Sandinistas will change only under outside pressure. A negotiated solution to the conflict that requires the United States to stop providing military assistance to them is unacceptable because they need U.S. military, economic and political support to survive. Thus, they agree with the United States on the root of the problem and its solution.

Nevertheless, these countries are ambivalent toward Washington. The United States cannot be too closely supported without undermining the still fragile domestic legitimacy of their governments. They also view U.S. policy toward the region as erratic and undependable. For these reasons, they need to hedge their bets in order not to irreparably damage their relations with the Sandinistas or the Contadora Four.

Toward the Contadora Four, their attitude is quite negative. Mexico, Venezuela, Colombia and Panama have little understanding of Central America, they feel, and are more interested in protecting their own interests and assuring the survival of the Sandinista government than in protecting them. Like the Contadora Four, these Central American countries want to avoid a regional war, but they doubt that the way to do it is by siding with the Sandinistas against the United States.

As the Contadora Four have become more involved with the specifics of a negotiated settlement, the Central American countries have become more resentful of what they regard as unwarranted intervention in their internal affairs. Costa Rica, El Salvador and Honduras believe that current trends are in their favor; Contadora, therefore, is seen as increasingly obstructionist. This resentment is directed most against Mexico, which is their "Colossus of the North."

Despite the general consensus that Costa Rica, Honduras and El Salvador share, there are some differences. As with the four Contadora countries, these variations grow out of the different historical experiences and current realities of each country.

*Costa Rica.* Costa Rica is unique in Central America as the only institutionalized democracy without a military establishment. Costa Rica also has a tradition of distrust of Nicaragua, stemming from Somoza's repeated attempts to intervene in his neighbor's internal affairs. Anti-Somoza sentiments ultimately led Costa Rica to join with Venezuela, Colombia, Panama and Mexico to help oust the dictator. Costa Rica, however, soon found the Sandinistas to be authoritarian and interventionist as well.

Officially neutral toward the Central American conflict, Costa Rica is not ideologically neutral; it is profoundly anti-communist. This helps explain the unofficial support that Costa Rica has given to Edén Pastora, the former Sandinista and current leader of the Nicaraguan rebel group that operates in the border region between Costa Rica and Nicaragua. Costa Rica also supports the need to democratize the Nicaraguan government and incorporate the rebels into the political system. It does not want a Contadora agreement that allows the further consolidation of a communist regime in Nicaragua. Costa Rica distrusts the ability of any treaty to contain the expansionist tendencies of the Sandinistas and believes, as does the United States, that democratization and internal reconciliation are the best guarantors against the export of revolution by the Sandinistas. Finally, without an agreement that integrates the contras into Nicaraguan politics, Costa Rica fears it will receive thousands of refugees in addition to the approximately 40,000 that it already hosts.

*El Salvador.* The government of El Salvador is engaged in a civil war and needs uninterrupted military assistance from the United States in order to hold its own against the guerrillas, let alone defeat them. The government also needs to prevent the Sandinistas, the Cubans and their other allies from supplying the rebels with training, munitions and other supplies. Therefore, the Salvadoran government is most concerned with the security-related issues of the Contadora process. It supports an end to arms trafficking and is against provisions that would limit military assistance from the United States to El Salvador.

El Salvador also supports the need for internal reconciliation and democratization in Nicaragua. It opposes a double standard implicit in much of the Contadora discussions: the belief that pressure is legitimate if used to get the Salvadoran government to democratize, but is interventionist and illegitimate if applied to the Nicaraguan goverment. Although the process has not yet gone far, the Duarte government has held talks with the Salvadoran guerrillas and sees no reason why the Sandinistas should not be required to do the same with their guerrillas.

*Honduras.* As the only immediate neighbor of Nicaragua with a military establishment, Honduras is the one most concerned with the strength and size of the Nicaraguan armed forces. Thus, Honduras took the lead in Central America in opposing the September 1984 Acta, which provided for a freeze of military force levels. Honduras does not want a freeze, since that would freeze Nicaragua's military superiority over Honduras. It wants reduction.

A reduction would also assuage Honduran fears over the growing strength of the Salvadoran military. Although Honduras and El Salvador are currently cooperating with each other, they have traditionally been competitors, if not enemies. The perception of a common threat from the Sandinistas has enabled them to bury their differences for the moment. The Hondurans believe, however, that the chances of Honduran-Salvadoran cooperation enduring would be increased if El Salvador's armed forces were not allowed to become vastly superior to those of Honduras. As the country from which most of the contras operate, Honduras is also strongly supportive of a treaty that does not abandon the Nicaraguan rebels. Like Costa Rica, it supports talks between the contras and the Sandinistas leading to the eventual incorporation of the former into the Nicaraguan political process.

Finally, like El Salvador, Honduras fears a treaty that would deprive it of U.S. military support, and has thus sought a bilateral military agreement with the United States. At the same time, Honduras does not wish to be taken for granted, and so periodically attempts to negotiate more favorable terms of cooperation with the United States.

Why had the Central American allies of the United States originally seemed willing to accept the September Acta that Washington opposed? In part, they were posturing. They had serious problems with the Acta, but they chose to adopt a positive stance in order to impress favorably a group of European foreign ministers scheduled to meet in San José, Costa Rica, on September 28, 1984, to discuss economic assistance for the region. They believed that their objections to the Acta could be concealed for the time being, since they were convinced that Nicaragua would reject it, They were wrong. Nicaragua's unexpected acceptance of the Acta, on the condition that it not be changed in any way, led them to withdraw their support and to draft the Act of Tegucigalpa, which more accurately reflected their interests.

*Guatemala.* Since October 1984, when Honduras called together the other Central American governments to draft a substitute treaty, Guatemala has sought to distance itself from the others. Appearances are deceiving. The Guatemalan government is as anti-Sandinista as the other three Central American governments. It also does not want to freeze arms levels with Central America at current levels, thereby giving Nicaragua an advantage. It too wants an end to arms shipments to guerrilla movements, and it does not want the United States to withdraw from the region. Furthermore, although Guatemala sent only a vice minister to the October meeting of foreign ministers and failed to endorse the draft treaty publicly, the vice minister participated actively in its drafting.

Guatemala's ambivalence is explained by its unique situation. It is the only Central American country that shares a border with Mexico, the country that has been most sympathetic to the Sandinistas. Relations between Guatemala and Mexico have never been easy. The Guatemalan government's anti-guerrilla campaign created a serious refugee problem in southern Mexico. Because some refugee camps were used as safe havens for the Guatemalan guerrillas, Guatemala wanted the camps removed from the border. To achieve Mexico's cooperation, Guatemala needed to improve its relations with its neighbor.

The Guatemalan government also had been upset with the United States for some time, largely because of U.S. criticism of its human rights performance and the related cutoff of economic and military assistance. Although Guatemala basically agrees with the United States on Nicaragua and its potential threat to the region, it wants the United States to pay a price for its cooperation with the other Central American countries.

Finally, the behavior of Guatemala's military rulers has made the country a pariah within Latin America. The civilian governments of Latin America all publicly supported the efforts of the Contadora Four and regarded the opposition of Honduras, Costa Rica and El Salvador to the September Acta as an obstructionist move masterminded by the United States. By withholding public support from the October draft treaty, Guatemala could partially reintegrate itself into Latin America.

*VI*

Nicaragua has consistently preferred bilateral over miltilateral negotiations to resolve the conflict in Central America. It has believed it could better protect its interests by dealing with its neighbors individually and avoid the issues of democratization/ national reconciliation and regional arms control. A series of bilateral agreements would also make it more difficult for the United States to coordinate its policies with its Central American allies. Facing a Central American refusal to accept bilateral negotiations, and therefore a choice between multilateral negotiations or nothing, Nicaragua reluctantly joined the Contadora process. Negotiations would help forestall a U.S. invasion, which the Sandinistas regarded as otherwise inevitable. And multilateral negotiations could possibly produce a treaty that would legitimize the Sandinista regime and formally circumscribe the U.S. military role in Central America.

The Nicaraguan government, however, does not have faith that a multilateral treaty would constrain Washington. It therefore demanded bilateral talks with the United States, toward the goal of a separate U.S.-Nicaragua treaty that would, among other things, prohibit the United States from invading Nicaragua. When the talks began in Manzanillo in June 1984, Nicaragua's purpose was to preclude U.S. support for the contras. Nicaragua was willing to make a number of concessions to achieve the goal; it saw the contras as the main obstacle to the rapid consolidation of Sandinista rule. In the course of the talks, Nicaragua therefore agreed in principle to send home its Cuban advisers, refrain from supporting guerrilla movements in neighboring countries and prohibit the installation of foreign bases on its territory.

The issues of internal reconciliation and the democratization of the regime were raised by the United States in the first meeting. The Sandinista position, however, was that internal reconciliation between the government and unarmed opposition groups was already occurring, and that the government would never talk with the contras, who were traitors. They added later that there was no need to discuss democratization since Nicaragua already had a democratically elected president and a pluralistic political system. Finally, the Sandinista government argued that the current internal reconciliation and democratization demands went beyond those that former Assistant Secretary of State Thomas Enders had originally stated to the Sandinistas in August 1981.

At that time, the United States had not insisted on talks between the Sandinistas and the rebels. Enders had demanded that the Sandinistas stop sending arms to El Salvador, cease their own military buildup, loosen their ties with Cuba and the Soviets, and generally increase political and economic pluralism. In exchange, the United States would resume economic aid and not help the rebels.

The United States ultimately suspended the Manzanillo talks in January 1985, after the ninth session. It argued that Nicaragua was using the talks to extricate itself from Contadora and was exploiting fears among Washington's Central American friends of a separate deal between the United States and Nicaragua. Finally, the United States argued that it was demanding more from the Sandinistas than Assistant Secretary Enders had because Nicaragua had become more authoritarian and allied with the Soviet Union since 1981.

The Nicaraguans claimed that the United States suspended the Manzanillo talks because progress toward an acceptable treaty *was* being made, and the United States had no intention of negotiating a settlement of its conflict with Nicaragua. Since the suspension of the talks, Nicaragua ostentatiously sent 100 Cuban soldiers home and agreed to halt both the military draft and the acquisition of new weapons systems. It hoped that these gestures would keep the U.S. Congress from supporting the contras and pressure the United States to resume bilateral talks. President Ortega's trip to Moscow undermined the strategy; Congress voted in favor of humanitarian aid for the contras, and Nicaragua then reversed its positions on the draft and the acquisition of new weapons systems.

Within Contadora, Nicaragua holds firm in its support for the September 1984 Acta, as originally drafted, and continues to press for a resumption of bilateral talks with the United States. In the meantime, it has intensified its military campaign against the Nicaraguan rebels. Nicaragua continues to refuse to talk with the contras or consider additional steps to democratize its political system. Instead, the Sandinistas have tightened their control over the country. They also continue to argue that they have the right to ally with the Soviet Union, Cuba or any other country and to take whatever steps are necessary to protect themselves against their enemies. Nicaragua has reversed its position before. Whether it will do so again will depend on internal and external pressures on the regime.

*VII*

Contadora is stalemated once again. The immediate stumbling block concerns timing; Nicaragua first wants an end to U.S. support for the contras, and then it would be willing to negotiate both the terms and timetables of other issues such as a reduction in the number of military advisers, arms control and maneuvers.

The other Central American countries want "simultaneity." Agreement must first be reached on all outstanding issues and all should then enter into effect simultaneously. The Nicaraguans do not like the Tegucigalpa draft treaty because they do not want to negotiate under military pressure. The other Central American countries do not like the September Acta because they are convinced that the Sandinistas will not negotiate in good faith if the contras are first disbanded and the U.S. military presence in the region is reduced.

Even if the disagreement over timing could be resolved, much work remains to be done to convert agreement on principles into the detailed provisions of a negotiated settlement. To their credit, Contadora's numerous working groups are already giving serious attention to the question of how to stop arms trafficking and outside support for so-called liberation movements of the right and left. The negotiators are also grappling with the problem of how to verify arms levels, military reductions and the like.

Even if these details are worked out, the problem of what happens if and when treaty provisions are violated still remains. None of the Contadora countries wants the United States to act unilaterally. On the other hand, the regional powers have traditionally been reluctant, if not opposed, to taking collective action, including military action. They cannot have it both ways.

If the Contadora Four want a negotiated settlement in Central America that will be more than cosmetic, they must be willing to take responsibility for assuring compliance with the treaty. They cannot continue to hide behind the principle of nonintervention. They must be prepared to intervene collectively, including militarily, against violators of the treaty.

Once a treaty draft is available that resolves the timing issue and deals adequately with the problems of verification and enforcement, the problems of internal reconciliation and democratization will remain. At that point, what happens at the negotiating table will depend on what is happening on the ground—and in Washington.

If the Sandinista government is able to resist pressure from the contras, either because it has won the timing issue or because of its own military capabilities, it will also be strong enough to maintain political control of Nicaragua and to refuse to sign a treaty providing for democratization and internal reconciliation. In such a situation, the U.S. government would be hard put to justify an invasion and the casualties and high political costs that it would entail. More likely, the United States would eventually decide to drop its demand for democratization and internal reconciliation and settle instead for the kinds of security arrangements that are currently being worked out by Contadora. It would not be an ideal solution. Contadora would have produced a negotiated settlement of the Central American conflict, but the United States would have accepted the consolidation of another communist regime in the Western hemisphere.

## LOSING CENTRAL AMERICA[4]

One of the keys to the outcome of the Nicaraguan conflict is the anomalous reaction to it around the world. All it takes to appreciate that anomaly—which is "no accident" and is not generically unique to Nicaragua—is a brief rehearsal of the basic facts.

A civil war, then, is taking place in Nicaragua. On one side are the Sandinista party (FSLN) and the Nicaraguan government, which the FSLN acquired by fraud and holds by force. The FSLN is a Marxist-Leninist party closely allied with the Soviet Union and Cuba. It receives large amounts of Soviet aid which it is using to build the biggest armed forces in Central America. Since it seized power after the overthrow of Somoza in 1979, between five and ten thousand operatives have come from the Communist bloc and other states involved in international terrorism to help the Sandinistas set up their military and internal-security programs (about one foreigner for every 50 people in Nicaragua's non-farm labor force).

[4]Reprint of an article by Max Singer, president of the Potomac Organization, a consulting firm in Washington, D.C., and a founder and former president of the Hudson Institute. *Commentary*. Jl. '86. pp. 11–14. Copyright 1986 Commentary Magazine Inc. Reprinted from *Commentary*, July 1986, by permission; all rights reserved.

Externally, the Sandinistas have committed aggression by means of armed subversion against their three neighbors (El Salvador, Honduras, and Costa Rica). At home, they have attacked the free trade unions and all other independent institutions; they are trying to replace the Catholic Church with an atheistic "church of the poor"; they have persecuted the black and Indian minority population; and they have undermined the economy. They have also established an elaborate secret-police apparatus which makes extensive use of torture and murder, and now holds 6,500 political prisoners in inhuman conditions (in addition to 2,500 of Somoza's National Guardsmen who have been held for more than seven years already).

The other side in the Nicaraguan civil war—usually called the *"contras"**—includes virtually the whole spectrum of Nicaraguan political life from Left to Right, all sectors of society, and the largest volunteer (unpaid) peasant army raised in Latin America in fifty years. The aims of this popular-resistance movement, whose leadership had been part of the fight against Somoza, are democracy, independence, and freedom of religion, plus some vague economic and social reforms.

Ranged on the side of the Sandinistas are Mexico, the major Latin American democracies, Canada, the European democracies (except Germany), and the Socialist International. Some of their support—including hundreds of millions of dollars—goes directly to the Sandinistas. Some of it takes the form of backing the so-called Contadora process, the diplomatic effort organized by Mexico and aimed at a settlement which would destroy the *contras* in exchange for promises by the Sandinistas to refrain from external aggression and perhaps also to move toward internal pluralism.**

In the U.S. almost the entire Democratic party and most of the mainstream church organizations are also lined up behind the Sandinistas. On the other hand, the U.S. government, some private American citizens, and other countries acting in secret (probably including Israel and Taiwan) are on the side of the

*Often the name *"contras"* is used by their enemies as shorthand for "counterrevolutionary." But here it is used the way Jeane J. Kirkpatrick uses it, to stand for "counter-tyranny."

**Originally the Contadora countries were Mexico, Panama, Colombia, and Venezuela. Recently Argentina, Brazil, Peru, and Uruguay have been added as the "Contadora support group." Five Central American countries (Nicaragua, El Salvador, Honduras, Costa Rica, and Guatemala) have also been associated with the process.

*contras*. A majority of the members of the Organization of American States (OAS), representing the whole of Latin America, also favors the *contras*, but the issue has not been brought up in the OAS and so this group has not played a prominent role in the debate over Nicaragua.

This description of the Nicaraguan conflict must sound like madness to anyone unfamiliar with the facts. In a civil war pitting a communist tyranny supported by the Soviet Union and the terrorist powers against a popular, nationalist democratic group supported by the United States, why should most of the democracies side with the Communists? Why should the victims and potential victims of Sandinista aggression oppose the Sandinistas' enemies? Why should Christian organizations side with the party that persecutes the Christian faithful? Obviously most of the people in the democratic world who are lined up with the Communiists must see the facts differently from the way they are summarized above.

Some, of course, do. But many of the key participants in the debate recognize, at least privately, the truth of some such description as I have just given. Others simply regard the truth about Nicaragua as irrelevant—their position is determined by other concerns.

In trying to understand why the *contras* have so little political support from those who might have expected to side with them, we can begin with Europe.

When the Sandinistas came to power in 1979 they engaged the hopes and sympathy of people throughout Western Europe because they were part of a broad Nicaraguan coalition committed to democracy and national independence. The *contras*, on the other hand, had a dark birth—as a small-scale effort by the CIA, using former Somoza National Guard officers, to create a thorn in the side of the FSLN and to inhibit or serve as a bargaining chip in limiting Nicaraguan support of the Communist guerrillas in El Salvador.

By now the Sandinistas have clearly betrayed the democratic promises they originally made. Conversely, as I have already noted, the *contras* have been a genuinely indigenous popular movement whose political leadership mainly consists not of former Somocistas but of former allies of the Sandinistas in the revolution that overthrew Somoza. Nevertheless, the outdated perceptions of 1979 continue to influence opinion in Western Europe.

One reason for the persistence of these outdated perceptions is that Europeans tend to deal with Central America not on the merits but as an expression of their attitudes toward the United States. But an even more critical reason the Europeans have not realized what is happening is the confusion of messages from Nicaragua's neighbors. There is a wolf among the sheep in Central America, but the sheep are not acting in the way an inocent observer would expect sheep to act when a wolf is in their midst. They are not uniting against the common danger, or crying together for outsiders to save them from the wolf. On the contrary, many Central American voices are going along with Mexico's program to protect the Sandinistas from the *contras*.

Of course the Contadora countries do not say that their aim is to protect the Sandinistas from the *contras*. They say that Central America should settle its disputes peacefully and without foreign interference. But the members of the Contadora group know that there is much more foreign interference on the side of the Sandinistas than on the side of the *contras*. They know that they will not be able substantially to reduce this foreign help to the Sandinistas. They know that the *contras* cannnot survive against Soviet guns without U.S. aid. They know that the Sandinistas will never really share power with democratic elements in Nicaragua. Thus they are in effect working to eliminate the *contras* and leave the Sandinistas fully in power.

But why should they do this?

A large part of the answer has to do with the unresolved dependency relationships of these countries with the U.S.

Dependency on the U.S. is a pervasive influence on events in Latin America, often serving as an excuse for passivity in the face of danger, frequently manifesting itself in ritualistic denial. For example, some of the most sophisticated and "anti-American" Mexicans today think they can afford to oppose the U.S. (thereby demonstrating their supposed independence) and cooperate with the Sandinistas (thereby pacifying the Communists and other leftist elements within their own country) because if the worst were to come to the worst, the U.S. would never let Mexico fall into Communist hands.

Costa Rica is another example. A solid majority of Costa Ricans and their political leaders know the facts about the conflict in Nicaragua. Accordingly, they oppose and are afraid of the

Sandinistas and prefer the resistance. (They are also very pro-American.) The two major newspapers (*La Nación* and *La Repúblicia*) have strongly argued for some time that Costa Rica will be in grave danger if the Sandinistas are allowed to consolidate their power. When Luis Alberto Monge was President of Costa Rica, he told many people, including the Kissinger Commission, that he thought so, too. There is every reason to believe that this was truly his view. Nevertheless Monge often made statements, and his government often took actions, that he knew would help the Sandinistas. Conversely, Costa Rica was rarely active in organized opposition to the Sandinistas.

Now Monge has been succeeded as President by Oscar Arias, a member of his own party, Partido de Liberación Nacional (PLN). Before his election, Arias indicated both privately and publicly that he shared Monge's ideas about the Nicaraguan civil war. Yet Arias, together with the President of Guatemala, Mario Vinicio Cerezo, is moving toward the Mexican position.

Undoubtedly dependency is a major factor in this shift. Even apart from the use of force (and Costa Rica has no army), Costa Ricans are not accustomed to assuming responsibility for their own security. In general, their normal behavior is to wait and see what the U.S. is going to do before taking a position, and when they see how hard it is for the Reagan administration to get congressional approval for military aid to the *contras*, they begin to wonder whether the U.S. will stick with the Nicaraguan resistance.

But there are reasons that go beyond dependency. For one thing, important elements of the PLN, including such distinguished democratic figures as José Figueres and Daniel Oduber, are explicitly or in effect Sandinista supporters. Some are genuine believers; some (particularly among the younger men) think that if Costa Rica refrains from working against the Sandinistas, Nicaragua will refrain from threatening Costa Rica; some are being manipulated by personal and financial pressures; some fear retaliation of various kinds for anti-Sandinista activity (the Mexicans arranged to have a recent Costa Rican Foreign Minister—Fernando Volio—fired because he took strong anti-Sandinista positions); some think that the Sandinistas are going to win and that it is therefore useless and dangerous to act against them.

In each of the *contadora* countries there are local circumstances that help explain why those governments, none of which is pro-Sandinista, are working to isolate the *contras*. And each of the Latin American governments realizes that it would not get any special advantage from saving Nicaragua from the Sandinistas, while any government that were to go out front to support the *contras* would certainly have to pay a special price. It would be jumped on not only by the Left but also by all those who have been led to believe that the only basis for supporting the *contras* is extreme conservatism or obeisance to the U.S. How could a government justify spending the political capital that would have to be committed to such an extraneous controversy—especially since U.S. support for the *contras* seems neither effective nor reliable?

The same pattern of incentives applies in Europe, and the stand of the European democracies thus reinforces the tendency of the Latin American countries to passivity.

This failure of the democracies, both in Europe and in Latin America, to speak clearly against the Sandinistas and for the *contras* is bound to have a profound impact on the people of Nicaragua themselves.

There are several different "audiences" in Nicaragua, each of which has to try to figure out who is likely to end up in control of the country. The first audience is the general population who can in small ways help either the *contras* or the Sandinistas or can stay strictly neutral. Second is the part of the urban population that might try to start a clandestine resistance movement against the brutal, state-of-the-art security apparatus that East Germans and others have provided to the FSLN. Third are those who might in a crisis participate in a "general uprising." Fourth are the troops of the Sandinista army who will fight either well or poorly when they get into heavy combat with the *contras*, depending to some extent on how they see the legitimacy and future of the Sandinista regime. (So far these Sandinista troops have mostly fought poorly.) Finally there are the Sandinistas themselves.

Most discussion of what will influence the actions of Nicaraguans have emphasized factors like Sandinista repression, living conditions, perceptions about *contra* leadership and policy, etc. But Nicaraguans would be superhuman if their actions were not also strongly influenced by who looks to them like the winner. Most people are reluctant to risk torture, death, or even loss of income, when there seems little chance of success.

How do prospects look today to those in Nicaragua who are deciding how to bet their lives and who know all too well that the *contras* will be defeated unless they get a continuous supply of military assistance from the U.S.?

Probably they can prudently bet that President Reagan will continue to believe in the *contra* cause. But from a distance the struggles in Congress over *contra* aid must have produced some doubt as to whether the President would have enough political capital to win a series of such battles. And the Nicaraguan trying to judge the reliability of U.S. aid cannot take much comfort from the tides of the debate in Congress or the country so far.

It is true that by 1985 congressional and much other influential opinion in the U.S. had clearly begun to recognize the truth about the Sandinista regime, and to turn away from supporting it. But this must be a very limited source of reassurance to someone who is wondering about the reliability of the U.S. First he must be concerned about the five-year period that elapsed before the U.S. policy debate caught up with the facts of the Nicaraguan conflict: safety requires a faster response. Second, it must worry him that many of those in the U.S. who have recently lost their illusions about the Sandinistas now have nearly equally false information about the *contras*—much of it from the same sources that propagated their former views.

Any Nicaraguan trying to judge the reliability of the U.S. commitment to the *contras* must be struck by how few of the Congressmen who have recently become disillusioned with the Sandinistas seem to have drawn any conclusions from their experience. They are not acting as if they were angry at having been deceived for years, or as if they were concerned about the continuing power and consequences of the system responsible for the long success of the Sandinista deception. And those who have been anxiously following our political struggle over *contra* aid must be frustrated by how much more the outcome is influenced by extraneous elements in U.S. politics than by the reality in Nicaragua.

As for the Sandinistas themselves, so far they have been able to have it both ways. They speak and act like Communists, brutally suppressing democratic organizations, but they are treated with great respect by most of the democratic world. They do not need to feel at all isolated, and they have not been forced to choose between Communism and the West. They must be greatly reassured by the steady stream of encouragement from all the democracies.

Think how different it is for an Afghan government official at an international conference. Unlike the Sandinistas, who are regarded as heroes, Afghan officials are despised because they represent a brutal regime held in power by Soviet troops against a popular nationalist force. Of course there are no Soviet troops as such in Nicaragua, but there are hundreds of millions of dollars worth of Soviet arms and nearly half as many Communist-bloc foreigners (including East Germans and Bulgarians) per capita in Nicaragua supporting Sandinista repression as there are Soviets in Afghanistan supporting the Afghan Communist party. If this similarity between the two situations were reflected in the treatment of the Sandinistas—if, that is, they began to be greeted with the moral contempt that is generally directed by the democracies at the Afghan Communists—it is reasonable to wonder how many defections or other strains might materialize among them.

Think also how great a boost it would be for the morale of the *contras* if they were accorded the same kind of international respect and sympathy that the anti-Communists Afghan *mujaheddin* get from the democracies—even though, ironically, the commitment of the *contras* to democratic values is far greater than that of the *mujaheddin*.

There is, however, little hope any longer that the democracies can be turned away from their support of the Communist side in the Nicaraguan civil war. The case is too hard to make without the Central Americans, especially Costa Rica.

Given this problem, and given all the opposition in Congress to the *contras*, President Reagan will find it hard, if not impossible, to dissuade those in Honduras who feel that their most prudent course is to limit *contra* use of Honduran territory. If the Hondurans were to take steps in this direction, the smell of defeat might begin to hang over the *contras*, and the resulting downward momentum could destroy them faster than we could act to save them.

With this accomplished, the Sandinistas would be able to consolidate their power at home and would be ready to move in one of two directions abroad. They might decide to step up the guerrilla war in El Salvador and Guatemala, perhaps maneuvering so that the armies of those countries felt forced to take power again.

The guerrillas, heavily supported from Nicaragua, including "disguised" Nicaraguan personnel, would be in a good position to defeat such politically isolated post-coup governments, in the kind of long drawn-out political-military struggle we have seen before.

Alternatively, the Sandinistas could first go after Costa Rica and Honduras. There the technique would probably be to use groups that were not themselves Communist but were sympathetic and vulnerable to Communist control, and which with Sandinista, Mexican, and Cuban help could obtain power without Nicaragua's army crossing the border. The majority of the people would want to resist, but they would be divided and sapped by doubt of their chances, and any cry to Washington would be drowned out by strong local voices telling us that our "help" was unwanted and unneeded.

Unless we were lucky, there would be no point in this process at which the U.S. could turn the tide, for we too would be divided and sapped by doubt—not so much of our chances as of whether the Sandinistas had "really" broken their agreement. Either way, thanks to a combination of European apathy, Mexican cynicism, Central American dependency, Communist skill and energy, and U.S. disunity, Central America would within five or ten years be as Communist as Eastern Europe. Not only would additional millions of poor souls be doomed to live under totalitarian tyranny, but a great opportunity would also have been lost to demonstrate that people willing to fight for their freedom can successfully resist the Communist coalition and the juggernaut of lies, deceit, and brutality it always sets in motion.

---

## CHASING RAINBOWS: A FUTILE SEARCH FOR REGIONAL PEACE[5]

---

Peace in Central America has become as elusive as a rainbow. The latest initiative vanished on June 6, the deadline set for a treaty proposed by the Contadora countries—Colombia, Mexico,

[5]Reprint of an excerpt from the Third World Media Service "South" of London written by Maria Elena Hurtado. *World Press Review.* S. '86. p. 24. Copyright 1986 World Press Review, Inc. Reprinted with permission.

Panama and Venezuela—and the support group of Argentina,
Brazil, Peru and Uruguay when all met in Panama in April.

The disappointment was acute, because there had been glim-
mers of hope. The illusion lasted until the summit meeting of
Central American presidents in Guatemala in May. Because of
the presence of President Daniel Ortega of Nicaragua, President
Oscar Arias of Costa Rica objected to a reference in the leaders'
final declaration to the region's "democratically elected" governments. Earlier at a preparatory meeting for the summit, Nicaragua, Honduras, Costa Rica, Guatemala and El Salvador had
approved a draft that included such a reference. Apparently,
someone had put pressure on the Costa Rican president to make
such an objection.

The Costa Ricans have much to think about in their dealings
with Managua. In the 1950s, during the Somoza years, Nicaragua
invaded Costa Rica, which nevertheless felt betrayed when the
Sandinistas took control of the revolution that overthrew the Somoza dictatorship in 1979. San José had backed the social democrats. Recent relations have been soured by border incidents, in
one of which two Costa Rican guards were killed when Nicaraguan soldiers clashed with *contras* operating out of San José.

There are 150,000 political refugees, most of them Nicaraguans, in Costa Rica—a country of only 2.5 million. Local businessmen say Nicaragua has undermined the economy by making
Central America a high-risk region for investment.

In the final analysis, though, there are gains to be had from
an anti-Sandinista stance. U.S. aid to Costa Rica, which totaled
less than $200 million for 1962 through 1979, has exceeded $179
million a year since 1983. A leading Costa Rican economist describes the Sandinistas as the country's "best industry."

Honduras has even more reason to fear peace in the region.
It is getting $182 million in U.S. aid this year in return for allow-
ing 12,000 *contras* to operate out of the country.

Although it is at the center of the regional storm, Honduras
has maintained a dialogue with the Nicaraguans—which is more
than the Costa Ricans have managed to do. There is an element
of "hear no evil, see no evil" in the policies pursued by Tegucigalpa—notably its refusal to allow its well-trained army to become
involved in clashes between Sandinista soldiers and the *contras*.

Honduras is uncomfortable about the military strength of
Nicaragua. President Ortega has declared his willingness to make

concessions. He distinguishes between offensive and defensive weapons, which may provide some room for maneuver.

U.S. military exercises in Honduras are another bone of contention. Even if this sensitive issue is resolved, a way must be found to insure compliance with any deal on arms reduction—a problem in past discussions.

The larger Latin American countries have been able to exert leverage in Central America through Contadora. Their influence would greatly diminish if the peace treaty were signed. Now a proposed Central American parliament threatens to sign it.

Washington may find a regional parliament easier to influence than Contadora. It is already saying that the parliament would put Nicaragua's democratic intentions to the test—particularly because members will be chosen in direct elections, providing an opportunity to press the Sandinistas to agree to participation in the parliament by the *contras*.

# BIBLIOGRAPHY

An asterisk (*) preceding a reference indicates that the article or part of it has been reprinted in this book.

## BOOKS AND PAMPHLETS

Adams, Faith. Nicaragua: struggling with change. Dillon Press. '86.

Americas Watch Committee (U.S.). Human rights in Nicaragua: 1985–1986. Americas Watch Committee. '86.

Amnesty International. The Republic of Nicaragua: an Amnesty International report including the findings of a mission to Nicaragua, 10–15 May 1976. Amnesty International Publications. '77.

Amnesty International USA. Nicaragua, background briefing: persistence of Public Order Law detentions and trials. Amnesty International USA. '82.

Arnove, Robert F. Education and revolution in Nicaragua. Praeger. '86.

Belli, Gioconda and Zimmerman, Marc. Nicaragua in reconstruction and at war. The people speak: a collage of chronology, analysis, poetry, etc. portraying insurrection, reconstruction, cultural revolution and U.S. intervention. MEP Publications. '85.

Belli, Humberto, Calero, Adolfo, and Montealegre, Haroldo. Three Nicaraguans on the betrayal of their revolution. The Louis Lehrman Auditorium, the Heritage Foundation, October 11, 1984. Arthur Spitzer Institute for Hemispheric Development of the Heritage Foundation. '85.

Berg, Terry and Cohn, Betsy. A chronology of U.S.–Nicaraguan relations, policy and impact. Central American Historical Institute. '83.

Bermann, Karl. Under the big stick: Nicaragua and the United States since 1848. South End Press. '86.

Berrigan, Daniel. Steadfastness of the saints: a journal of peace and war in Central and North America. Orbis, Dove Communications. '85.

Black, George. Triumph of the people: the Sandinista revolution in Nicaragua. London: Zed Press. '81.

Black, George and Bevan, John. The loss of fear: education in Nicaragua before and after the revolution. Nicaragua Solidarity Campaign, World University Service. '80.

Booth, John A. The end and the beginning: the Nicaraguan revolution. Westview Press. '85. (2nd ed, rev. and updated)

Borge, Tomas. Carlos, the dawn is no longer beyond our reach: the prison journals of Tomas Borge remembering Carlos Fonseca, founder of the FSLN. New Star Books. '84.

Borge, Tomas. Sandinistas speak. Pathfinder Press. '82.

Brody, Reed. Contra terror in Nicaragua: report of a fact-finding mission, September 1984–January 1985. South End Press. '85.

Buvollen, H. P. Nicaragua: revolution in a disintegrated nation. International Peace Research Institute. '85.

Cabestrero, Teofilo. Blood of the innocent: victims of the Contras' war in Nicaragua. Orbis Books, Catholic Institute for International Relations. '85.

Cabezas, Omar. Fire from the mountain: the making of a Sandinista. Crown. '85.

Camejo, Pedro and Murphy, Fred. The Nicaraguan revolution. Pathfinder Press. '79.

Campaign for Political Rights (U.S.). Transcript of U.S. covert operations against Nicaragua. A public forum, Thursday, May 27, 1982, Dirksen Senate Office Building, Washington, D.C. Campaign for Political Rights. '82.

Cardenal, Ernesto and Cohen, Jonathan. With Walker in Nicaragua and other early poems, 1949–1954. Wesleyan University Press. '84.

Cayetano Carpio, Salvador, Payeras, Mario, and Wheelock, Jaime. Listen, companero: conversations with Central American revolutionary leaders, El Salvador, Guatemala, Nicaragua. Center for the Study of the Americas. Solidarity Publications. '83.

Chinchilla, Norma Stoltz. Women in revolutionary movements: the case of Nicaragua. Women in International Development, Michigan State University. '83.

*Christian, Shirley. Nicaragua: revolution in the family. Random House. '85.

Cohn, Betsy, Roberts, Charles, and Berg, Terry. U.S.-Nicaraguan relations: chronology of policy and impact, January 1981–January 1984. Central American Historical Institute, Intercultural Center, Georgetown University. '84.

Collins, Joseph. Nicaragua: what difference could a revolution make? Institute for Food and Development Policy. '85.

Crawley, Eduardo. Dictators never die: a portrait of Nicaragua and the Somoza dynasty. St. Martin's Press. '79.

Crawley, Eduardo. Nicaragua in perspective. St. Martin's Press. '84. (rev. ed.)

Denny, Harold Norman. Dollars for bullets: the story of American rule in Nicaragua. Greenwood Press. '80.

Dickey, Christopher. With the Contras: a reporter in the wilds of Nicaragua. Simon and Schuster. '85.

Diederich, Bernard. Somoza and the legacy of U.S. involvement in Central America. Dutton. '81.

*Dixon, Marlene and Jonas, Susanne. Nicaragua under siege. Synthesis Publications. '84.

Eich, Dieter and Rincon, Carlos. The Contras: interviews with anti-Sandinistas. Synthesis Publications. '85.

Elman, Richard M. Cocktails at Somoza's: a reporter's sketchbook of events in revolutionary Nicaragua. Apple-Wood Books. '82.

EPICA Task Force. Nicaragua: a people's revolution. The Task Force. '80.

Fagen, Richard R. The Nicaraguan revolution: a personal report. Institute for Policy Studies. '81.

Ferlinghetti, Lawrence. Seven days in Nicaragua libre. City Lights Books. '84.

Fogel, D. Revolution in Central America. Ism Press. '85.

Fonseca Amador, Carlos. Long live Sandino. Dept. of Propaganda and Political Education of the FSLN. '84. (2nd ed.)

Frappier, Jon, Talamante, Olga, and Thomas, Polly. Democracy in Nicaragua: an eyewitness report on the 1984 election and popular democracy in Nicaragua. U.S. Out of Central America. '85.

Grossman, Karl. Nicaragua: America's new Vietnam? Permanent Press. '84.

Hanmer, Trudy J. Nicaragua. F. Watts. '86.

Heyward, Carter, Gilson, Ann, and the Amanecida Collective. Revolutionary forgiveness: the call of Nicaragua. Orbis Books. '86.

Hodges, Donald Clark. Intellectual foundations of the Nicaraguan revolution. University of Texas Press. '86.

Houston, Robert. The nation thief. Pantheon Books. '84.

Ibarra Grijalva, Domingo. The last night of General Augusto C. Sandino. Vantage Press. '73.

Inter-American Commission on Human Rights. Report on the situation of human rights in Nicaragua: findings of the on-site observation in the Republic of Nicaragua, October 3-12, 1978. General Secretariat, Organization of American States. '78.

International Justice Fund. Role of the Nicaraguan and the United States governments in the relocation of the Miskito Indians and subsequent developments on the Atlantic Coast. The Fund. '84.

Jones, Jeffrey. Brigadista: harvest and war in Nicaragua. Praeger. '86.

Karmali, Jan, O'Shaughnessy, Hugh, and Pollak, Andrew. Nicaragua: dictatorship and revolution. Latin America Bureau. '79.

*Levie, Alvin. Nicaragua: the people speak. Bergin & Garvey. '85.

Macaulay, Neill. The Sandino affair. Duke University Press. '85.

Marcus, Bruce. Nicaragua: the Sandinista People's Revolution; speeches by Sandinista leaders. Pathfinder Press. '85.

McGinnis, James. Solidarity with the people of Nicaragua. Orbis Books. '85.

Meyer, Harvey Kessler. Historical dictionary of Nicaragua. Scarecrow Press. '72.

Millett, Richard. Guardians of the dynasty. Orbis Books. '77.

Munck, Ronaldo. Revolutionary trends in Latin America. Centre for Developing-Area Studies, McGill University. '84.

Nicaragua/Junta de Gobierno de Reconstruccion Nacional/Direccion de Divulgacion y Prensa. C.I.A. conspiracy in Nicaragua. Direccion General de Divulgacion y Prensa de la J.G.R.N. '83.

Nogales Mendez, Rafael de. The looting of Nicaragua. R. M. McBride & Company. '28.

Nolan, David. The ideology of the Sandinistas and the Nicaraguan revolution. Institute of Interamerican Studies, Graduate School of International Studies, University of Miami. '84.

O'Shaughnessy, Laura Nuzzi and Serra, Luis H. The church and revolution in Nicaragua. Ohio University, Center for International Studies, Latin America Studies Program. '86.

Payne, Douglas W. The democratic mask: the consolidation of the Sandinista revolution. Freedom House. '85.

Randall, Margaret and Alexander, Floyce. Risking a somersault in the air: conversations with Nicaraguan writers. Solidarity Publications. '84.

Randall, Margaret and Yanz, Lynda. Sandino's daughters: testimonies of Nicaraguan women in struggle. New Star Books. '81.

Reed, Roger. Nicaraguan military operations and covert activities in Latin America. Council for Inter-American Security. '82.

Rosset, Peter and Vandermeer, John. The Nicaragua reader: documents of a revolution under fire. Grove Press, '83.

Rosset, Peter and Vandermeer, John. Nicaragua: unfinished revolution. Grove Press. '86.

Rudolph, James D. Nicaragua: a country study by John Morris Ryan. Foreign Area Studies, the American University, for sale by the Supt. of Docs., U.S. G.P.O. '82. (2nd ed: edited by James D. Rudolph)

*Schroeder, Richard C. Decision on Nicaragua. Editorial Research Reports. Vol. 1, no. 8, '86.

Selser, Gregorio. Sandino. Monthly Review Press. '81.

Selva, Salomon de la and Arellano, Jorge Eduardo. Sandino: free country or death. Biblioteca Nacional de Nicaragua. '84.

Sims, Harold. Sandinista Nicaragua: pragmatism in a political economy in formation. Institute for the Study of Human Issues. '82.

Somoza, Anastasio. Communist-Cuban aggression versus the socio-economic development of Nicaragua. Secretaria de Informacion y Prensa de la Presidencia de la Republica. '77.

Somoza, Anastasio and Cox, Jack. Nicaragua betrayed. Western Islands. '80.

Spalding, Rose J. The political economy of revolutionary Nicaragua. Allen & Unwin. '86.

Stansifer, Charles L. Cultural policy in the old and the new Nicaragua. American Universities Field Staff. '81.

Tierney, John. Somozas and Sandinistas: the U.S. and Nicaragua in the twentieth century. Council for Inter-American Security. '82.

Tijerino, Doris and Randall, Margaret. Inside the Nicaraguan revolution. New Star Books. '78.

Unitarian Universalist Service Committee. American principles sacrificed; U.S. foreign policy in Central America: report of a fact finding mission to El Salvador and Nicaragua. The Committee. '83.

United States/Congress/House/Committee on Foreign Affairs. Concerning U.S. military and paramilitary operations in Nicaragua: markup before the Committee on Foreign Affairs, House of Representatives, Ninety-eighth Congress, first session, on H.R. 2760, May 18, June 6 and 7, 1983. U.S. G.P.O. '83.

United States/Congress/House/Committee on Foreign Affairs/Subcommittee on Inter-American Affairs. Review of the Presidential certification of Nicaragua's connection to terrorism: hearing before the Subcommittee on Inter-American Affairs of the Committee on Foreign Affairs, House of Representatives, Ninety-sixth Congress, September 30, 1980. U.S. G.P.O. '80.

United States/Congress/House/Committee on Foreign Affairs/Subcommittee on Western Hemisphere Affairs. U.S. support for the Contras: hearing before the Subcommittee on Western Hemisphere Affairs of the Committee on Foreign Affairs, House of Representatives, Ninety-ninth Congress, first session, April 16, 17, and 18. U.S. G.P.O. '85.

United States/Congress/House/Committee on International Relations/Subcommittee on International Development. Rethinking United States foreign policy toward the developing world: Nicaragua; hearing before the Subcommittee on International Development of the Committee on International Relations, House of Representatives, Ninety-fifth Congress, first session. U.S. G.P.O. '78.

United States/Congress/Senate/Committee on Foreign Relations. U.S. policy toward Nicaragua and Central America: hearing before the Committee on Foreign Relations, United States Senate, Ninety-eighth Congress, first session, April 12, 1983. U.S. G.P.O. '83.

United States/Congress/Senate/Committee on Foreign Relations/ Subcommittee on Western Hemisphere Affairs. Human rights in Nicaragua: hearings before the Subcommittee on Western Hemisphere Affairs of the Committee on Foreign Relations, United States Senate, Ninety-seventh Congress, second session, February 25 and March 1, 1982. U.S. G.P.O. '83.

United States/Dept. of State/Bureau of Public Affairs. The Sandinista military build-up. U.S. Dept. of State, Bureau of Public Affairs. '85. (rev May 1985)

United States/Dept. of State/Office of Public Communication/Editorial Division. Revolution beyond our borders: Sandinista intervention in Central America. U.S. Dept. of State, Bureau of Public Affairs. '85.

Vanderlaan, Mary B. Revolution and foreign policy in Nicaragua. Westview Press. '86.

*Walker, Thomas W. Nicaragua: the first five years. Praeger. '85.

Walker, Thomas W. Nicaragua: the land of Sandino. Westview Press. '86. (2nd ed. rev and updated)

Walker, Thomas W. Nicaragua in revolution. Praeger. '82.

Walker, William. The war in Nicaragua. University of Arizona Press. '85.

Wall, James T. Manifest Destiny denied: America's first intervention in Nicaragua. University Press of America. '81.

Weber, Henri. Nicaragua: the Sandinist revolution. Verso. '81.

Weissberg, Arnold. Nicaragua: an introduction to the Sandinista revolution. Pathfinder Press. '82.

Wheelock, Jaime and Harnecker, Marta. Nicaragua: the great challenge. Alternative Views. '84.

White, Gordon, Young, Kate, and Fitgerald, Valpy. Nicaragua after the revolution: problems and prospects. '85.

Woodward, Ralph Lee and Herstein, Sheila R. Nicaragua. Clio Press. '83.

Zwerling, Philip and Martin, Connie. Nicaragua: a new kind of revolution. L. Hill. '85.

## PERIODICALS

Nicaragua's revolution. America. 149:362-3. D. 10, '83.

Christ of the Americas. Nouwen, Henri. America. 150:293-302. Ap. 21, '84.

Church and state in Nicaragua. America. 151:21-2. Jl. 21-28, '84.

U.S. policy in Nicaragua. America. 152:205-6. Mr. 16, '85.

Sandinista crackdown: their lies and ours. America. 153:269-70. N. 2, '85.

*An interview with Miguel d'Escoto Brockman, foreign minister of Nicaragua. Stahel, Thomas H. America. 153:318-23. N. 16, '85.

The Contadora alternative. America. 154:178-9. Mr. 8, '86.

A report on Nicaragua. Oppenheim, Frank M. America. 154:183-5. Mr. 8, '86.

Saying no to the president. America. 154:258. Ap. 5, '86.

*The man who made the Yanquis go home. Bain, David Haward. American Heritage. 36:50-61. Ag./S. '85.

*Icy day at the ICJ. Franck, Thomas M. Am. J. Int'l L. 79:379-84. Ap. '85.

Nicaragua v. United States as a precedent. Kirgis, Frederic L., Jr. Am. J. Int'l L. 79:652-7. Jl. '85.

Nicaragua and international law: the academic and the real. D'Amato, Anthony. Am. J. Int'l L. 79:657-64. Jl. '85.

Nicaragua v. United States: constitutionality of U.S. modification of ICJ jurisdiction. Glennon, Michael J. Am. J. Int'l L. 79:682-9. Jl. '85.

Litigation implications of the U.S. withdrawal from the Nicaragua case. Highet, Keith. Am. J. Int'l L. 79:992-1005. O. '85.

Intervention under article 63 of the ICJ statute in the phase of preliminary proceedings: the Salvadoran incident. Sztucki, Jerzy. Am. J. Int'l L. 79:1005-36. O. '85.

*God and man in Nicaragua. O'Brien, Conor Cruise. The Atlantic. 258:50-60+. Ag. '86.

Wider unrest narrows support for Nicaragua's revolution. Bussey, John. Business Week. p. 46+. Ja. 24, '83.

How Washington's allies are aiding the Sandinistas. Heard, Joyce and Kruckewitt, Joan. Business Week. p. 45. Jl. 29, '85.

The contras are giving Reagan less bang for the buck. Robbins, Carla Anne and Boyd, Larry. Business Week. p. 41. D. 23, '85.

Reagan will have to go to the mat to get more contra aid. Fly, Richard. Business Week. p. 41. Mr. 10, '86.

$100 million won't begin to buy a contra victory. Javetski, Bill and Boyd, Larry. Business Week. p. 55. Ag. 25, '86.

Jurisdiction of the I.C.J.—admissibility of Nicaragua's application in Case Concerning Military and Paramilitary Activities in and against Nicaragua. Loeper, Sabine. Cambridge L. J. 44:183-8. Jl. '85.

U.S. Nicaraguan policy. The Center Magazine. 18:2-8. N./D. '85.

The unbending Pope in Nicaragua. Wilde, Margaret D. The Christian Century. 100:264-5. Mr. 23-30, '83.

A faithless response to Contadora (U.S.-Nicaragua). Wilde, Margaret D. The Christian Century. 101:1052-3. N. 14, '84.

Nicaragua: on saving us from ourselves. Brown, Robert McAfee. The Christian Century. 102:6-7. Ja. 2-9, '85.

Letting go of the middle. Wilde, Margaret D. The Christian Century. 102:852-3. O. 2, '85.

'Humanitarian aid' at work. Hostetter, Doug. The Christian Century. 102:885-6. O. 9, '85.

The Tutu/d'Escoto dilemma: nonviolence and justice. Green, Clifford. The Christian Century. 102:921-3. O. 16, '85.

Nicaraguan images: a visitor's notebook. Brown, Robert McAfee. The Christian Century. 103:235-8. Mr. 5, '86.

The contra debate: an issue of control. Wall, James M. The Christian Century. 103:283-4. Mr. 19-26, '86.

Public-policy debate evaporates in images. Wall, James M. The Christian Century. 103:315-16. Ap. 2, '86.

Church vs. contra aid. The Christian Century. 103:353-4. Ap. 9, '86.

Contras vs. Sandinistas: what should the U.S. do? Spring, Beth. Christianity Today. 30:36+. Ap. 18, '86.

Nicaragua, the United States, and the World Court. Chayes, Abram. Colum. L. Rev. 85:1445-82. N. '85.

*Losing Central America. Singer, Max. Commentary. 82:11-14. Jl. '86.

Perspectives on Nicaragua. Commonweal. 110:234-44. Ap. 22, '83.

Should we go to war with Nicaragua? Commonweal. 112:355-6. Je. 21, '85.

The battle for Nicaragua. Sheehan, Edward R. F. Commonweal. 113:259-61, 264-8. My. 9, '86.

Central American policy: the dangerous drift. Hehir, J. Bryan. Commonweal. 113:425+. Ag. 15, '86.

*Is the Reagan administration policy toward Nicaragua sound? (pro). East, John P. Congressional Digest. 63:266+. N. '84.

*Is the Reagan administration policy toward Nicaragua sound? (con). Kennedy, Edward Moore. Congressional Digest. 63:267+. N. '84.

The U.S., the law, and Nicaragua. Moore, John Norton. Current (Washington, D.C.). 275:17-24. S. '85.

Fantasies and facts: the Soviet Union and Nicaragua. Leiken, Robert S. Current History. 83:314-17+. O. '84.

*United States policy in Central America: a choice denied. Kenworthy, Eldon. Current History. 84:97-100+. Mr. '85.

*Nicaragua under siege. Colburn, Forrest D. Current History. 84:105-8+. Mr. '85.

Neutrality Costa Rican style. Lincoln, Jennie K. Current History. 84:118-21+. Mr. '85.

Nicaragua's frustrated revolution. Millett, Richard. Current History. 85:5-8+. Ja. '86.

Confusing victims and victimizers: Nicaragua and the reinterpretation of international law. Friedlander, Robert A. Den. J. Int'l L. & Pol'y. 14:87-96. Spring/Summer '85.

Nicaragua: threat to peace in Central America. Enders, Thomas O. Department of State Bulletin. 83:76-80. Je. '83.

Nicaragua: a threat to democracy. Bush, George. Department of State Bulletin. 85:22-4. My. '85.

Nicaragua peace proposal. Reagan, Ronald. Department of State Bulletin. 85:9-10. Je. '85.

Central America. Reagan, Ronald. Department of State Bulletin. 85:11-12. Je. '85.

Restoring bipartisanship in foreign affairs. Shultz, George Pratt. Department of State Bulletin. 85:39-42. Jl. '85.

Economic sanctions against Nicaragua. Reagan, Ronald. Department of State Bulletin. 85:74-7. Jl. '85.

Nicaragua. Reagan, Ronald. Department of State Bulletin. 85:88. Ag. '85.

*The United States and the World Court. Sofaer, Abraham D. Department of State Bulletin. Current Policy no. 769. D. '85.

U.S. terminates acceptance of ICJ compulsory jurisdiction. Department of State Bulletin. 86:67-71. Ja. '86.

Nicaragua. Reagan, Ronald. Department of State Bulletin. 86:23-4. F. '86.

Nicaragua: will democracy prevail? Shultz, George Pratt. Department of State Bulletin. 86:32-9. Ap. '86.

Permanent dictatorship in Nicaragua? Abrams, Elliott. Department of State Bulletin. 86:83. Ap. '86.

Central America and U.S. security. Reagan, Ronald. Department of State Bulletin. 86:28-32. My. '86.

*Nicaragua and the future of Central America. Shultz, George Pratt. Department of State Bulletin. 86:37-40. My. '86.

Assistance for Nicaraguan democratic resistance. Reagan, Ronald. Department of State Bulletin. 86:81-6. My. '86.

Captured weapons displayed at the State Department. Reagan, Ronald. Department of State Bulletin. 86:87. My. '86.

How the Russians look at Managua. Smith, Adam. Esquire. 100:15-16. N. '83.

Nicaragua. Forbes, Malcolm S., Jr. Forbes. 137:23. F. 10, '86.

Yes, they have no bananas. Field, Alan M. Forbes. 138:76+. Ag. 25, '86.

Nicaragua's imperiled revolution. Cruz, Arturo. Foreign Affairs. 61:1031-47. Summer '83.

At war with Nicaragua. Ullman, Richard H. Foreign Affairs. 62:39-58. Fall '83.

U.S. policy and Central American realities. Cruz, Arturo. Foreign Affairs. 62:201-3. Fall '83.

*Demystifying Contadora. Purcell, Susan Kaufman. Foreign Affairs. 64:74–95. Fall '85.

Resist romanticism. Gleijeses, Piero. Foreign Policy. 54:122–38. Spring '84.

America's diplomatic charade. Gutman, Roy. Foreign Policy. 56:3–23. Fall '84.

Nicaragua and U.S. foreign policy, 1928. Harper's. 268:44. Je. '84.

The children's hour. Goldman, Francisco. Harper's. 269:69–74. O. '84.

Elements of CIA style. Harper's. 270:16. Ja. '85.

With the 'contras'. Eich, Dieter and Rincon, Carlos. Harper's. 271:27–8+. O. '85.

Abusing human rights abuse. Harper's. 271:21–4. N. '85.

A C.I.A. man in Nicaragua. Anderson, Jon Lee. Life. 8:24–8. F. '85.

Military and Paramilitary Activities in and against Nicaragua: the International Court of Justice's jurisdictional dilemma. Loy. L. A. Int'l & Comp. L. J. 7:379–408. '84.

The Sandinista offensive. Mitchell, Jared. Maclean's. 96:21–2. Ap. 4, '83.

The gathering clouds of war. Ross, Val. Maclean's. 96:18–20+. Ag. 1, '83.

Nicaragua: the fire next time. Ellman, Paul. Maclean's. 96:40. O. 24, '83.

Managua moves to limit the dangers. North, David. Maclean's. 96:42. D. 5, '83.

Dealing with Nicaragua. Mackenzie, Hilary. Maclean's. 98:11. My. 20, '85.

A first-round setback for Reagan's contras. McDonald, Marci. Maclean's. 99:32–3. Mr. 31, '86.

The contras—close up. Levin, Bob. Maclean's. 99:34. Mr. 31, '86.

Revolution under siege. Levin, Bob. Maclean's. 99:16–17. Jl. 28, '86.

Solidarity with the Sandinists. Grass, Günter. The Nation. 236:300–3. Mr. 12, '83.

The selling of military intervention. Hitchens, Christopher. The Nation. 237:129+. Ag. 20–27, '83.

With Sandino in Nicaragua. Beals, Carleton. The Nation. 238:76. Ja. 28, '84.

Mirror of our midlife crisis. Davis, Peter. The Nation. 238:76–88. Ja. 28, '84.

Sandinista fiesta. Kopkind, Andrew. The Nation. 238:243–4. Mr. 3, '84.

Contempt of court. The Nation. 240:99–100. F. 2, '85.

Who's funding the contras? Cockburn, Alexander. The Nation. 240:134–5. F. 9, '85.

The rollback of the revolution. Nusser, Nancy. The Nation. 240:370–1. Mr. 30, '85.

Hard questions on Nicaragua. Massing, Michael. The Nation. 240:395-8. Ap. 6, '85.

Reading Nicaragua. Sklar, Holly. The Nation. 241:185-9. S. 7, '85.

Nicaragua: news from nowhere. Cockburn, Alexander. The Nation. 241:702-3. D. 28, '85-Ja. 4, '86.

Nicaragua's disloyal opposition. Jenkins, Tony. The Nation. 242:505+. Ap. 12, '86.

Nicaragua: nation in conflict. Edwards, Mike. National Geographic. 168:776-811. D. '85.

The WCC in Nicaragua. Novak, Michael. National Review. 36:46. Mr. 9, '84.

A mess in Nicaragua. Buckley, William F. National Review. 36:54-5. My. 18, '84.

Who was right? National Review. 36:55. Jl. 27, '84.

They used to call it the resistance. Buckley, William F. National Review. 36:54. N. 30, '84.

To save a country. National Review. 37:18-19. Ap. 5, '85.

Nicaragua, another Vietnam. Buckley, William F. National Review. 38:63. Ap. 11, '86.

Managua's Mexican standoff. Singer, Max. National Review. 38:39. Je. 6, '86.

Cautious optimism in Nicaragua. Brumberg, Abraham. The New Leader. 67:5-11. Ap. 30, '84.

Reagan's contrary campaign. Goodman, Walter. The New Leader. 69:9-10. F. 24, '86.

Sandinistas besieged. Hennican, Ellis. The New Republic. 188:13-14+. Mr. 7, '83.

Path to disaster? Kondracke, Morton. The New Republic. 188:8-9. Ap. 25, '83.

Nicaraguan nettle. Krauthammer, Charles. The New Republic. 188:15-16. My. 9, '83.

Darkening Nicaragua. Radosh, Ronald. The New Republic. 188:7-12. O. 24, '83.

Nicaragua's untold story. Leiken, Robert S. The New Republic. 191:16-17. O. 8, '84.

The Reagahnev doctrine. The New Republic. 192:4+. Ap. 29, '85.

Contra dance. Morley, Jefferson. The New Republic. 192:12-14. My. 13, '85.

The Sandinista path. Zaid, Gabriel. The New Republic. 192:10-17. My. 20, '85.

The people's happiness. Lane, Charles. The New Republic. 192:12-13. My. 20, '85.

Another choice in Nicaragua. Aronson, Bernard. The New Republic. 192:21-3. My. 27, '85.

*Confessions of a 'contra'. Chamorro, Edgar. The New Republic. 193:18-23. Ag. 5, '85.

The Sandinista lobby. Barnes, Fred. The New Republic. 194:11-14. Ja. 20, '86.

Managua's game. Cruz, Arturo, Jr. The New Republic. 194:17-19. Mr. 10, '86.

*The case for the contras. The New Republic. 194:7-9. Mr. 24, '86.

Contra delusion. Morley, Jefferson. The New Republic. 194:14-16. Mr. 31, '86.

*Reform the contras. Leiken, Robert S. The New Republic. 194:18-20. Mr. 31, '86.

Contra for a day. Barnes, Fred. The New Republic. 194:13-16. Ap. 7, '86.

Is Ortega stupid? Krauthammer, Charles. The New Republic. 194:6+. Ap. 21, '86.

Bleeding Nicaragua. Walzer, Michael. The New Republic. 194:15-16. Ap. 28, '86.

Human rights in Nicaragua. Shea, Nina H. The New Republic. 195:21-3. S. 1, '86.

Playing dominoes. Kramer, Michael. New York. 16:23-4+. Ap. 11, '83.

Whose counterrevolution is it anyway? Kramer, Michael. New York. 16:16+. Je. 6, '83.

What to do about Nicaragua. Kramer, Michael. New York. 18:37-9. Ap. 15, '85.

Developments at the International Court of Justice: provisional measures and jurisdiction in the Nicaragua case. Malloy, Michael P. N. Y. L. Sch. J. Int'l & Comp. L. 6:55-91. '84.

The Nicaraguan tangle. Leiken, Robert S. The New York Review of Books. 32:55-64. D. 5, '85.

The battle for Nicaragua. Leiken, Robert S. The New York Review of Books. 33:43-52. Mr. 13, '86.

The US and the contras. Neier, Aryeh. The New York Review of Books. 33:3-4+. Ap. 10, '86.

'Contra' justice. Neier, Aryeh. The New York Review of Books. 33:50-1. My. 29, '86.

Scenes from Nicaragua. Kempton, Murray. The New York Review of Books. 33:5-6+. Ag. 14, '86.

Nicaragua: the beleaguered revolution. Kinzer, Stephen. The New York Times Magazine. pp. 22-8+. Ag. 28, '83.

In Nicaragua. Vargas Llosa, Mario. The New York Times Magazine. pp. 36-42+. Ap. 28, '85.

Manifest destiny. Pfaff, William. The New Yorker. 61:90+. My. 27, '85.

The secret war boils over. LeMoyne, James. Newsweek. 101:46-50. Ap. 11, '83.

Unmasking the death squads. Young, Jacob. Newsweek. 105:38. F. 4, '85.

Nicaragua: a war of words. Whitaker, Mark. Newsweek. 105:20-2. Mr. 11, '85.

The hottest game in town. Greenfield, Meg. Newsweek. 105:86. Mr. 11, '85.

How to handle Nicaragua. Watson, Russell. Newsweek. 105:38-9. Ap. 29, '85.

Sending Managua a message. Whitaker, Mark. Newsweek. 105:46-8. Je. 17, '85.

A plug for the contras. Deming, Angus. Newsweek. 107:29. Mr. 3, '86.

The contra crusade. Martz, Larry. Newsweek. 107:20+. Mr. 17, '86.

Guerrilla chic. Cooper, Nancy. Newsweek. 107:22. Mr. 17, '86.

Nicaragua's unholy war. Woodward, Kenneth L. Newsweek. 108:48. Ag. 4, '86.

Nicaragua and human rights. Dickey, Christopher. Newsweek. 108:19. Ag. 18, '86.

Our state, their revolution. Lens, Sidney. The Progressive. 47:14-15. S. '83.

Curbing a lawless government. Falk, Richard A. The Progressive. 48:13. Je. '84.

War of attrition. Armstrong, Robert. The Progressive. 49:20-2. D. '85.

Life under siege. Krajick, Kevin. The Progressive. 49:23-6. D. '85.

The front line. Ivins, Molly. The Progressive. 50:15. My. '86.

*The way of the Sandinistas. Landau, Saul. The Progressive. 50:21-5. Ag. '86.

A contra's story. Drucker, Linda. The Progressive. 50:25-8. Ag. '86.

Prisoners of an undeclared war. Landau, Saul. Rolling Stone. pp. 11-12. Ap. 14, '83.

U.S.-sponsored terrorism. Greider, William. Rolling Stone. pp. 13-14+. D. 6, '84.

Nicaragua at the turning point. Klein, Joe. Rolling Stone. pp. 37-8+. O. 10, '85.

Political tourism in Cuba and Nicaragua. Hollander, Paul. Society. 23:28-37. My./Je. '86.

Military and Paramilitary Activities in and against Nicaragua [1984 I.C.J. 169]. Johnson, D. H. N. Sydney L. Rev. 10:485-502. Mr. '85.

Uneasy over a secret war. Isaacson, Walter. Time. 121:10-12. My. 16, '83.

Yankees leave home. Time. 122:16. D. 19, '83.

Broadsides in a war of nerves. Russell, George. Time. 124:72-4. N. 26, '84.

Say uncle, says Reagan. Thomas, Evan. Time. 125:16-18. Mr. 4, '85.

The propaganda war. Russell, George. Time. 125:34-5. Mr. 11, '85.

The revolution is not finished. Smolowe, Jill. Time. 126:36. D. 30, '85.

Why Congress should approve contra aid. Talbott, Strobe. Time. 127:95-6. Mr. 24, '86.

Escalating the contra battle. Duffy, Michael. Time. 128:26. Jl. 7, '86.

55 speak in debate on Nicaragua. UN Chronicle. 20:8-22. My. '83.

Nicaragua complains of United States support for counter-revolutionaries. UN Chronicle. 20:31-2. N. '83.

*Contadora: peace process in Central America. UN Chronicle. 21:9-12. Mr. '84.

*Nicaragua's sovereignty and independence should not be jeopardized by military activities, International Court of Justice declares. UN Chronicle. 21:3-10. Ap. '84.

World Court finds it has jurisdiction in case of Nicaragua vs. United States. UN Chronicle. 21 no10-11:35-6. '84.

Security Council reaffirms support for Contadora efforts, calls on United States and Nicaragua to resume dialogue. UN Chronicle. 22 no5:16-21. '85.

Mr. Casey's covert war: the United States, Nicaragua, and international law. Friedlander, Robert A. U. Dayton L. Rev. 10:265-93. Winter '85.

A legal analysis of the United States' attempted withdrawal from the jurisdiction of the World Court in the proceedings initiated by Nicaragua. Hassan, Farooq. U. Dayton L. Rev. 10:295-318. Winter '85.

Nicaragua's leftist rulers—defiant as ever. Migdail, Carl J. U.S. News & World Report. 94:29-30. Mr. 14, '83.

U.S. aid to Nicaraguan rebels—lawmakers speak out. U.S. News & World Report. 94:29. My. 2, '83.

Nicaragua's contras face a rough road. U.S. News & World Report. 95:29-30. Ag. 29, '83.

Why U.S. snubs the World Court. U.S. News & World Report. 96:12. Ap. 23, '84.

What's behind Reagan strategy in Nicaragua? U.S. News & World Report. 96:27-9. Ap. 23, '84.

Nicaragua's rulers: can they survive? Wallace, James. U.S. News & World Report. 97:39-40. N. 5, '84.

The uphill struggle to salvage Nicaragua policy. Fromm, Joseph. U.S. News & World Report. 98:23-4. Ap. 29, '85.

Sandinistas to Reagan: we'll outlast you. Wallace, James. U.S. News & World Report. 98:28-9. Je. 3, '85.

The sad state of the contras. Horton, Bob. U.S. News & World Report. 100:32. Mr. 17, '86.

Treating gnats like dragons. Yoder, Edwin M. U.S. News & World Report. 100:13. Mr. 24, '86.

Bracing for the long haul. Wallace, James. U.S. News & World Report. 100:16–19. Mr. 24, '86.

Why contras are failing on home front. Robbins, Carla Anne. U.S. News & World Report. 100:18–19. Mr. 24, '86.

The key is Mexico, not Nicaragua. Broyles, William. U.S. News & World Report. 100:10. Mr. 31, '86.

What the Viet Cong should have taught us. Broyles, William. U.S. News & World Report. 100:10. Ap. 14, '86.

Contra policy? Where? Wallace, James. U.S. News & World Report. 100:26–7. Je. 2, '86.

Ortega woos—and maybe wins—new pals across U.S. Duffy, Brian. U.S. News & World Report. 101:26. Ag. 18, '86.

U.S. involvement in Central America: a historical lesson. Kornbluh, Peter R. USA Today (Periodical). 112:45–7. S. '83.

The U.S. and revolution in Nicaragua. Wolfe, James H. USA Today (Periodical). 114:9. Ja. '86.

The contra debate: defining American interests. Bresler, Robert J. USA Today (Periodical). 115:6–7. Jl. '86.

The United States and Nicaragua: reflections on the lawfulness of contemporary intervention. Joyner, Christopher C. Va. J. Int'l L. 25:621–89. Spring '85.

Peace and democracy in Nicaragua. Calero, Adolfo. Vital Speeches of the Day. 51:636–9. Ag. 1, '85.

Nicaragua: aiding the contras. Reagan, Ronald. Vital Speeches of the Day. 52:386–9. Ap. 15, '86.

Thirty myths about Nicaragua. Weinrod, W. Bruce. Vital Speeches of the Day. 52:454–66. My. 15, '86.

Whose revolution is this, anyway? The Washington Monthly. 17:14–15. Ap. '85.

Truth and myth in Nicaragua. Lane, Charles. The Washington Monthly. 17:50–2. Jl./Ag. '85.

Nicaragua faces elections. Niedergang, Marcel. World Press Review. 31:30–2. Jl. '84.

Nicaragua: an editor's exile. Balk, Alfred. World Press Review. 32:33–5. F. '85.

The Nicaragua embargo. Godwin, Peter. World Press Review. 32:47–8. Je. '85.

*Chasing rainbows: a futile search for regional peace. Hurtado, Maria Elena. World Press Review. p. 24 S. '86.

The Contadora approach to peace in Central America. Duran, Esperanza. The World Today. 40:347-54. Ag./S. '84.

United States armed intervention in Nicaragua and article 2(4) of the United Nations Charter. Bernheim, Carlos Tünnermann. Yale J. Int'l L. 11:104-38. Fall '85.